STUDIES

Mandy Esseen
Martin Phillips
John Ashton: Chief Examiner
Mike Edwards

www.heinemann.co.uk
✓ Free online support
✓ Useful weblinks
✓ 24 hour online ordering

01865 888118

Part of Pearson

Contents

6 Pop music 123

7 Advertising and marketing 145

8 Radio 171

9 External Assessment 181

10 Controlled Assessment 188

Glossary 229

CD-ROM contents

You will find a CD-ROM in the back of this student book. On it is an electronic version of this student book and a range of resources to help you with your GCSE Media Studies course. Wherever a resource appears, you will find detail on this in the student book in the 'CD-ROM Extra!' feature.

CD-ROM Extra!

Film Posters

Open the CD in the back of this book and click on the icon below to see examples of film posters.

Welcome to WJEC GCSE Media Studies. You have chosen to embark on a wonderful journey of investigation and creation in the fast-changing world of the modern media. This course will, we hope, equip you with the knowledge and skills to understand better how you interact with the contemporary media as a user and, crucially, develop your skills to create your own media, which can be used by others.

What will you be studying?

The following section outlines what your WJEC GCSE Media Studies course includes.

Media Concepts and Ideas

You will learn about these and constantly revisit them during your course. These Media Concepts and Ideas are:

- Media texts: genre, narrative and representation
- Media organisations
- Media audiences and users.

In all your investigations of media texts and practical production work, you will constantly engage and reflect on these Key Concepts.

The two central activities and convergent media

The course is based on two activities: *thinking about* the media and *making* the media.

1. Thinking about the media

You will do this through textual investigations, whether in print, broadcast or in the online environment. You will write, talk about and present your investigations in a wide variety of ways. You will often use the new technologies to report on what you have found.

2. Making the media

You will be active in making your own media by:

- researching texts and audiences
- visually researching
- storyboarding
- scripting
- planning layouts and displays for print and electronic media
- creating pitches and synopses.

Production:

- making short films and animations
- making newspapers or magazines
- creating film posters or CD covers
- making web pages
- making podcasts.

Editing your productions:

- targeting them at audiences and users
- thinking carefully about the consequences of making your own media in the convergent media environment and the uses others will make of your media products
- reflecting on how you produced your own converging media texts.

These two activities of *thinking about* the media and *making* the media are set in the context of what has become known as the **convergent media**. This essentially means that most media texts, whether films, newspapers, television or popular music, are now experienced by the user in a variety of ways, most often through the Internet or multimedia platforms. All the topics you study should therefore reflect this convergent nature and indeed your media production work will also reflect this.

The Case studies in this book provide a regular and explicit focus on convergent media in the context of the relevant chapter.

Key terms

Convergent media
Where more than one media is used for communicating a message.

How will you be assessed?

Your WJEC GCSE Media Studies course is assessed in two main sections: Controlled Assessment and External Assessment. In brief, your course looks like this:

Course component and outline	% of your GCSE	Marks (and Assessment Objectives)
Controlled Assessment **Two textual investigations:** • On two different media areas (one must be print-based) • Together worth 20% of your GCSE **One media production:** • Consisting of research, planning, the production and an evaluation • Worth 40% of your GCSE	60%	• Textual investigations: 40 marks in total (AO2) • Media production: 80 marks in total (AO3 and AO4)
External Assessment • Investigating – four questions • Planning – a series of tasks	40%	• 80 marks in total (AO1, AO2, AO3)

Controlled Assessment

During your course you will produce two textual investigations and a media production as part of your Controlled Assessment package.

You and your teacher will decide on the texts you study and the texts you research, plan and make. This means that both of you have some control over what you study and that you can be involved in shaping your course, so be prepared to offer ideas and resources which can be used.

The two textual investigations

Your teacher will provide you with titles for both of your investigations. For each investigation you will produce findings on one main text and findings from other linked texts. These findings will be presented in an appropriate manner, for example, a written report (with or without graphics), or a multimedia presentation (with or without sound). Better organised presentations will get better marks. Your teacher will provide guidance about how much evidence to present.

The media production

The media production includes four elements:

1. **Research** (10 marks)
   - You will provide evidence consisting of a minimum of two pieces and a maximum of four pieces of research.
   - You must not present the same findings as other candidates, though the research methods may be the same.
   - You can use research methods such as: textual annotation, audience research in the form of questionnaires and surveys, small-scale focus-group research (4–6 participants).
   - You will get better marks by explaining how the findings have been used in the final production and by using terminology appropriate to the text.

2. **Planning** (10 marks)
   - You will provide evidence of having used a minimum of two and a maximum of four planning techniques.
   - You must not present the same approach to planning as other candidates, though you may use the same technique.
   - Your teacher will help with other appropriate techniques you can use.
   - You will get better marks by explaining how the techniques have been used to develop the final production and by using terminology appropriate to the type of text.
3. **Production** (50 marks)
   - You will create your own media text which can be print, interactive or broadcast-based.
   - Your teacher will advise on the quantity and length of your text and will give you a list of options from which you can choose.
   - You can be in a group only for an audio and audio-visual production
   - You will get better marks for an original approach to the production rather than one which copies existing texts slavishly.
   - You should always try to create your own imagery (hand-drawn, photographed, computer-drawn or filmed). Where this is not possible then 'found' images (scanned or downloaded) can be used, though a high level of creative manipulation is expected for marks at the higher levels.
4. **Evaluation** (10 marks)

   You need to explain how your media production:
   - met your aims and purposes
   - used appropriate codes and conventions
   - used representations
   - was organised to appeal to and engage the audience/user
   - explored some of the organisational issues raised by the text.

   You will get more marks by presenting your viewpoints clearly and succinctly.

External Assessment

The External Assessment is a written examination lasting 2¼ hours. It is in two sections:

- **Section A**: This is based on a topic that you will have studied during your course. In particular, it focuses on how contemporary media is convergent.
- **Section B**: Here you will have to demonstrate planning and creative skills. Again, there is a particular focus on the convergent nature of contemporary media.

The External Assessment topic

For Section A of the External Assessment, you will study one of the topics listed below for a period of your course. You will develop your investigative skills by thinking about and studying a wide range of media texts from a variety of genres and forms from one of these topics:

- music
- television drama
- advertising
- animation
- science-fiction film
- lifestyle and celebrity
- news
- comedy.

Note that a new External Assessment topic is set by the Awarding Body, WJEC, every two years but it will be one from the above list.

Assessment Objectives

Assessment Objectives are the criteria that the Awarding Body, WJEC, uses to assess your capabilities. There are four Assessment Objectives in GCSE Media Studies. It is useful to remember what these are so that you are sure of covering them when you prepare for your exam and work on your textual investigations and media production. They are:

- **AO1: Knowledge and Understanding** – this is what you can remember and how you present your work. Using the right terminology, for example, or being able to deconstruct a media text thoroughly.
- **AO2: Analysis and Response** – this is being able to investigate and explore something rather than just describe it, and make your own responses to the media you are studying.
- **AO3: Research and Planning** – this covers all the planning you do to understand how and why something was created for the audience to experience and use.
- **AO4: Production and Evaluation** – here you will be expected to make media texts and be able to critically evaluate them.

Your teacher will be able to explain how these Assessment Objectives work in more detail, but don't forget about them, and remember that these are the objectives you will be tested against.

And finally ...

As students of the media you will often be asked when investigating media texts to make the familiar unfamiliar; to treat those everyday films, magazines, television programmes, computer games or web pages as objects of study and apply the concepts and ideas outlined in this book.

In making your own media texts you will use these investigations to produce exciting media products which could include short films, advertisements, newspapers and magazines or web pages. You have at your disposal an array of digital technologies from such familiar objects as mobile phones with cameras (you could make digital stories, or Bluetooth your pictures into 'comic life' to create your own comics) to Photoshop, to create stunning CD covers or film posters.

So, enjoy investigating and creating. Get active, get thinking, get making!

Film

Your learning

In this chapter you will learn about:

- film theory: genre, narrative, representation
- film technology in relation to film-making, marketing and viewing
- film promotion, looking especially at posters, trailers and websites
- the convergent media nature of film including marketing and distribution, advertising, magazines, the Internet and television
- studying films: making films and textual investigation – a case-study approach.

Genre

In film, exploring the ways certain **conventions** or **characteristics** are used to create style and appeal is important.

1. *Working on your own, write down your two favourite and two least favourite films.*

2. *Now combine your chosen films into two class lists.*
   - *Do the same types of film – such as adventure, fantasy, science fiction, romantic comedy and Westerns – appear on both lists?*
   - *Were the same types of film popular with both boys and girls?*

Genre conventions or **characteristics** The typical features in a film which show the audience what genre it is.

Genre A type of media text (programme, film, CD cover, etc.) with certain predictable characteristics.

Audience People who are reading, looking at, listening to or using a media text.

Did you find it easy to say what types of film were your favourites? If so, it is probably because you already know a lot about **genre** (a French word meaning 'type'). You can probably tell, from a few seconds of a TV trailer or even from a poster, what genre a new film is likely to be, and you will have certain expectations as a result.

What film genre do the following words suggest:

- explosions
- car chases
- time pressure?

You probably thought 'Action' before you even read the second word! Media producers rely on your ability to recognise genre when they promote new films, to arouse **audience** interest, expectation and anticipation.

Films are often a mix of several genres – known as cross-genres or **hybrid** genres – to attract the widest possible target audience. For example, *Cloverfield* (2008) seems to be a simple action movie aimed at fans of the action genre. However, it also uses the genre characteristics of:

- science fiction – the largely unseen threat is an alien monster
- documentary – the footage is shot on a documentary-style hand-held camera
- teen horror movie – the characters are all young people who face unexpected and tense threats.

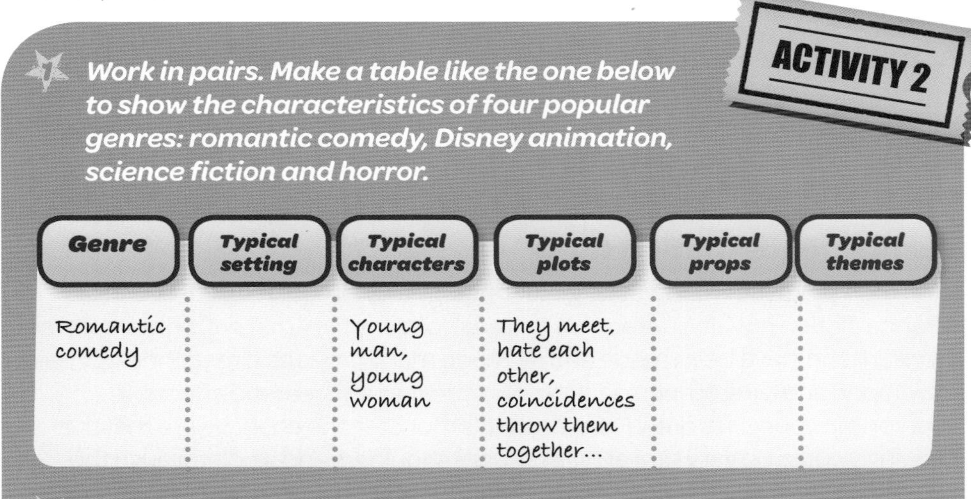

ACTIVITY 2

1. *Work in pairs. Make a table like the one below to show the characteristics of four popular genres: romantic comedy, Disney animation, science fiction and horror.*

Genre	Typical setting	Typical characters	Typical plots	Typical props	Typical themes
Romantic comedy		Young man, young woman	They meet, hate each other, coincidences throw them together...		

2. *Now share your answers with another pair. Add any good ideas that you missed.*

Key terms

Hybrid When at least two genres are brought together, for example, the superhero movie combines the genres of superhero comics and action films.

CD-ROM Extra!

Trailers

Open the CD in the back of this book and click on the icon below to open a link to see some examples of film trailers.

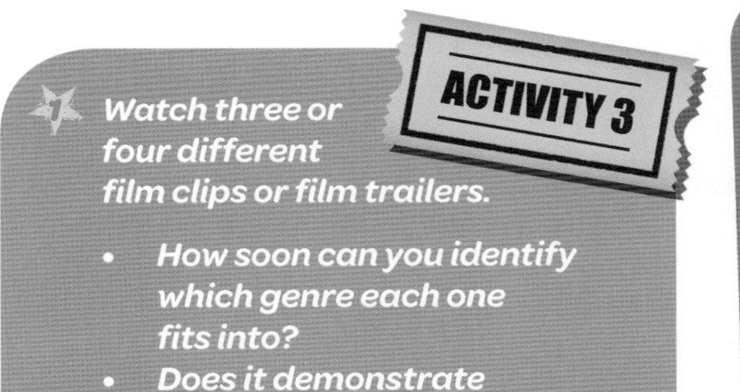

ACTIVITY 3

1. *Watch three or four different film clips or film trailers.*
   - *How soon can you identify which genre each one fits into?*
   - *Does it demonstrate cross-genre (hybrid) characteristics?*
   - *What type of audience will each one attract? For example, young or old, male or female?*

Science fiction is a genre that has at its heart some form of technology which is not yet possible, but which could be one day. It is a popular genre, although it has not always drawn the huge audiences it does today. For that reason, it is an interesting genre to study, to see how it has developed and from what roots.

The roots of science fiction

Literary heritage

Science-fiction novels were popular long before film was even invented. Early sci-fi novels include *Twenty Thousand Leagues Under the Sea* by Jules Verne (1870) and *The Time Machine* (1895) by H.G. Wells. Even earlier, Mary Shelley's *Frankenstein* was published in 1818 when she was only 21. It is an early example of a hybrid, it being part horror and part science fiction. It told the story of a scientist who discovered how to create life and make a creature in his own likeness, with terrible consequences.

Early science-fiction films

With their fantastic worlds, strange technology and almost magical events, science-fiction novels offered rich material for early film-makers. Some, such as *Frankenstein*, have been made and re-made many times as film technology has developed and offered increasingly sophisticated and realistic effects. If everyone in your class drew Frankenstein's monster, the chances are that the drawings would be very similar (with square shoulders and a bolt through the neck!) and based on the first film representation of the monster, played by Boris Karloff in 1933!

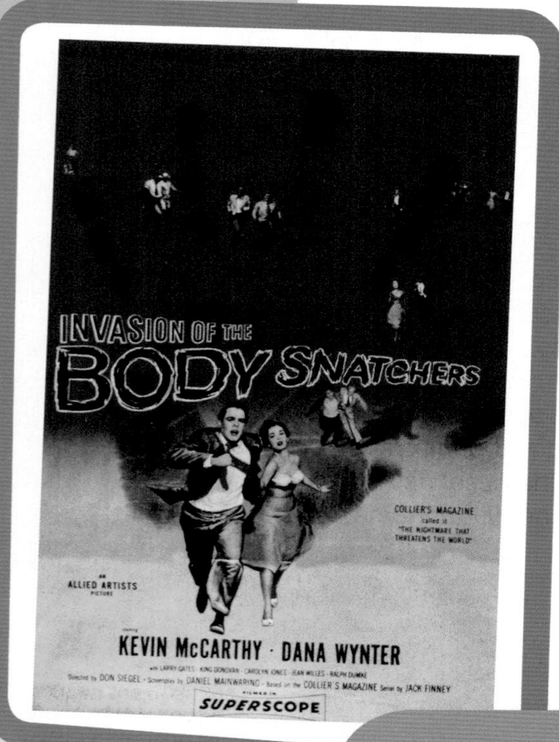

Science fiction as a social symbol

Because science-fiction narratives often include exploration, danger and new technology, they have been used to explore issues causing concern in society. For example:

- *Invasion of the Bodysnatchers* (1956) seemed to be about an alien invasion, but was also about the McCarthy trials in the 1950s, when many American citizens were questioned about their possible Communist sympathies.
- American science-fiction films in the 1950s and 1960s, such as *Dr Strangelove or: How I Learned to Stop Worrying and Love the Bomb* (1964), explored the fear that nuclear technology would result in the destruction of the world.
- The X-Men comics, and later the film trilogy, seem to be about humans and mutants, but are also texts that have been used to explore attitudes to prejudice, such as racial hatred.

ACTIVITY 4

If you can, look at some X-Men comics together with some scenes from X-Men the movie. How do these science-fiction texts communicate messages about human prejudice?

The blockbuster science-fiction film

Until the early 1990s, science-fiction film was regarded as a minority genre which only longstanding fans watched. Then James Cameron produced the special effects-driven *Terminator 2* in 1991, Steven Spielberg produced *Jurassic Park* in 1993 and Roland Emmerich wrote and directed *Stargate* in 1994. All these films were marketed to audiences as cross-genres of action with science fiction. With a big budget and special effects, Emmerich followed *Stargate* in 1996 with *Independence Day*, and science fiction was established as a hugely exciting and action-packed genre for teenagers.

Blockbuster A film that has a huge budget and is expected to be a hit, so-called because of the long queues around the block to see successful films.

Science-fiction films continue to be big hits today

ACTIVITY 5

1. *Using the Internet as a starting point, find out as much as you can about the big blockbuster science-fiction films from the past few years. Which directors and stars have become associated with science-fiction films?*
2. *Which science-fiction films do you think most teenagers prefer? Can you explain why?*
3. *Try to decide what top five ingredients make a science-fiction film really popular.*

Representations in science fiction

Key terms

Representation How people, places, events or ideas are represented or portrayed to audiences in media texts. Sometimes this is simplistically through stereotypes so the audience can see immediately what is meant, and sometimes the meanings are less obvious.

Stereotypical Showing groups of people in terms of certain widely held but over-simplified characteristics, for example, showing women as nagging housewives.

Representation is an important word in Media Studies. Representations of people are usually designed to make them as believable as possible, but if you look closely at representations of key social groups, such as women, men, teenagers, ethnic groups, old people, you will see that they are often quite **stereotypical**. Many representations of teenagers show them as being disrespectful, moody and selfish – this is obviously a very narrow view of teenagers!

ACTIVITY 6

1. *Look at a range of film clips in two or three science-fiction films. Try to identify different ways in which people are represented.*
2. *Now refine your observations by making a list to show how similar social groups (women, men, teenagers, ethnic groups, old people) are generally represented.*
3. *Try to suggest examples of representations that are not stereotypical but seem to be genuinely convincing and 'realistic'.*

When discussing character it is helpful to consider the views of Vladimir Propp, a theorist who wrote about characters in narratives. He suggested that every story had characters in certain roles: hero, heroine or princess, villain, donor or mentor and helper (see below to find out more about these roles). Science fiction can represent groups of people in unusual ways by allowing them to fulfil unexpected roles in societies that are wholly invented, such as the character of the alien.

Representations of women

Science fiction has offered women the opportunity to break away from the stereotypical role of the heroine as a helpless 'princess' who needs to be rescued by the hero. Ripley in Ridley Scott's *Alien* (1979) and Sarah Connor in *Terminator* (1984) were given lead roles who had real power and strength and were often central to the meaning and development of the narrative. It could be argued that such women play the hero role rather than the heroine.

Lara Croft in *Tomb Raider* – hero not heroine?

ACTIVITY 7

In small groups, find out about some or all of these characters. Present your findings as a display of images with accompanying factfiles.

- *Lara Croft in* Tomb Raider *(2001)*
- *Sarah Connor in* Terminator 2 *(1991)*
- *Ripley in* Alien Resurrection *(1997)*
- *Lyndsay in* The Abyss *(1989)*
- *Princess Amidala in* Star Wars I, II and III *(1999, 2002 and 2005)*
- *Trinity in* The Matrix *trilogy (1999–2003)*

Representations of aliens

One of the most interesting conventions of science fiction is the presence of some amazingly memorable aliens! Try jotting down as many as you can in one minute.

Sometimes taking 'human' form, sometimes robot, sometimes imaginative life-forms from other planets, aliens allow film-makers to explore different patterns of behaviour, language and customs. The essential thing about aliens is that they are different from us. It is not hard to see that aliens are often used as a symbol for themes of belonging and for being different. They can also be a way for film-makers to explore social problems, such as prejudice, in a subtle way.

ACTIVITY 8

Create your own alien. You can make it friendly or hostile, but you must label your design by pointing out key features that make it different from a human. Before you start, consider what you've already learned about the representations of aliens!

Extend your design by writing a paragraph describing how the alien responds to humans, and what would happen if it came to Earth.

*Other commonly found representations in science-fiction films are: scientists, **stock characters** and captains or other leadership figures. Choose one of these representations and investigate its role in one or two films of your choice. Share your findings with the class as a presentation or display.*

Key terms

Stock character A supporting character who is often quite stereotypical and whose job it is to support the lead characters, to be saved by them or to die!

Investigating science-fiction films

Investigating a film is similar to reading a book, and calls upon similar analytical skills. First, however, you must know the key features of film language, and then be able to work out what it means. Use this checklist to help you to look for the most important features in a science-fiction film:

- *Characters* (including aliens) will have clear roles and purposes in the narrative.
- *Costumes* are important – especially in future worlds.
- *Settings* (the locations where the action takes place) are part of the created world and often involve **special effects**.
- *Colours* are important and are often symbolic. For example, neon green often symbolises 'the alien'.
- *Soundtrack* is a vital clue to suggesting mood, theme and key moments.
- *Conventions* such as space, jargon, gadgets, weapons, etc. all build up the understanding of the narrative.
- *Special effects* may play a huge part – look out for animation, CGI (computer-generated imagery – see page 117, clever use of camera angles, action sequences.

Key terms

Special effects Exciting and dynamic visual or sound effects used to create impact in films.

Examiner's tip

Your investigation of science-fiction clips could form the basis of an excellent piece of genre or representation investigation for part of the Controlled Assessment.

ACTIVITY 9

Practise your exploration skills in science fiction. Watch clips from a range of science-fiction flms. Make notes on the conventions, themes and characters as you go, using a table like the one below. An example has been given to get you started.

Name of film	Conventions	Themes	Characters
Sunshine	Space travel Cut off from Earth	How far humans will go for new experiences	Captain Space crew

You could present your notes as an essay, report or presentation. Try to explain what common themes you recognised, what you noticed about characters and anything you noticed about different approaches to the science-fiction genre.

Key terms

Film pitch An idea for a new film which is presented to film producers. This usually involves ideas for a plot, possible actors, promotion and marketing.

Prepare a developed film pitch, based around the following idea:

New technology has made space travel even easier. Led by a female Captain and a male First Officer, NASA launches a revolutionary spaceship that can travel through the universe using the technique of 'space-folding' making it possible to travel vast distances. The journey is very exciting, and takes the crew to a new world where the inhabitants have strange but seemingly peaceful customs. The humans then realise that all is not as it first appeared and must work out a plan to escape and get back to Earth – but not without tragedy, love and an unexpected twist of fate before the end of the film.

1. ***Give your film a title and explain its meaning.***
2. ***Cast the main parts and explain your choices.***
3. ***Outline the narrative more fully, explaining all the interesting details.***
4. ***Design the film poster.***
5. ***If you are going to develop this work into a Controlled Assessment piece, plan the promotion campaign for the film. This could include: storyboard or trailer, merchandise designs, soundtrack CD cover and DVD cover.***

If you are stuck for a title, you may wish to use 'Beyond the stars' or 'Far from home'

Narrative

Understanding **narrative** is an important part of any Media Studies course – this applies to many media texts, and not just film.

Narrative A story or account.

How narratives are organised

When discussing narrative, it is helpful to consider Russian theorist Tzvetan Todorov. He devised a way of analysing narratives according to the way they move forward through different stages. Todorov suggested that many narratives, regardless of their genre, could be broken into specific stages for analysis. Read the stages below then the extract that follows.

Todorov's Narrative Stages

Equilibrium – the setting is established, key character(s) are introduced and the storyline is set up.

Disruption – oppositional character(s) appear and the story takes a particular direction.

Recognition of disruption – the lives of characters and events are interwoven. Tension builds throughout this section, which is often the longest.

Attempt to repair disruption – the highest point of tension after which there is a change in dynamic.

Reinstatement of equilibrium – matters are sorted out, problems are solved and questions answered.

Emily was tired of watching wimpy princes trying to get rid of the local dragon, so she decided to have a go herself. She soon came upon the dragon, who was singeing the top of a freckle-faced boy's head.

Being a resourceful princess, Emily set a trap for the dragon and then tricked him into following her.

'You're just a silly girl, and even though it's hardly worth it, I'm going to toast you to a crisp and have you for pudding!' boomed the dragon. Just then, the branches he was standing on gave way, and he fell down a very deep well, his fire put out once and for all.

Emily returned to the boy.

'What's your name?' she asked.

'Prince Matthew,' said the boy.

'That'll do nicely,' said Emily. 'Where do you live?'

'In Happy-Ever-After,' he replied.

'That'll do nicely too,' said Emily.

And with that, she and Matthew rode off together to Happy-Ever-After.

Narrative structure The way a story is organised and shaped in terms of time and events.

You may well ask why this children's fairy story is in a book on GCSE Media Studies. The answer is that the **narrative structure** suggested by Todorov fits this story perfectly.

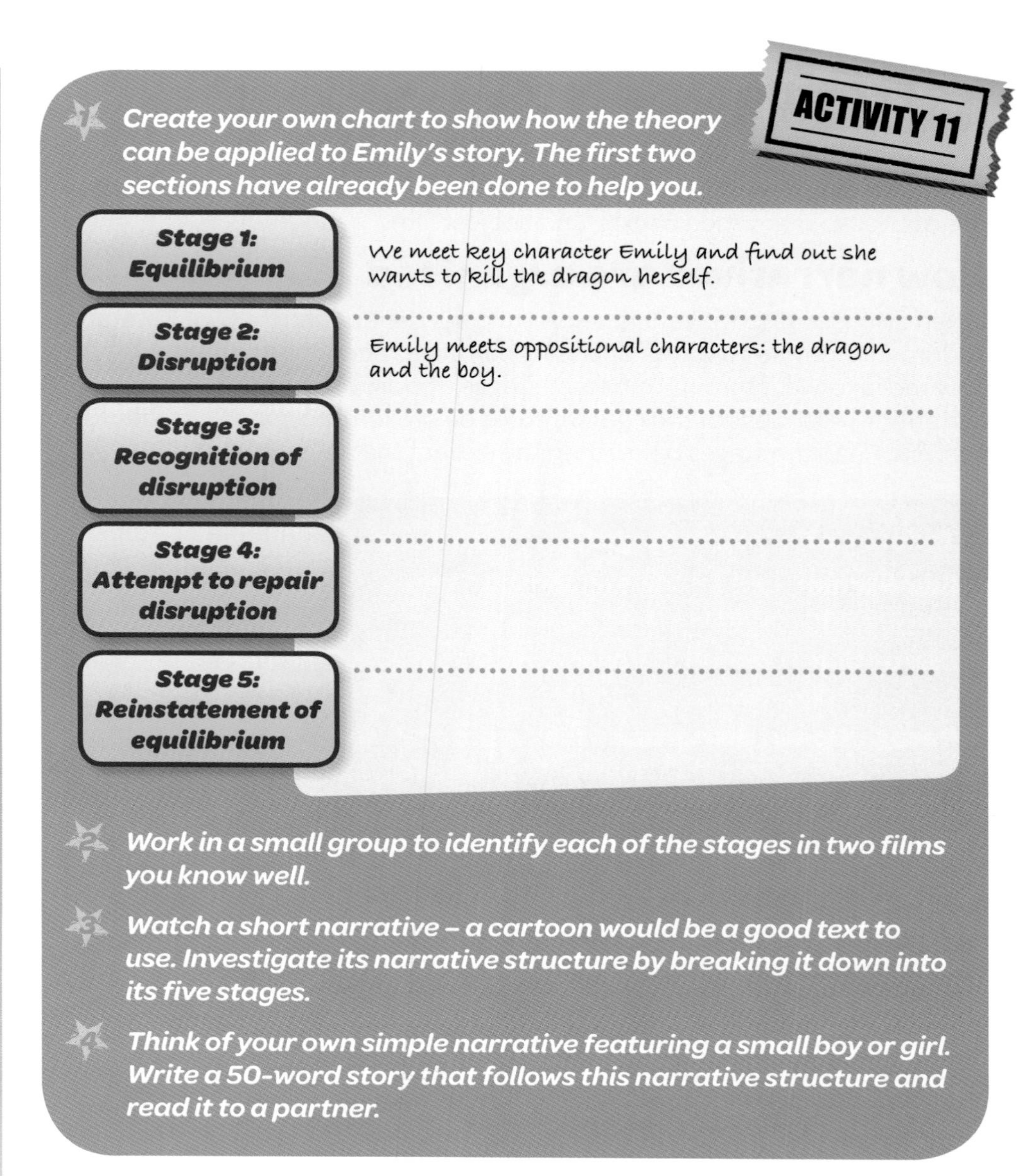

ACTIVITY 11

1. ***Create your own chart to show how the theory can be applied to Emily's story. The first two sections have already been done to help you.***

Stage 1: Equilibrium	We meet key character Emily and find out she wants to kill the dragon herself.
Stage 2: Disruption	Emily meets oppositional characters: the dragon and the boy.
Stage 3: Recognition of disruption	
Stage 4: Attempt to repair disruption	
Stage 5: Reinstatement of equilibrium	

2. ***Work in a small group to identify each of the stages in two films you know well.***
3. ***Watch a short narrative – a cartoon would be a good text to use. Investigate its narrative structure by breaking it down into its five stages.***
4. ***Think of your own simple narrative featuring a small boy or girl. Write a 50-word story that follows this narrative structure and read it to a partner.***

Playing with narratives

Not all narratives fit into the straightforward structure suggested by Todorov, especially if they are trying to do something different or unpredictable. For example, in the film *Back To The Future* (1985) directed by Steven Spielberg, a boy travels back in time to meet the scientist who invented time travel. The stages of the narrative in this film are not in chronological order. Can you think of any other examples of unpredictable narratives?

The correct term for something that does not fit a recognised theory is a **subversion**. You may recognise these subversion techniques:

- *Flashback* – where a section of the film is referred back to, for example, *The Incredible Hulk* (2008) directed by Louis Leterrier.
- *Flashforward* – where a section of the film from the future is shown before it would normally have happened, for example, *Inside Man* (2006) directed by Spike Lee.

Key terms

Subversion When a technique is used which does not fit a theory or the usual way of doing something (for example, when a twist takes the narrative in a new direction).

- *Twist* – where part of the film (often the end) is unpredictable or even shocking, for example, *The Happening* (2008) directed by M. Night Shyamalan.
- *Parallel narratives* – where the lives of characters move alongside each other for some of the film without them meeting, for example, *Crash* (2004) directed by Paul Haggis.

Audience involvement

Audiences enjoy texts most when they are really involved in them. When they are genuinely hooked into the text's narrative and development, it is as if they are actually part of it. You can see why this is so important – someone who is really involved in a text is much less likely to switch it off or put it back on the shelf.

Reading facial expression is crucial to understanding a character's reaction

Here are some techniques that help an audience to become involved or positioned in a film or television text.

- Point-of-view shots – the camera adopts the position of a character within the text. This can be an over-the-shoulder shot, looking at whatever the character is looking at, or a shot from the point of view of the character. This is particularly powerful when the character is experiencing a strong emotion – the viewer is more likely to feel their emotion when taking their point of view.
- Reaction shots – the camera moves to an extreme close-up of a character's face to show their reaction to something that has happened.
- Insert shots – this technique gives the audience extra or privileged information that one or more characters may not yet know, for example, in a two-set scene with two characters in different locations. The audience knows what is happening to each of them when the characters themselves do not.
- Shot reverse-shot – the camera alternates between two characters to show their building relationship (whether positive or negative), often as a conversation is taking place between them. This is a common technique in dramas where the inter-relationship between characters is important. The camera acts as a third person in shot reverse-shot, giving the audience the impression that they are turning their heads from one character to the other.

These three images demonstrate the shot reverse-shot technique

ACTIVITY 12

Divide into groups. Look again at Emily's story on page 9. Each group should prepare to re-tell the story, using one or more subversions. Change the original version so that the narrative no longer follows the same path. The following suggestions may help you:

- ***Flashback – start the story from the moment when Emily is facing the dragon.***
- ***Flashforward – begin the story with a dream sequence in which Emily faces a fire-breathing beast.***
- ***Twist – Emily does not have to be human!***
- ***Parallel narratives – tell Emily's story side by side with Prince Matthew's (or the dragon's) story. This could make the audience feel differently towards them.***

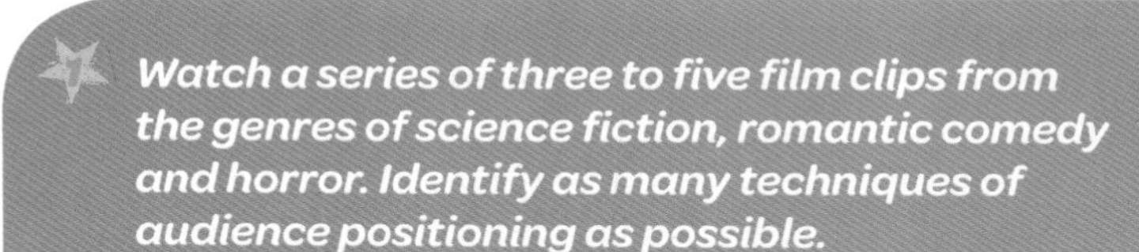

1. ***Watch a series of three to five film clips from the genres of science fiction, romantic comedy and horror. Identify as many techniques of audience positioning as possible.***
2. ***Using a still camera, create a series of shots which demonstrate each of the audience positioning techniques. Display them in your classroom with an imaginary narrative situation written underneath each one. You can see an example in the photographs on page 11.***

A minicam

Additional camera terms and definitions

A lot of time is spent on setting up every scene in a film. It is important to position the cameras in just the right way to capture on film exactly what the director wants the audience to see. In addition to the techniques mentioned already, here are some other camera shots that you will be able to identify in the films you study.

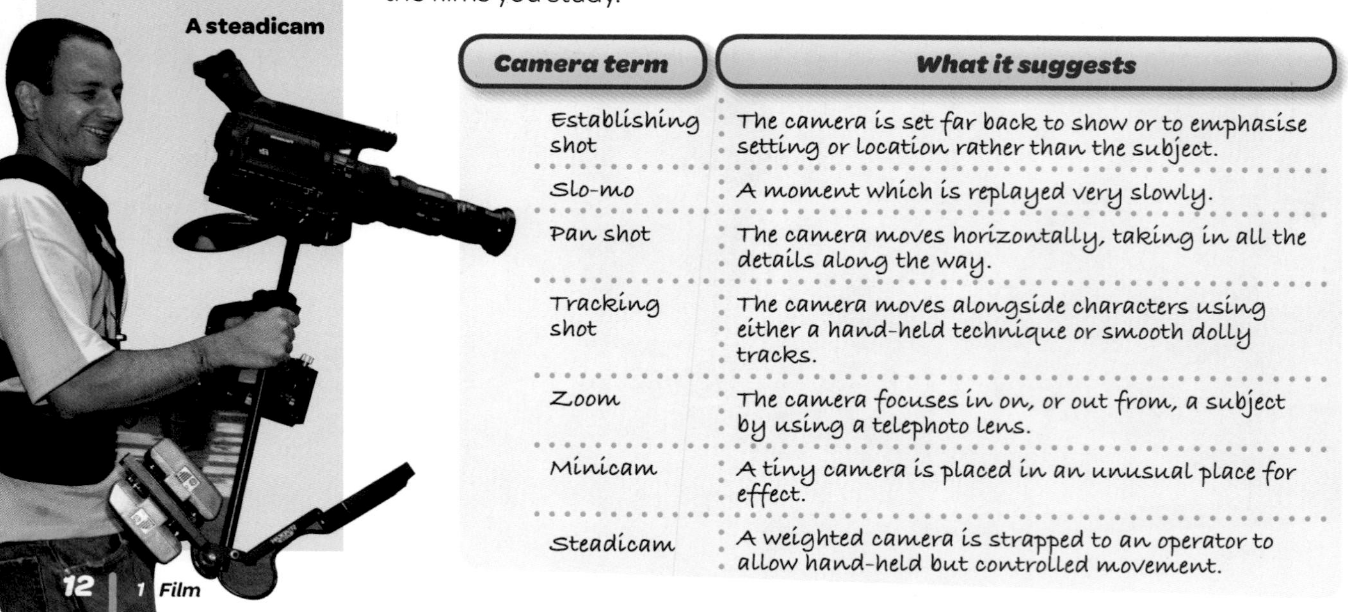

A steadicam

Camera term	What it suggests
Establishing shot	The camera is set far back to show or to emphasise setting or location rather than the subject.
Slo-mo	A moment which is replayed very slowly.
Pan shot	The camera moves horizontally, taking in all the details along the way.
Tracking shot	The camera moves alongside characters using either a hand-held technique or smooth dolly tracks.
Zoom	The camera focuses in on, or out from, a subject by using a telephoto lens.
Minicam	A tiny camera is placed in an unusual place for effect.
Steadicam	A weighted camera is strapped to an operator to allow hand-held but controlled movement.

Intertextuality

Have you ever experienced the thrill of watching a film and recognising a reference to another film? This type of link between two texts is known as an **intertextual reference**.

Do you recognise the phrase 'I'll be back'? Where have you heard it? It is, of course, used in all *Terminator* films, but has also been used intertextually in other films such as *Last Action Hero* (1993) when Arnold Schwarzenegger says 'I'll be back... Ha! Bet you didn't expect me to say that!'

The UK Film Council reported in 2007 that 'I'll be back' is the most often used line from a film in everyday conversation!

Intertextual references can be visual as well. You can find a good example of this in *Toy Story 2* (1999). The toys are riding around Al's toy barn in a Barbie tour guide car and Rex the dinosaur is running behind them, his reflection clearly seen in the wing mirror. This is an intertextual reference to the scene in *Jurassic Park* (1993) when the T-rex can be seen in the wing mirror chasing the tour guide vehicle – in this case, with the intention of eating the passengers!

The story of *Bridget Jones's Diary* (2001) is full of intertextual references to Jane Austen's *Pride and Prejudice*, although the settings and the characters of the heroines could hardly be more different. The basic storyline is similar: girl meets and hates boy but after many mishaps realises his true worth and marries him.

Key terms

Intertextual reference When one media text mimics or refers to another media text in a way that many consumers will recognise.

TIP

Using a chart, table or annotation to present textual investigation for research and planning tasks will help you to control the presentation of the investigation.

ACTIVITY 14

1. *Watch the first ten minutes of one of these films:* Star Wars IV: A New Hope *(1997),* The Truman Show *(1998) or* Saving Private Ryan *(1998). Look for evidence of genre characteristics, narrative structure, audience positioning and carefully set-up camerawork.*
2. *Present your findings as a table, chart, report or essay. For example, you could set out your findings in a table like the one below.*

Film	Genre characteristics	Narrative structure	Audience positioning	Camerawork
The Truman Show	Orchestral music, realistic setting and convincing dress codes suggest a drama			The camera is used in very unusual ways – first as a way of positioning the film audience, but also (through secret mini-cameras) to show what the TV audience are seeing

Film technology

Film-making technology

Today most directors use small, light (and very portable) cameras for filming, which also allows for digital editing software to be used. Such editing is known as non-linear editing, which means that footage can be shot, cut up and ordered out of sequence on a computer. Because it is fairly easy to use, it has led to a massive rise in low-budget, independent films being made. You may be an independent film-maker yourself, or you may have simple film-making technology in your school or college. (See the Controlled Assessment chapter pages 194–199, which include ideas and tips for film-making.)

Film-viewing technology

Screen size, sound quality and the comfort of film viewing have changed remarkably over time. Look at and discuss the three different film-viewing places pictured below. How do these different places affect your appreciation of the film?

A traditional Odeon cinema

The IMAX cinema in London

A state-of-the-art home cinema system

Film flashback

When you look at any key area of Media Studies, it is always a good idea to understand its background. For film, it is important to have a grasp of how the film industry's technology has changed over time in response to changing patterns of audience response and expectations.

Charlie Chaplin in the silent film *The Gold Rush* (1925)

1894

First moving pictures were screened to audiences. They were very short and featured actual events happening, so they were called 'actualities'. Examples included *The Sneeze* and *The Kiss*.

Early 1900s

Films became longer and began to tell stories. Some even used early special effects. A good example is *A Trip to the Moon* (1902) by Georges Méliès. Films were silent, with on-screen text.

Hollywood began to dominate film production by setting up powerful (and rich) film studios. This was known as the Studio System.

1927

The first 'talking' film – *The Jazz Singer* – was released, changing film production for ever.

1930s

The first films to use Technicolor were produced. Two good examples were Oscar contenders *Gone with the Wind* and *The Wizard of Oz* in 1939.

1950s

The popularity of epic films resulted in screens being bigger – an early form of today's widescreen technology.

1977

Star Wars IV: A New Hope was the first film to use Dolby surround sound.

1982

Disney's *Tron* was the first film to use CGI (computer-generated imagery).

1999

Star Wars I: The Phantom Menace was the first film to be filmed mostly using digital cameras – which meant that digital editing was used too.

2001

We will see more developments that will make films seem increasingly realistic. IMAX 3D screens will use Sony's new stereoscopic Real-D technology to make film viewing a virtual reality experience!

2008

Christopher Nolan's *The Dark Knight* was the first film to use IMAX technology in the shooting of the film.

21st century

Peter Jackson used breakthrough CGI technology, called motion-capture animation, to create the realistic character Gollum for *The Lord of the Rings* trilogy. He did this by putting sensors on actor Andy Serkis and recording his movements onto a computer-generated character.

CGI was used to create this sabre-toothed tiger in the 2008 film *10,000 BC*

Film promotion and marketing in the 21st century

Film posters

Posters and trailers have been used to promote films for many years, but the nature of film marketing and promotion has changed a great deal since the 1990s. However, posters are still a vital part of the marketing process, so it is always worthwhile studying their key **conventions**.

Poster conventions

- an eye-catching image or images – often related to characters (and the stars in the film) or the setting of the film
- the title of the film, carefully constructed in terms of font style, colour, size and placement: a lot of thought goes into the title – it is meant to be memorable, and also to suggest the genre of the film
- a tagline for the film – which is like the catchy slogans of advertisements – offering another clue to the genre and main themes or content of the film
- the names of well-known or key people connected to the film. These are usually the lead actors but may also be the director or producer.
- **endorsements** from other media productions (for example, *Empire* magazine) giving their comments such as 'an unmissable film'
- details of any award nominations or awards that the film has already won. These will be placed clearly on the poster.
- The production 'blurb' – information, in tiny print, that lists the production and distribution companies as well as other information.

Key terms

Conventions The typical characteristics of a particular type of text.

Endorsement Giving approval to something.

CD-ROM Extra!

Film posters

Open the CD in the back of this book and click on the icon below to see enlarged versions of the film posters on page 17.

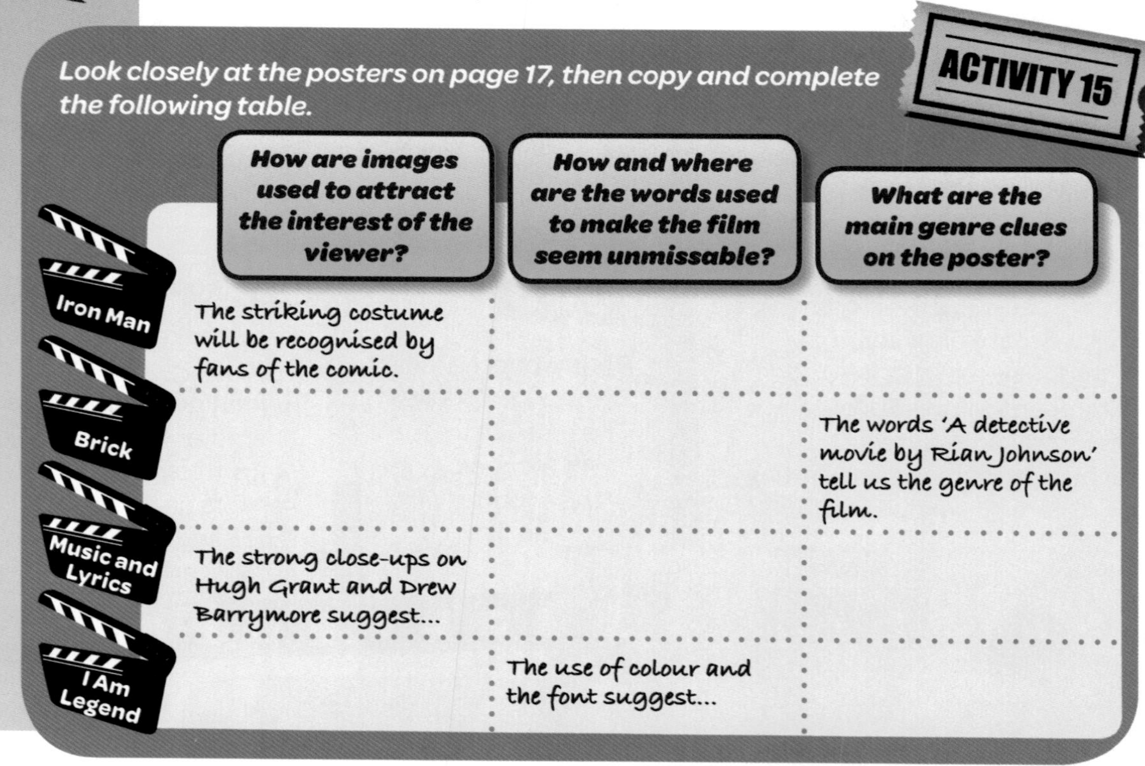

ACTIVITY 15

Look closely at the posters on page 17, then copy and complete the following table.

	How are images used to attract the interest of the viewer?	How and where are the words used to make the film seem unmissable?	What are the main genre clues on the poster?
Iron Man	The striking costume will be recognised by fans of the comic.		
Brick			The words 'A detective movie by Rian Johnson' tell us the genre of the film.
Music and Lyrics	The strong close-ups on Hugh Grant and Drew Barrymore suggest...		
I Am Legend		The use of colour and the font suggest...	

DOWNEY JR.
HOWARD
BRIDGES
PALTROW
IRON MAN
5.2.08

THE BRAIN
"The foil with the inside track."
BRICK
A detective movie by Rian Johnson
brickmovie.net
FOCUS
WINNER | SPECIAL JURY PRIZE | ORIGINALITY OF VISION | SUNDANCE 2005

hugh grant drew barrymore
music and lyrics
VALENTINE'S DAY

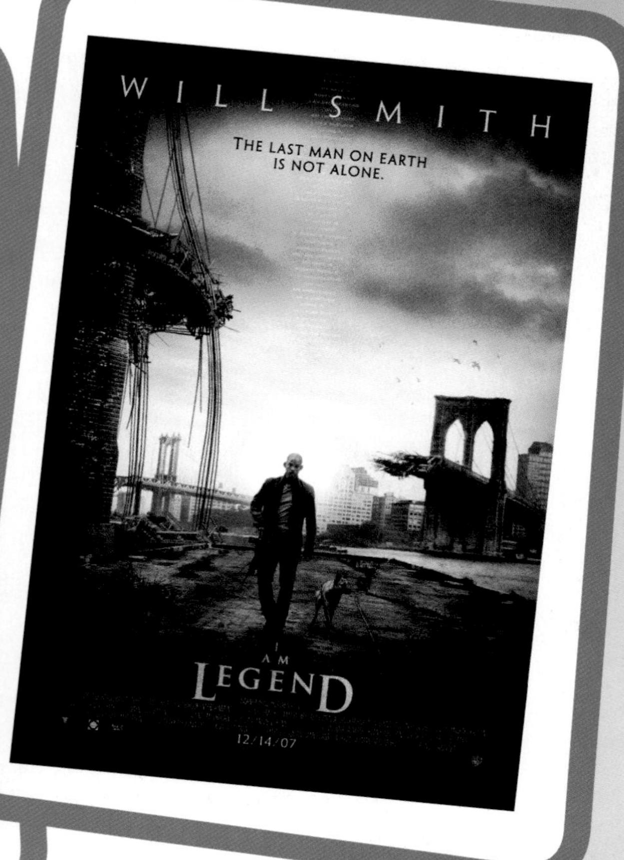
WILL SMITH
THE LAST MAN ON EARTH IS NOT ALONE.
I AM LEGEND
12/14/07

ACTIVITY 16

Using your table from Activity 15, compare how at least two of the posters on page 17 use different techniques to appeal to their audiences.

As you present your answer, it might help you to think about where you might see film posters. For example, an obvious place is in the cinema itself, where they are usually to be found on walls, or blown up to become 3D cardboard displays. However, they also appear on billboards or bus shelters.

Film trailers

Trailers are an important part of film marketing. They are similar to advertisements in that they promote a product – in this case the film. Trailers often have big budgets because film studios understand that the trailer is one of the most important ways of creating immediate interest in a film before it is released. Like posters, there are often several versions of trailers made – the earlier ones are known as 'teaser' trailers, because they are meant to tease audiences with only a few exciting details. Closer to the release date, trailers give more information, including the all-important release date.

Look closely at the following list of trailer conventions:

Trailer conventions

- Trailers include key moments from the film which are not placed in the sequence of the film, and do not give away any crucial plot details (some trailers are criticised for giving away too many details).
- The title of the film is not usually put on screen until the end of the trailer, often followed by a release date.
- The names of the main stars are put on screen early on in the trailer. This is important as it lets audiences know who they can expect to see in the film. Audiences will often decide they want to see a film just because of the stars in it.
- Sometimes the names of the director and/or producer are included, with phrases such as 'from the director/makers of....' This helps the audience to make connections between the film being trailed and previously successful and recognised films.
- Many mainstream films will use a powerful voice-over that draws our attention to the key points of the film.
- On-screen text gives important information about the film, including the stars, director/producers, tag line, title and release date. Notice the style of this text and how it is often accompanied by a musical beat.
- Music is essential in trailers as it can suggest the genre, style and plot of the film. Look at how music is used cleverly to bring all the elements of the trailer together.

1. *Watch at least four film trailers. Choose one of them and make a timeline of the key moments in it.*
2. *Watch all four trailers again. Give each one a star award (five stars is the highest rating) according to how much you feel you want to see the film after watching the trailer. Explain your reasons for giving the awards.*
3. *Choose one trailer again. Use the Internet to find the promotional poster that corresponds to the film trailer you've chosen.*
   - *Make a table like the one below to show the main similarities and differences between the poster and the trailer. Some ideas for the* I Am Legend *film trailer have already been given to get you started.*
   - *Can you suggest reasons for the similarities and differences?*

	Poster	Trailer
How stars/characters are represented	A single image of the lead star is shown as the central image – the film is using the star's 'pull' to attract audiences.	The lead star is shown in a series of shots with other actors – the trailer shows us how the star interacts with others and what his/her character type is.
Use of	The poster uses a classic black serif font that suggests the serious and realistic nature of the film – it also supports the idea of the word 'Legend' being grand and memorable.	
Genre clues		
Narrative clues		
Characters and relationships		

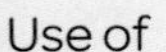

Trailers

Open the CD in the back of this book and click on the icon below to open a link to see some examples of film trailers.

Key terms

Typography The choice of font style and size, graphic design and layout.

CD-ROM **Extra!**

Indiana Jones

Open the CD in the back of this book and click on the icon below to open a link to the Indiana Jones website.

HTML

Film websites – the Internet

This section has already pointed out the importance of Internet technology in film marketing. Most films today have their own websites with 'extra features' to interest audiences, such as games, facts and trivia about the film, background details on the stars and hyperlinks to the director's commentary, etc.

The Indiana Jones website generates huge interest as the films have been so popular

Film-related websites are also important in giving information to film fans. For example, imdb.com is one of the most visited websites. If you visit the site you will see that you can find out details of any film:

- that has been made
- is being made at the moment
- is planned for production in the near future.

You can research actors, directors, producers or any other film-related personnel. It is an extremely educational (and quite addictive) site.

CD-ROM **Extra!**

imdb.com

Open the CD in the back of this book and click on the icon below to open a link to imdb.com.

HTML

ACTIVITY 18

This activity encourages you to visit and use imdb.com. When the home page comes up, simply look in the search box menu and select the word 'Titles' for a film or 'Names' for a star or director, then type in the title or name in the box next to it to start your search.

You could create 'factfiles' as a class and make a display of the details you discover.

Film-related magazines also have their own websites that are popular with audiences. *Empire* magazine, for example, offers readers and non-readers of the print-based magazine the chance to subscribe to empireonline.co.uk. This site is a weekly updated review of newest releases, awards and 'in-production' projects. It is rapidly becoming more popular than the magazine itself!

Choose an unreleased film and find out as much as you can about it from your chosen website. Ask yourself the following questions.

- ***Does the site try to influence your opinions about the film in some way?***
- ***Are there interactive links within the site to, for example, trailers or interviews?***
- ***Does the site give any exclusive information or gossip about films/stars/directors, etc?***

What are the strengths and weaknesses of the site?

Practise your research skills. Think of a director or actor. Look them up on imdb.com and write down any new information you have gained about them. You could present your findings in a short presentation to your class, including clips of films with which they have been associated.

Compare your research with information given in a film-related magazine. What are the main similarities and differences between the two media areas relating to film?

Distribution

Distribution varies from film to film. Films with big budgets may, in Britain, start with release in big London cinemas and then go on general release. Films which are less highly financed will appear at selected cinemas. Some films never make it to the cinema and go 'straight to DVD', either because their quality is thought to be poor, or because there is no money to promote them.

Spending huge amounts of money on making and promoting a film which is expected to be a blockbuster is no guarantee of box-office success. There have been many expensive flops, for example, *Waterworld* (1995), starring Kevin Costner. The film, which was said to have cost over $150 million to make, was disliked by the critics and was not an immediate success with the public (although it is believed to have made money eventually through DVD sales etc.).

Leonardo DiCaprio signing autographs for fans (2007)

There have been surprise successes too. The box office success of *William Shakespeare's Romeo and Juliet* (1996), directed by Baz Luhrmann, was so unexpected that not enough prints of the film were available! One of its stars, Leonardo DiCaprio, became a box-office draw and appeared soon after in the successful film *Titanic* (1997) which won 11 Oscars.

British film *The Full Monty* (1997) was a surprise hit for another reason. It was a low-budget film, so little money was spent on publicity and there was limited distribution. It proved to be a huge hit, mainly because people who saw it found it funny and moving, and told their friends to go and see it. Before long, the film was packing out the cinemas all over Britain and it enjoyed success in the USA too.

Film classification

Before any film can be shown in the cinema or sold as a video or DVD, it must be assessed by a regulatory body to decide which age group it is suitable for. The BBFC classifies films, while OFCOM rates videos and DVDs. You can see the BBFC classification scheme below.

Universal: suitable for everyone.

Video release particularly suitable for pre-school children.

Parental Guidance: anyone can see the film, although some material may be unsuitable for children.

Children under 12 can see the film only if accompanied by an adult.

Not suitable for people under 15.

Not suitable for people under 18.

Video can only be sold through a licensed sex shop.

ACTIVITY 20

Many critics and parents have suggested that the film The Dark Knight *should have been given a 15 certificate instead of a 12A because of its suggestions of violence rather than actual violence. One scene of particular concern was when The Joker holds a knife in a man's mouth, although the audience never sees any actual violence.*

Why do you think suggested violence could have a harmful effect on some audiences?

CD-ROM Extra!

The Dark Knight podcast

Open the CD in the back of this book and click on the icon below to listen to a podcast on **The Dark Knight.**

Film podcasts

Podcasts are audio or audio-visual files which are distributed through downloading or streaming to mobile MP3 players or personal computers. Links to the podcast are usually found on the podcast's website, and are often free to download.

Podcasts are proving to be increasingly relevant in the media area of film. As well as channel re-broadcasting podcasts such as BBC iPlayer, which offer users chances to see films on TV they have missed, film distribution companies sometimes use podcasts as a way of promoting new films, making interviews with stars available and offering film fans a way of responding to new films.

In addition, and making the most of the popularity of film review magazines such as *Empire* and TV review shows, there is a growing interest in film review podcasts. BBC iPlayer, for example, broadcasts a review podcast in its Arts, Media and Culture section, although the most popular example is the Mark Kermode and Simon Mayo Film Reviews podcast. Broadcast originally on Radio 5 Live, the podcast which is free to download is continuing to attract growing numbers of a wide range of users.

ACTIVITY 21

Click on the Mark Kermode and Simon Mayo Radio 5 Film Review podcast link on the CD-ROM and listen to the discussion.

1. *Discuss in a small group the main films reviewed in the podcast. What factors do you think Mark Kermode looks for in a good film? What factors make him critical of a film?*
2. *Working with a partner, choose two films – one of which you both love, and one of which you do not rate highly. Record yourselves discussing the films, as if it were going to be a new podcast, giving reasons for your opinions, and backing them up with references to other films too.*
3. *Share your recordings as a class, and make suggestions to each potential podcaster on ways to improve the quality/ humour/ clarity of the podcast.*

CD-ROM Extra!

Film podcasts

Open the CD in the back of this book and click on the icon below to open a link to BBC Radio 5's Mark Kermode and Simon Mayo's Film Review podcast website.

This case study considers the convergent media aspects of the film industry.

Merchandise

Films sometimes use promotional toys, gadgets, clothing, franchise deals with food companies, etc. to help market themselves. Sometimes we can own a film, wear a film, take our pens to school in the film pencil case and even *eat* the film! For example, McDonald's often have a deal with Disney where they will pay Disney for the right to give away small film-related toys with their Happy Meals, thus making the meals more appealing and selling more of them. As a result, both McDonald's and Disney profit from the arrangement.

It has been claimed that the global sales of Harry Potter merchandise have made J.K. Rowling almost as much money as the sales of the books themselves. Harry Potter has become a worldwide name thanks, in part, to such a successful international marketing campaign.

Advertisements

Visiting the cinema is an experience that is pleasurable on many levels. Not only do we have the opportunity to watch eagerly awaited films on huge screens with surround sound while sitting in a comfortable seat (with a specially shaped armrest to hold a large fizzy drink!), we can also see the latest big budget advertisements – often as a version made especially for cinema viewing – as well as 'forthcoming releases' (trailers).

When media industries set up relationships with each other (for example, the advertising and film industries), and where each industry offers something to the other, it is called media synergy. Advertisers pay film distributors to advertise their products before their films are screened and, as a result, there is more money for films to be made.

Magazines

Film-related magazines also have an industry relationship with film distributors (another example of media synergy). Distributors are responsible for the marketing of a film and also for setting the release date. They buy space in film magazines to help promote their film and, in return, the magazine sells more copies based on the amount of 'inside information' on up and coming films. Sometimes this can lead to magazines running two different front covers in order to promote sales even more. For example, at the end of 2006, *Narnia: The Lion, the Witch and the Wardrobe* was due to be released on 8 December, while *King Kong* was due to be released on 15 December. *Empire* magazine ran one version of the December issue with a lion on the front, and another version with a gorilla.

The TAGLINE uses the BUZZ WORDS 'amazing' and 'special edition' to make the audience feel that they are getting something unique and valuable. The phrase 'sci-fi' stands out in blue to make a link between the whole edition and the genre of science fiction.

The TITLE BLOCK is red SANS SERIF font on a blue background which suggests both technology and masculinity. The tagline above also links the title block to the genre of science fiction.

A typical Empire magazine cover

The WEBSITE makes it possible for the audience to connect to the publishing company and to see more details about the magazine online.

The words 'Meet the new Spock and Kirk' are like an instruction. Film fans may recognise the names of the characters as the Captain and First Officer of the famous Starship *Enterprise*.

The CENTRAL IMAGE uses a challenging DIRECT MODE OF ADDRESS of two actors looking straight at the reader in character.

The title of the film acts as ANCHORAGE text for the central image which may call on their FORE-KNOWLEDGE of the huge TV show and film franchise.

A special Blu-Ray guide emphasises the magazine as leading the way with film technology and quality films.

A series of PUFFS are used to inform readers about articles connected to key film areas: behind the scenes insights, reviews and polls.

★CASE STUDY★ ACTIVITY

Look at the film pages in a range of magazines. These could include* Empire, Total Film, Total DVD, Heat, the Guardian Weekend *magazine, etc. Discuss how films are marketed in these magazines. You might like to consider the following areas:

- ***How many pages are there in the magazine?***
- ***Who is the likely target audience of the magazine?***
- ***How many pages are devoted to film?***
- ***How many films are given space in the magazine?***
- ***Choose one or two films that are found in most, if not all, the magazines. Compare the different responses of the reviewers to each film.***
- ***Choose your favourite review from one of the magazines. Explore its style and the techniques it uses to appeal to its readers.***

What have you learned?

In this chapter you have learned about:

Texts

- Investigating narratives
- Investigating and comparing posters and trailers
- Exploring websites
- Looking at the construction of film magazine covers

Media language

Genre

- How film genres use clear characteristics to allow audiences to classify and engage with them
- How sub-genres and cross-genres develop
- Case study genre – science fiction. How genres develop over time
- How to include an understanding of genre in coursework

Narrative

- How linear narratives are organised
- How non-linear narratives use subversions
- The importance of character types and their function in narratives
- The importance of audience positioning in narratives

Representation

- How representations lead to stereotyping
- How different social groups can be categorised through representation
- The representation of women in science fiction
- The representation of social issues and events in science fiction

Audiences

- Thinking about target audiences
- Considering audience appeal
- Exploring audience responses and needs
- Discussing the effects of film classification on audiences

Organisational issues

- Film technology in relation to film-making, marketing and viewing
- The key dates of the film industry
- Film promotion, looking especially at posters, trailers and websites

Convergent media

- The convergent nature of film including:
  - marketing and distribution
  - advertising
  - magazines
  - the Internet
  - television

2 Television

Your learning

In this chapter you will learn about:

- television history – public service and commercial broadcasting
- TV production
- the regulation of TV channels and programmes
- channel identity
- investigating opening sequences
- television genres and their appeal to audiences
- the convergent nature of television

ACTIVITY 1

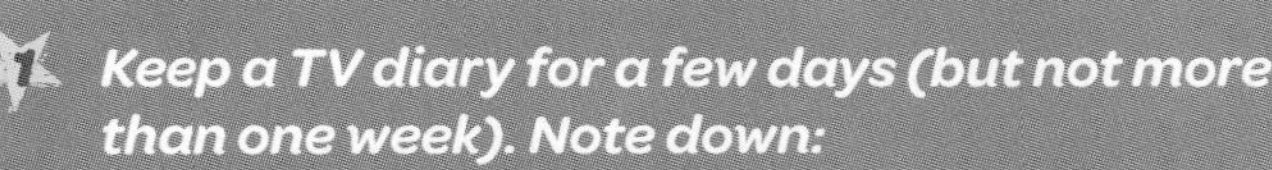

1. *Keep a TV diary for a few days (but not more than one week). Note down:*
   - *when you watch and for how long*
   - *which programmes you actively try to see*
   - *where you watch*
   - *whether you watch alone or with others.*
2. *What would you miss most if you had to spend three months without television:*
   - *particular programmes or types of programme*
   - *the coverage of particular events*
   - *particular channels?*
3. *Do you think having access to the Internet makes having a television unnecessary? What are the main attractions of each?*

Television – a brief history and introduction

Key terms

Target audience
A specific group of people that each media text is aimed at.

From Activity 1, what did you learn about your own viewing habits? Most programmes attract quite specific audiences, and many of the programmes you watch will be aimed at you, the **target audience**. Other programmes you watch are influenced by other factors. For example, you may not have as much choice about what you watch if you are watching television with your family. Who is in charge of the remote control in your home?

If you watch a media text such as a TV programme with focus and attention, it is called *primary* consumption. If you are doing something else (such as homework) while the television is on, it is called *secondary* consumption.

Secondary viewing

1. *Discuss the results of your TV diary (from Activity 1) with some classmates. You may well have many findings that are similar, but you will also find it interesting to discuss the differences.*
2. *Conduct a class survey to find out which channels you watch most frequently.*
3. *Each person should choose their top three favourites out of the following channels and award three marks to the first choice, two to the second and one to the third. Then add up the class marks for each channel.*
4. - *BBC1*
   - *Five*
   - *MTV*
   - *BBC2*
   - *Sky One*
   - *Film Four*
   - *ITV1*
   - *Sky Sports channels*
   - *E4*
   - *Channel 4/S4C*
5. *Which channel logo do you prefer and why?*

Did you find it hard to imagine life without television? You may well have several television sets in your home, including one in your bedroom! Your TV diary will already have shown you how often you turn to the television for your media entertainment.

Less than 60 years ago, it would have been unusual for a family to have even one 20 cm wide black-and-white television set – and it could only transmit one channel! To get a clear idea of the major developments in television history, look at the timeline on the next page.

Television is less than 100 years old

UK television timeline

1922: First BBC radio broadcast

1927: Philo Farnsworth is credited with the invention of the 'television scanning tube', although he first had the idea in 1921 when he was only 14

1936: First BBC television transmission – public service broadcasting financed the licence fee

1939–1945: Second World War – television suspended. Audiences heard news through radio and BBC newsreels

1953: Elizabeth II's coronation. The first mass TV audience. Huge sales of TV sets (often on hire purchase)

1955: ITV first transmitted – commercial broadcasting through advertising revenue

1964: BBC2 first transmitted

1967: First colour TV transmission

1982: C4/S4C first transmitted

1989: Satellite TV first transmitted

1997: C5 first transmitted

1999: First digital broadcasting

2000+: Flat-screen, plasma and HD viewing technology

2002: Digital freeview boxes first introduced

By 2012: Digital transmission only – no more analogue signal

Key terms

Public service broadcaster A channel funded by a licence fee that has to provide a choice of programmes to appeal to all social groups, for example, BBC1.

BBC Charter The official permission from the government for the BBC to charge a licence fee in return for quality programming.

CD-ROM Extra!

Stephen Fry's podcast

Open the CD in the back of this book and click on the icon below to open a link to Stephen Fry's podcasts. Listen to Episode 4, Broadcasting, where he discusses the BBC.

HTML

When the BBC first began transmitting radio programmes in the 1920s and television in the 1930s, it was as a **public service broadcaster**. This means that, in return for the payment of a licence fee, the BBC will provide viewers with a service of programmes. These, the **BBC Charter** states, are guaranteed to 'inform, educate and entertain' and to appeal to as wide an audience as possible. This is known as the *public service remit*.

When ITV first began transmitting television programmes in the 1950s, it was as an independent **commercial broadcaster**. Independent television channels are paid money in return for time slots that advertisers use to promote their products. Such time slots vary in price depending on whether they are during **peak time** (6.00 p.m. to 10.30 p.m.) or not.

ACTIVITY 3

1. *Look at the television schedule for any day of the week in a TV listings magazine. Count up how many programmes on BBC1 and BBC2 are informative, educational and/or entertaining (you may wish to look at the information on the Uses and Gratifications Theory on page 76 before tackling this activity).*
2. *Now look at the programmes that are on the commercial channels listed in Activity 2 during peak time. Can you identify any types of programme which are especially popular?*
3. *Discuss as a class or in small groups whether the BBC should be allowed to continue charging a licence fee. Use information from this activity and the class survey. Start by looking back at your schedules and try to find out what programmes the BBC offers that are different from commercial channels. You may also want to interview your teachers and ask them about their views on the BBC.*

What do you think would happen to viewing choices if every channel was funded by advertising revenue? Advertisers are most interested in buying time slots around or during peak time programmes, when most people are watching. This puts pressure on commercial broadcasting channels to produce more and more of the types of programme that are most popular. What could be the effects of this?

Television production

Television programmes are either made directly by television companies or commissioned from smaller freelance companies. Every role in the making of a TV programme is important – ranging from those in **pre-production** through to **production** and **post-production**. Look at the list of some of the key roles shown on the next page – which ones do you think are the most important? You will find a more thorough list on the CD-ROM.

Key terms

Commercial broadcaster A channel funded by money from advertising, for example, ITV.

Peak time The hours between 6.00 p.m. and 10.30 p.m. when most people are watching television and viewing figures are at their highest.

Key terms

Pre-production Activities at the beginning of the production process, e.g. ideas, bids for finance, storyboards, scriptwriting, planning and designing, set construction, casting and rehearsals.

Production Shooting in purpose-built sets or in outside locations.

Post-production Activities at the end of the production process, e.g. editing, sound dubbing, credits, marketing and promotion, focus groups, trailers, articles and features.

Key roles in television production

Executive producer
arranges finance and oversees the whole project, including editorial decisions.

Producer/Director
is responsible for the setting up and shooting of every scene.

Researcher
for example, ensures all details of location, sets, props and costume are appropriate and accurate for the style and time period of the programme.

Scriptwriter
writes the script for the programme; this could be from an original idea or an adaptation.

Camera operator
responsible for setting up every shot in a scene. This may involve working with other operators for techniques such as shot reverse-shot.

Editor
takes the 'raw footage' shot each day and edits it into a sequence of scenes that tell the story. This can also involve adding music, fades and dissolves.

Production assistant
looks after all administration, including scripts and running orders.

Actors/performers
create believable characters. The success of a programme can depend on audiences appreciating the actors' performances – they are often the most memorable feature of a programme. This also applies to presenters. The most successful programmes usually mean stardom (and pay rises!) for the lead actors or presenters.

All of the above roles are important at different times and in different ways. Ultimately, it is the performance in front of the camera which attracts and keeps audiences, but for those performances to be outstanding, the team behind the camera need to have first done their specialist jobs. A television production is a complex task and planning is absolutely vital. However, some things are unpredictable, no matter how good the plan.

What can go wrong

- Multiple takes are often needed to 'get it right' in front of the camera – look at 'blooper' programmes, which are about moments when actors and presenters do not get it right.
- Live audiences: unpredictability on the part of guests and audiences and having to manage large numbers.
- The weather: some programmes have to be cancelled or postponed if weather conditions are not just right.
- *Eastenders* is filmed three months ahead but it is designed to look as though it is happening today. This is difficult when seasons change in that time!
- Illness or scandal: a key character or presenter may be too ill to appear or may be involved in some public scandal.
- Skill and teamwork are needed to get over production problems as they arise. For example, in *Doctor Who*, the eruption of Vesuvius in Pompeii in AD79 was filmed in 2008 in South Wales!

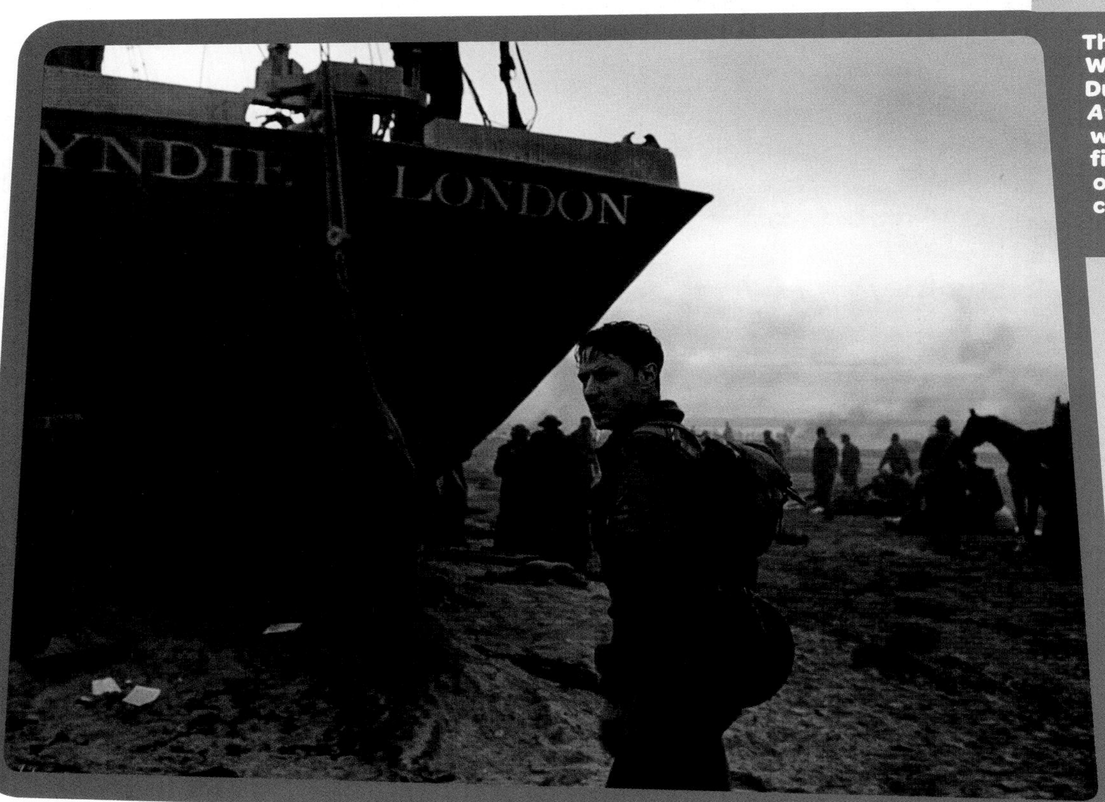

The powerful WWII scenes at Dunkirk in the film *Atonement* (2007) were actually filmed at Redcar on the North-East coast of England

Television regulation

Whenever you study a media industry, it is always important to consider how the industry is regulated in order to protect audiences from potentially offensive or harmful material.

ACTIVITY 4

How do television broadcasters try to protect audiences from seeing harmful material? Make a list of all the ways you can think of that television broadcasters try to do this. For example, scheduling a programme after 9 p.m. or issuing warnings of disturbing images at the beginning of a programme.

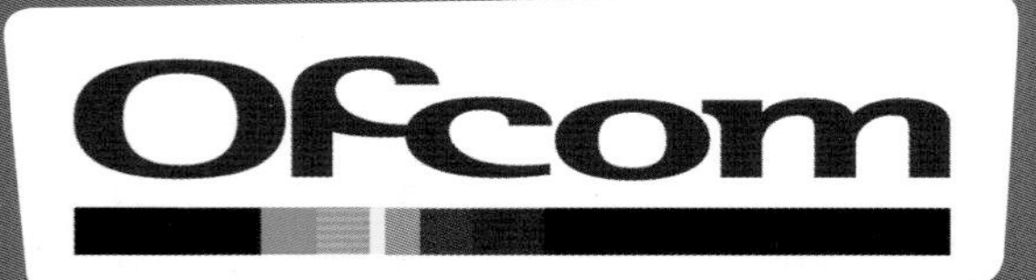

The regulatory body, Ofcom, has the responsibility of ensuring that TV and radio audiences are protected in areas such as taste, decency, fairness and privacy. If Ofcom decides that a programme does not uphold these standards, they can insist either that a programme is cancelled or that a warning is given at the beginning of the show.

The most vulnerable group in terms of being potentially affected by programme content is young children. Terrestrial television stations use the **watershed** to give parents the chance to ensure their children do not see adult material, such as explicit language or violence. Do you think broadcasters ever stretch the watershed agreement?

One problem that Ofcom faces is how to regulate television programmes that are increasingly viewed over the Internet. There is no clear regulation of programmes that are **downloaded**, and this means there is a chance of audiences, especially children, seeing programmes that would normally be censored by Ofcom.

Key terms

Watershed An agreement between terrestrial channels not to show explicit material until after 9 p.m.

Download Any file that is available on a remote server to be downloaded to a home computer. YouTube is an example of a file-sharing website.

8.00 Holby City

Change of Heart. The desecration of his wife's grave leaves Linden deeply upset. Jac, meanwhile, probes Joseph for news from South Africa, before a turn for the worse sees her rushed into theatre.

Michael Spence **Hari Dhillon**
Jac Naylor **Rosie Marcel**
Mark Williams **Robert Powell**
Connie Beauchamp **Amanda Mealing**
Elliot Hope **Paul Bradley**
Joseph Byrne **Luke Roberts**
Linden Cullen **Duncan Pow**
Maddy Young **Nadine Lewington**
Donna Jackson **Jaye Jacobs**
Daisha Anderson **Rebecca Grant**
Jayne Grayson **Stella Gonet**
Jamie Norton **Dominic Colchester**
Barry Carter **Francis Magee**
India Carter **Christina Baily**
Liam Harris **Craig Stein**

Writer David Lawrence; Producer Jane Wallbank
Director Daikin Marsh (S) (AD) 6536

Amanda Mealing answers One Final Question: page 162

9.00 Criminal Justice

RT CHOICE **DRAMA OF THE WEEK**

2/5. Newly arrived in prison, Ben has already but unwittingly made a deadly enemy. Meanwhile his defence team strikes a deal with the prosecution – but it's one that will require him to tell a lie. Continues tomorrow at 9pm.

For cast see Wednesday/Thursday (S) (AD) 6772

8.00 Today at Wimbledon

The ladies' quarter-final action plus a preview of tomorrow's corresponding men's matches. 4178

Repeated tomorrow at 10.30am (S)

Watch again over the next seven days, after 12 midnight, at www.bbc.co.uk/iplayer

9.00 Duncan Bannatyne Takes On Tobacco

RT CHOICE **DOCUMENTARY OF THE WEEK**

Multi-millionaire *Dragons' Den* veteran Duncan Bannatyne, himself a former smoker, travels to Africa to find out why increasing numbers of young people are taking up the habit. There he meets children as young as ten who not only smoke, but try to make their living from selling cigarettes. Having gathered evidence of one British-based firm's extraordinary marketing practices, the uncompromising Scot prepares to confront the company on his return to Britain. Showing in the *This World* documentary strand.

Director Alison Pinkney; Producer Debbie Christie (S) (AD) 7642

Channel identity

All television channels try to create a recognisable channel identity for themselves, so that audiences will feel a sense of familiarity and loyalty to the station. They create this identity by using:

- short snippets of music
- special graphics using the channel logo (called screen idents)
- seasonal idents
- certain types of programme, including flagship programmes for which the channel is known.

BBC1 is famous for its series *Strictly Come Dancing*

The identity of BBC1

The BBC is the oldest and most established broadcaster in the UK. As a public service broadcaster, BBC channels try to convey a high-quality image to their audiences, in order for them to feel the licence fee is worthwhile. They convey this image by creating a strong channel identity.

A recent series of on-screen **idents** for the BBC has been based on the symbol of a circle. Peter Fincham, Controller for BBC 1 in 2008 said, 'In an increasingly competitive marketplace, a channel needs to stand out from the crowd and I believe our new identity is just what's needed for BBC 1. The circle, which is at the heart of this campaign, has been familiar to BBC 1 viewers over the years, but what we've got here is modern, forward looking and surprising.'

The on screen idents are set in everyday and realistic locations, but show people or animals doing extraordinary things. The idents cover everything from daredevil motorbikes to synchronised hippos. It's warm and it's dynamic.

Key terms

Ident Like a logo, an instantly recognisable feature of the film, character or company, for example, the Hulk's green fists.

Other features of the BBC

- The BBC is well known for particular programmes, such as news and current affairs, documentaries, drama, sport and children's programmes.
- The BBC promotes itself in creative ways. In 1997 the BBC used Lou Reed's song 'Perfect Day' to show how the BBC promotes different types of music. The promo ended with the text on screen: 'Whatever your musical taste, it is catered for by BBC Radio and Television.'
- Flagship programmes include *The Evening News*, *Blue Peter*, *Doctor Who*, *Eastenders* and any big budget period/classic dramas.
- There are special promotions for forthcoming programmes, for example, Wimbledon, Christmas specials and even especially dramatic episodes of familiar programmes such as *Eastenders* or *Doctor Who*.

CD-ROM Extra!

BBC PERFECT DAY PROMOTION

Open the CD in the back of this book and click on the icon below to open a link to the BBC's Perfect Day promotion.

ACTIVITY 5

Explore the BBC website. It is one of the most visited websites in the world and is updated every minute. You may like to think about the following:

- *What are the most eye-catching features on the page?*
- *What is the lead story? If you check again later, has the story changed in some way?*
- *There are several interactive features on the site. Play with some of them and give your verdict!*
- *Experiment with how iPlayer works. Why do you think this is a good feature for the BBC to promote?*
- *Follow a link to a radio-related link, for example, 'The Best of Chris Moyles' podcast . How does it relate to the radio station itself?*
- *Scroll to the bottom of the site, and open the 'About The BBC' link. Read through this information – you will find it supports this chapter on television very well.*
- *Present or discuss your findings and opinions about the site.*

A Channel 4 on-screen ident

Channel 4

Channel 4 started in 1982 and had a reputation from the start for making challenging programmes that targeted a wide range of audiences. It is a commercial broadcaster, but has a strong public service image. The original, animated logo using early computer technology came to be seen as the embodiment of a channel that was constantly re-inventing itself and challenging the expectations of its viewers.

More recent on-screen idents have seen the Channel 4 logo being created out of unusual objects, such as skyscrapers, hedges and electricity pylons. You could try creating a new ident for Channel 4 or another channel.

Other features of Channel 4

Channel 4:

- is the only terrestrial channel deliberately to target teenagers with programmes such as *T4* and *The Tube*
- has launched sister channels that have their own identity:
  - More 4 is for serious programming
  - E4 is for lighter and youth programming
  - Film 4 is a dedicated film channel
  - 4Music is an independent radio channel
  - 4oD is an 'on demand' service that allows viewers to see any programmes from the last 30 days

- is more independent than the BBC and is able to take more risks in subject matter with, for example, controversial documentaries
- airs popular big-budget American dramas such as *The OC*, *ER*, *Entourage*, *One Tree Hill* and *Brothers and Sisters*
- launched a new music channel – 4Music – on Friday 15 August 2008
- makes and funds films
- has flagship programmes – *Hollyoaks*, *Skins*, *Richard and Judy*, *Friends*, *Big Brother*, *Channel 4 News*.

CD-ROM Extra!

Channel 4 website

Open the CD in the back of this book and click on the icon below to open a link to the Channel 4 website.

Explore the Channel 4 website. It is a site that really reflects the identity of the channel itself. You may like to think about the following:

- ***How is the page organised?***
- ***How are audiences encouraged to interact with the site (and even with Channel 4 itself)?***
- ***Scroll to the bottom of the site and open the 'Advertising on 4' link. Read through this information – what do you learn about Channel 4 as a commercial broadcaster?***
- ***Scroll to the bottom of the site, and open the 'About C4' link. You will find the information supports this chapter on television very well.***
- ***Stay inside the 'About C4' link. Under the 'Useful Links' tab, open the '4 Producers' link, and then click on 'Commissioning'. Here you will find some fascinating material which tells you how and why Channel 4 makes certain programmes.***
- ***Present or discuss what you have learned about Channel 4.***

Investigating opening sequences

Consider the key concepts of **genre**, **narrative** and **representation** in relation to television programmes. In many ways we could say that:

- genre shapes the codes/key features in a television programme
- narrative shapes the structure and organisation of the programme
- representation shapes the messages for the audiences of the programme.

Investigating television **opening (or title) sequences** is a useful way of thinking about the ways in which programmes as a whole are constructed with meanings for their target audiences. They are used to create instant identity and appeal.

Key terms

Genre A type of media text (programme, film, popular music, etc.) with certain predictable characteristics.

Narrative A story or account.

Representation How people, places, events or ideas are represented or portrayed to audiences in media texts. Sometimes this is simplistically through stereotypes so the audience can see immediately what is meant, and sometimes the meanings are less obvious.

Opening (or title) sequence A series of shots and music or graphics that appear at the start of a programme or film.

ACTIVITY 7

Look at the still frame shot from the opening sequence of Coronation Street. What clues does it give you about the programme? Copy and complete the table below (you'll see that some examples have been added to get you started). If you are able to watch the opening, you'll be able to pick out many more points!

What you can see	Clues about the programme
The camera shows us the key features of the area: the terraced housing and cobbled streets.	Establishes that the programme is set in a traditional area with a sense of community.
The title of the programme.	Coronation Street is written in a white, traditional font to emphasise the traditional nature of the programme.

Just from the still frames of an opening sequence, it is possible to start making observations about genre, narrative and representation.

Television genres and audiences

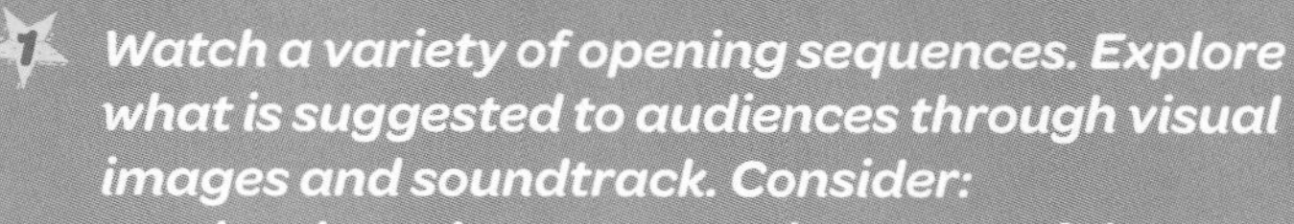

1. *Watch a variety of opening sequences. Explore what is suggested to audiences through visual images and soundtrack. Consider:*
   - *the clues that suggest the genre of the programme*
   - *how location and time are established*
   - *how groups of people are represented, if at all*
   - *how the soundtrack gives clues about the content of the programme*
   - *how any lettering used relates to the style of the programme.*
2. **Storyboard** *the opening sequence of a news or current affairs programme set in your local area (see pages 106–107 in Chapter 5 if you need help with storyboarding). Think about all the features you looked out for in the sequences you watched. You might like to think about:*
   - *the kinds of issue and event that local viewers would be interested in*
   - *the presenter of the programme*
   - *the style of reporting*
   - *music and graphics that reflect the style of the programme*
   - *the role of local residents.*

ACTIVITY 9

1. *Look at a daily TV schedule in a newspaper. Focus on BBC1, BBC2, ITV1, C4 and Five. List all the genres that you can find, such as situation comedy and news. Make a note of how many of each you can find. Discuss the genres that are most popular with teenagers.*
2. *In small groups, think of a new TV programme aimed at and featuring teenagers. Write down what genre the programme belongs to and when it will be shown. Add any other important details, such as what will happen and who will feature in it. If you wish, you could develop the news/current affairs programme idea from the previous activity.*
3. *Present your ideas to the rest of the class and listen to the ideas of other groups.*
4. *Think about all the ideas put forward. What were the most noticeable similarities and differences? Were there any particularly popular genres of programme? Why might that be?*

Storyboard The key moments of a story shown using images and notes – see the example on page 107.

EXAMINER'S TIP

Put your storyboard from Activity 8 into a folder. This could be included in your final Controlled Assessment folder as planning work.

EXAMINER'S TIP

Activity 9 is a good example of active research. You can use your findings in a number of ways for your Controlled Assessment folder. It is also a good exercise for External Assessment practice when you will have to discuss your given media topics in different ways.

Scheduling

You will probably notice that some television genres are more popular than others, and that these are often scheduled during peak time. Scheduling is an important strategy that broadcasters use to encourage as many people as possible to watch their channel. Techniques used to do this include:

- *Hammocking* – a new or less popular programme is scheduled between two high ratings (very popular) programmes. The idea is that viewers will keep watching the new programme after the first one has finished since they will be waiting for the third programme anyway.
- *Pre-echoing* – high ratings programmes are often advertised days before they are scheduled and early on during the actual day of transmission. This is to create a sense of excitement and expectation in audiences and also to attract new audiences.
- *Theming* – having special theme days, or theme weeks, such as 'Shark Week'.
- *Stacking* – grouping together programmes with similar appeal to 'sweep' the viewer along from one programme to the next.
- *Bridging* – when a channel tries to prevent the audience from changing channels on the hour or half hour. This can be achieved by:
  - having a programme already under way and something compelling happening at the 'changing point'
  - running a programme late so that people 'hang around' and miss the start of other programmes
  - advertising the next programme during the credits of the previous one.

E4

8.00 Friends
Series seven. Rachel bumps into an old college friend. (S) (AD)
8.30 Chandler turns to Joey and Ross for some much-needed help. (S)
9.00 Scrubs
New. 9/11; series seven. *My Dumb Luck* The board attempts to force Dr Kelso into retirement and JD and Turk try to show up Dr Cox when he is unable to diagnose a patient. (S)
www.radiotimes.com/scrubs
9.30 My Name Is Earl
9/22; series three. *Randy in Charge* Earl creates a sketch to deter kids from a life of crime. (S) (AD)

The Uses and Gratifications Theory

TV programmes are produced by teams of people who conduct extensive **market research** in order to find out what different audiences want to see on television. They are aware that audiences use the media to satisfy certain needs or requirements. Blumler and Katz discuss audience demand in their Theory of Uses and Gratifications (see page 76). To summarise, they suggest that audiences need to:

- be INFORMED and EDUCATED about the world
- IDENTIFY with characters and situations
- be ENTERTAINED
- use the media as a talking point for SOCIAL INTERACTION
- ESCAPE from their daily lives.

Key terms

Market research Finding out what audiences like or dislike about aspects of the media through interviews, surveys and focus groups.

1. *Look again at a TV schedule. Can you identify any obvious scheduling techniques? For example, can you spot channels using the hammocking technique?*
2. *Now apply the Uses and Gratifications Theory to the television programmes and genres you have just identified. This will help you see which audience needs are being met by each genre. Put your answers for each television programme you have chosen into a table like the one below, adding ticks where appropriate.*

	Inform	Identify	Entertain	Social interaction	Escape
Uses					
Gratifications					

Television drama

Television drama is a hugely popular television genre, attracting wide-ranging audiences simply because there are so many different dramas to choose from in terms of both style and content. Since it is such a large genre, it is useful to divide it up further into **sub-genres** such as crime drama, medical drama and docu-drama, in order to look at it more closely.

Key terms

Sub-genre Genres can be divided into sub-genres, for example, teen comedies are a sub-genre of comedy (see Chapter 1: Film for further details).

TV Drama

Crime drama

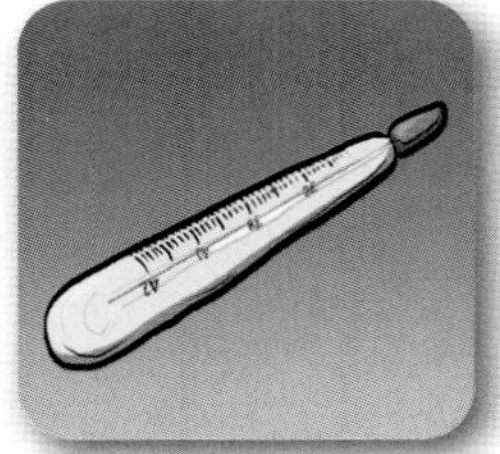

Medical drama

Docu-drama

***Desperate Housewives* is a very popular television drama**

ACTIVITY 11

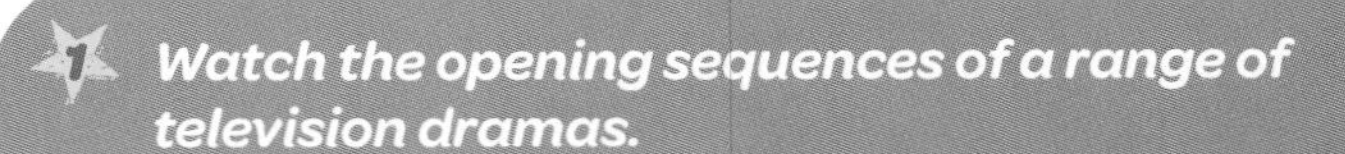

1. *Watch the opening sequences of a range of television dramas.*

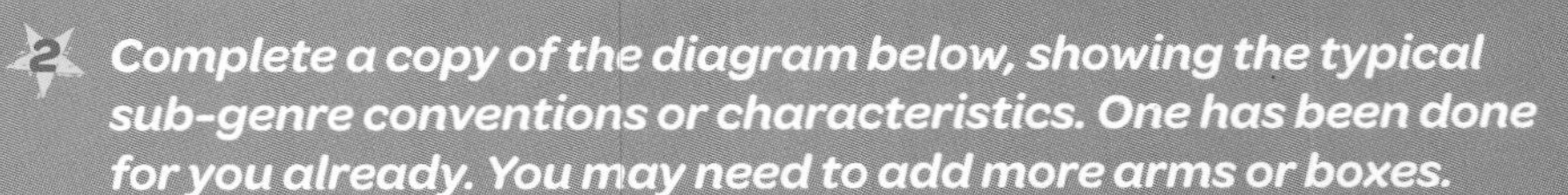

2. *Complete a copy of the diagram below, showing the typical sub-genre conventions or characteristics. One has been done for you already. You may need to add more arms or boxes.*

TV Drama

Crime drama

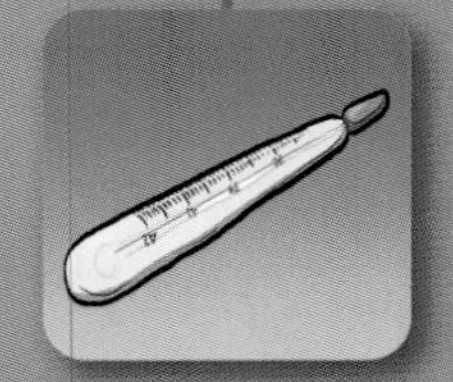

Medical drama

Docu-drama

3. *What other impressions do you get from the opening sequences? Try to add in more notes on your diagram about any of the following areas: music, striking images, on-screen text.*

4. *Discuss with a partner what storylines are suggested by the openings. What clues tell you the kinds of story that will be important in the programmes? Look out for where the camera spends extra time, giving importance to certain moments and particular characters and their stories.*

***Coronation Street* villain**

Camerawork

Some types of camera shot are used a lot in television drama. The aim is to make it seem as though the audience is either 'there' in the scene through point-of-view shots or 'looking on' through the use of lots of close-ups and shots through windows and doors. (You may like to look at the section on audience involvement on page 11 in Chapter 1: Film.)

Characters

Having central characters that the audience can get to know well is essential to television drama. These may play certain roles in the story, for example, heroes, villains and helpers (see page 103). However, often, realistic characters are harder to categorise into character types, since in real life people tend not to be heroes and villains!

Play a game with a partner. (Alternatively, you could make this a whole-class activity with rounds and a final winner.)

1. *Each person must choose two characters from different well-known television drama series.*
2. *Think of three facts about each character and give them one by one to your partner as clues, starting with the most difficult. Your partner must guess who your chosen characters are. Award 5 points for guessing with just one clue, 3 for two guesses and 1 for three guesses.*

Exploring character can focus our attention on one or more of the following important areas:

- the character's role in the drama
- their relationship with other characters
- the ways that the actor brings the character to life:
  - use of voice or accent
  - movement and gesture
  - emotional power to engage with the audience.
- the impact of the character on audiences over a long period of time.

The audience can usually spot two main types of character in a drama – those who are less important and are there for 'padding', and those around whom the main narrative(s) centre. For example, in a medical drama the patients are only shown for part of one programme, whereas the hospital staff are seen week after week. The less important characters are less developed and often more **stereotyped** than the main characters or **central protagonists**.

Characters in soap operas become very familiar to their audiences

Setting

The location of a TV drama is important in establishing a sense of a real place where the story can exist. Many regional features may well appear, such as landmarks and the local accent, dress and customs of those who live there.

Ramsey Street – the famous setting for the Australian soap *Neighbours*

Key terms

Stereotyping Grouping people together according to simple shared characteristics, without allowing for any individual uniqueness.

Central protagonists Key characters around whom the text and narrative are centred.

These features are included to encourage a strong sense of engagement with the world of the drama, the characters and their lives. Fans of TV drama sometimes write to their favourite characters, forgetting that they are played by actors and do not really exist!

One of the most important features of the majority of television dramas is that they create realistic worlds that audiences can believe in.

Soap opera

Soap opera is one of the most popular sub-genres of drama on television. It has its own set of conventions, all of which are designed to make viewers believe that the world of the programme really exists.

Radio soap opera *The Archers* is the world's longest running radio soap and was first aired in 1950

Soap operas began as serialised dramas, first on radio and later on television, paid for by washing-powder manufacturers. It became clear that the audience for daytime soap operas – housewives at home during the day – also enjoyed dramas based in hospital wards and in doctors' surgeries. Before long, soap operas appeared during peak-time viewing. Early examples included *The Archers* on Radio 4 and *Coronation Street* on ITV, which became popular in the 1960s and still have appeal today.

Recent UK soap operas include *Eastenders*, which began broadcasting on BBC1 in 1985, and *Hollyoaks* on Channel 4, which began life in 1995. *Desperate Housewives* and *Ugly Betty* on Channel 4 are popular American dramas that also have large followings.

Ugly Betty is popular with teenage audiences

ACTIVITY 13

Find out more about soap operas. Research the most important and popular soaps and how they have developed since they were first transmitted.
For each series, try to find out:

- ***when the series started***
- ***where it is set***
- ***any ways in which the series has changed over the years.***

Soap operas usually have a **multi-stranded narrative** where there is more than one story in one episode. The most important narrative in any particular episode usually acts as a cliff-hanger to keep audiences interested until the next episode. These narratives are interwoven or mixed together; it is possible to draw a special chart called a **cross-plot** to make it easier to investigate how the narrative works and which characters are given the most screen time.

Key terms

Multi-stranded narrative When a television drama follows more than one storyline and also connects or interweaves them.

Cross-plot A way of tracking different storylines through a single episode of a TV drama series.

Use the chart below to help you create your own cross-plot of an episode of your favourite soap opera. The cross-plot outlined is from a fictitious episode of a soap opera set in Cardiff.

1. *Start by watching the episode and making a list of all the scenes featured and what happens in them. There could well be more than 15.*
2. *Draw a chart like the one below that includes the main characters and three to five of the most important storylines in the boxes on the left. Make a column for each scene.*
3. *Put an X in each scene where a character from a particular storyline is featured.*
4. *If a character also appears briefly in another scene/storyline, put a small asterisk (*) in that scene.*

The Bay 17/09/2009	scene 1	scene 2	scene 3	scene 4	scene 5	scene 6	scene 7	scene 8	scene 9	scene 10
STORY 1 – James Burgess The rugby tickets	✗		✗	*		✗		✗		✗
STORY 2 – Carys and Chris The misunderstanding			✗		✗		✗		✗	
STORY 3 – Mrs Hendrikson Bomb scare at the assembly building		✗	*	✗					*	

Now that you have created your own cross-plot, you can investigate the ways in which the different storylines are interwoven, and how certain storylines dominate the episode.

- What do you notice about the pace and frequency of scenes towards the end of the episode?
- Which storyline does the episode end on?
- Why do some characters appear in more than one storyline?

Other important characteristics to look for when investigating soap opera are:

- a strong sense of realism in the setting and atmosphere
- a difference between the stable, regular characters (usually the inhabitants of the town/area/district) and the visiting characters who are just there for one or two episodes (usually visitors to the central location, as well as friends, relatives and 'love interests' of the inhabitants)
- sets that are carefully planned to be as believable as possible; décor, props and the behaviour of people in them are designed to convince the audience that they really do exist
- a central meeting place where characters can join together and interact
- episodes that usually follow the pattern of a normal day, i.e. morning until night.

EXAMINER'S TIP

Activity 15 may well become an excellent investigating piece of Controlled Assessment.

1. ***You could now watch two different British soap operas, trying to identify as many of the above characteristics as you can.***
2. ***If you have time, you could also watch one popular British soap opera and one American soap or drama. Then compare the storylines, characters and settings. Try to think of reasons to explain the main differences between them.***

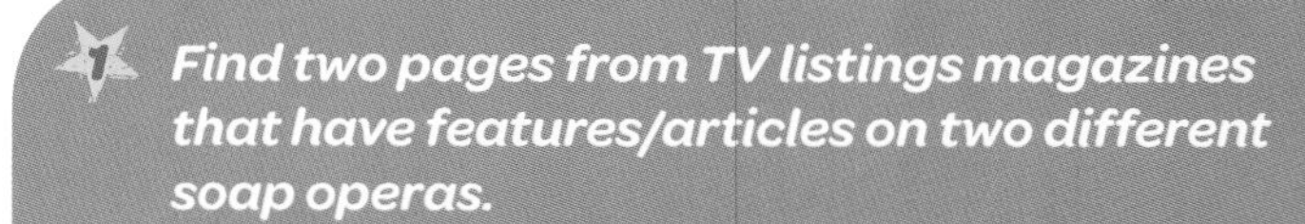

1. ***Find two pages from TV listings magazines that have features/articles on two different soap operas.***
2. ***Stick them onto A3 paper and annotate them, pointing out all their typical features and the ways the dramas have been made to seem interesting and appealing, for example, by focusing on the dramatic developments in the storyline of a regular character to encourage viewers to want to see what happens to them.***

Lifestyle programmes

There has been a huge explosion in the number of lifestyle programmes in the last 20 years and more recently there have been lifestyle satellite channels such as Discovery, Lifestyle and UKTV Food that only screen lifestyle programmes.

A lifestyle programme might be described as one that focuses on home, garden, food and family concerns. They have proved popular with a range of audiences, especially since the early 1990s. The main target audience for these programmes tends to be homeowners, but programme-makers keep trying to make them appeal to teenagers too.

Most terrestrial channels have their own food programmes, and while DIY shows are usually screened during the day, food programmes are often screened during peak time since they attract a high number of viewers.

Food programmes were originally targeted at 'housewives at home', and many still appeal mostly to female viewers who are traditionally seen as the 'food preparers'. But more recently there has been such a rise in male celebrity chefs, that male viewers have become more interested in cooking! And the number of boys taking Food Technology GCSE courses has increased recently by more than 30 per cent.

ACTIVITY 17

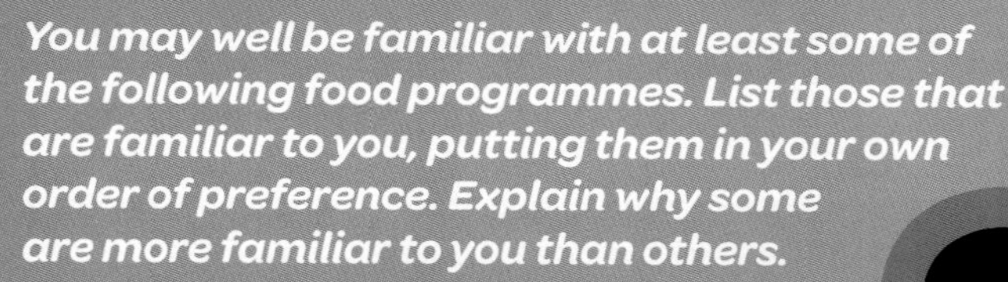

1. ***You may well be familiar with at least some of the following food programmes. List those that are familiar to you, putting them in your own order of preference. Explain why some are more familiar to you than others.***
   - **Masterchef**
   - **Ramsay's Kitchen Nightmares**
   - **Nigella Express**
   - **The F Word**
   - **Saturday Kitchen**
   - **Delia**
   - **Jamie at Home**
   - **Hell's Kitchen**
   - **Ready, Steady, Cook**

2. ***Lifestyle programmes are not often targeted at teenagers, but this is not because teenagers are not interested in their family, their surroundings or the food they eat! Outline your own lifestyle programme that you feel will appeal to a teenage audience. Think about the following aspects of the programme:***
   - ***the presenter***
   - ***the main focus areas***
   - ***the music and guests***
   - ***the channel and scheduling***
   - ***the production values – are these programmes expensive to make?***

TELEVISION WEBSITES

This case study discusses some of the convergent media aspects of television websites. The Internet has had a very big impact on television and is a good example of media convergence. In the same way that magazines and newspapers have their own interactive websites, television channels and even television programmes have their own sites that are full of extra facts, information and interactive games.

Skins

This chapter has already looked in some detail at the BBC and C4 websites, but most individual programmes also have their own websites.

CASE STUDY ACTIVITY A

Look at the information below on the Skins website. Then, choosing either the Skins website or another programme website, explore it. Present your findings, explaining how the website makes connections to the programme and yet also offers something different.

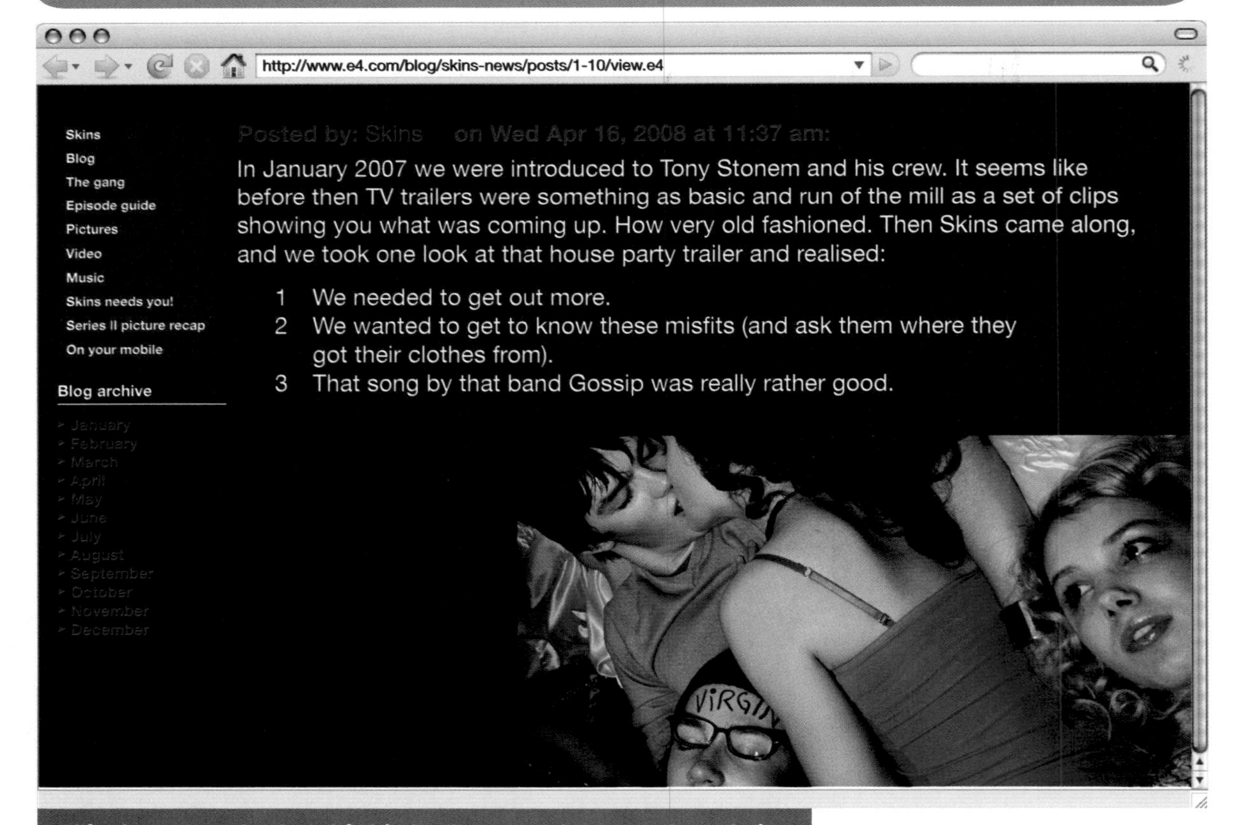

Skins **has proved to be a big hit, both as a TV drama and a website**

Big Brother

Love it or hate it, everyone has heard of the reality television show *Big Brother*. Screened on Channel 4, along with sister programmes on E4, the show has helped to make reality television one of the most popular television genres of the 21st century.

Big Brother*'s popularity*

From May to September 2008, *Big Brother 9* was transmitted every day to an average of 5 million viewers, which was perceived as a disappointment compared to the ratings of previous years. Nevertheless, *Big Brother* has proved itself a guaranteed audience attraction for Channel 4 and Endemol (its production company) for a number of years, and is part of Channel 4's identity, combining an eye with the Channel 4 logo.

The reality TV show began in 2000 and was the first of its kind in terms of the genre of reality TV. Since then, the show has been transmitted each summer with its simple formula of a group of 'ordinary' people who have been thrown together in 'the Big Brother house' completing tasks and bidding for public approval, with those least popular being voted out each Friday evening, during an 'eviction show'.

The show is referred to by Endemol UK executive Tim Hincks as a 'banker' for the channel , 'just like Wimbledon or *EastEnders* is to the BBC'.

Convergent media in Big Brother

Part of *Big Brother*'s appeal is its effective use of media convergence to self-publicise. It transmits partner programmes alongside the main show on C4 – 'Big Brother's Little Brother', 'Big Brother's Big Mouth', 'Diary Room Uncut' and 'Big Brother's Big Ears' are all screened on E4 and are designed to target a younger audience as they are more 'edgy' and controversial – often being screened after the watershed.

Big Brother*'s website*

Big Brother runs a successful website throughout the duration of the show's run. When the programme began in 2000, the *Big Brother* website accounted for 99.8 per cent of all traffic and was accessed by over 2 million visitors, one in five of all UK home surfers (according to research firm Net Value).

CD-ROM Extra!

Big Brother website

Open the CD in the back of this book and click on the icon below to open a link to the Big Brother website.

HTML

Today the site is highly interactive and invites the comments and opinions of site users. It includes a mixture of audio sound bites, video clips and text news reports on the housemates, as well as links to other C4 programmes and interactive games.

★CASE STUDY★ ACTIVITY B

Visit the* Big Brother *website. What do you think is its most interesting feature?

What have you learned?

In this chapter you have learned about:

Texts

- Investigating openings
- Investigating narratives
- Looking at the construction of drama, soap and lifestyle programmes

Media language

Genre

- How television genres use clear characteristics to allow audiences to classify and engage with them
- How sub-genres and cross-genres develop
- Case study genres – television drama, soap opera and lifestyle programmes
- Convergent case study – *Big Brother*. How programmes develop and change over time

Narrative

- The construction of television narratives
- How to use cross-plotting to investigate narrative construction

Representation

- How different social groups are represented in programmes
- The representation of characters, settings and issues in different genres
- The changing nature of representations on television

Audiences

- Who is watching and when
- Considering audience appeal
- Investigating audience responses and needs

Organisational issues

- Television regulation
- Television technology in relation to production and key roles in making programmes
- Public service and commercial broadcasting
- Scheduling techniques

Convergent media

- The convergent nature of television including:
  - channel identity
  - magazines and comics
  - the effects of advertising revenue
  - related websites

Your learning

In this chapter you will learn about:

- the different use of codes and conventions by media organisations who present the news
- how audiences are targeted and retained by news media organisations
- the changes in the news media brought about by new technology
- how the content of the news is influenced both by the institutions or organisations that produce it and by those that provide news stories
- how the representation of individuals and groups in the news is only one of many possible presentations.

News – an introduction

News is big business. A desire to find out what is happening in the world seems to be an important part of many people's daily lives. Some people get this from newspapers, others from the television, radio or the Internet. So why are we all so interested in one form of news or another? It's probably because human beings have an in-built love of stories: news stories sit alongside soap operas, novels and Hollywood movies as narratives, or stories.

Once they have found out about what is happening, people will often quickly form an opinion about the events of the time. Should the Prime Minister resign? Is knife crime among young people a sign that society is collapsing into chaos? Is *Big Brother* a good thing? The news keeps us thinking about these issues, which we then discuss with our friends at school, in the hairdressers, in the café, in the taxi or wherever. Now we can even share our views with the whole world by blogging, although this can have its downside, as American journalist Ed Murrow points out:

> ***'Just because your voice can now reach halfway round the world, it doesn't mean you're wiser than when it only reached to the end of the bar!'***

EXAMINER'S TIP

You should consider the convergent aspects of news throughout your course.

Key terms

Circulation The number of copies of a newspaper which are sold.

Readership The number of people who read the paper. This is usually higher than circulation, as several people can read the same paper.

With a group of at least two others, explore your own news consumption by discussing the following questions:

1. ***What sort of news do you watch, read and listen to? This might include: celebrity stories, crime stories, political stories, local stories.***
2. ***How many of the following news media do you use and how often do you use them?***
   - ***National TV news. Do you usually watch one particular channel? If so, why?***
   - ***Local TV news.***
   - ***The Internet. Which sites?***
   - ***National newspapers. Which ones?***
   - ***Local newspapers. Which ones?***
   - ***National radio. Which stations?***
   - ***Local radio. Which stations?***
   - ***Do you find local or national news more interesting?***

Newspapers

Despite competition from TV, radio and the Internet, 300 years after the first newspaper was produced, a printed daily newspaper is not yet a thing of the past. It is true that there is a constant and steady decline in the **circulation** of newspapers. All but one of the main national dailies sold fewer copies in the year up to June 2008. Some are in steeper decline than others.

The only 'winner' is the *Sun,* which showed an increase of 0.81 per cent, while its main rival, the *Daily Mirror,* was down by 5.97 per cent on the previous year. However, in June 2008, ten and a half million national daily newspapers were still sold in the UK every day. This means that the **readership** of these papers could be 20 million or more – a third of the population of the country.

This photograph appeared in the *Illustrated London News* in 1892. It shows the Duke of York (later King George V) and other officers on board *HMS Melampus*

A recent survey asked adults aged 16–34 which words they associated with each of radio, television and newspapers.

- Newspapers were thought to be 'informative', 'serious' and 'influential' by more people than radio and television.
- 42 per cent agreed that 'newspapers are an important part of daily life'.

A timeline of the British press

Today's newspapers are colourful, full of pictures and have Internet versions. This constitutes a big change which has happened very quickly. For the first 200 years of their 300-year history, newspapers were mostly printed with a few black and white pictures.

1702
First daily paper *Daily Courant* founded (last published in 1735).

1785
The Times is first published: UK's oldest surviving daily newspaper.

1791
Observer founded: UK's oldest surviving Sunday newspaper.

1806
First use of illustration in *The Times*: Admiral Lord Nelson's funeral.

1832
First recorded British newspaper cartoon, published in *Bell's New Weekly Messenger*.

1844
First story based on telegraphed news printed in *The Times*: birth of a son to Queen Victoria at Windsor.

1855
Repeal of the Stamp Act opens the way for cheap, mass-circulation newspapers and modern newspaper design, using spacing and headlines.

1889
Early use of photographs: Cambridge and Oxford boat crews, in *Illustrated London News*.

1900
Daily Express launched: first national daily to put news on the front page.

1903
Daily Mirror launched: first daily illustrated exclusively with photographs.

1963
Sunday Times launches a magazine-style colour supplement.

1987
First women editors of national newspapers in modern times: Wendy Henry (*News of the World*) and Eve Pollard (*Sunday Mirror*).

1991
Press Complaints Commission replaces the Press Council for more effective press self-regulation.

1994
Electronic Telegraph launched: first British national on the Internet.

1999
Metro launched: a daily newspaper distributed free to travellers on the London Underground.

2003
The first broadsheets go tabloid: the *Independent* and *The Times*.

2008
All major newspapers now have Internet versions which are fast becoming more important than the printed versions.

As photography became an important part of the way people could perceive the world, newspapers adapted and the 'pictorial' content gradually increased. The industry remained male-dominated until recently. Competition from other media eventually forced changes on a reluctant press.

Key terms

Broadsheets Traditionally, newspapers printed in a large format (pages of 37 cm by 58 cm); they are considered to be more serious in content than tabloids.

Tabloids Traditionally, newspapers with pages half the size of broadsheets; they are usually more highly illustrated and can be less serious in their tone and content than broadsheets.

Demograph The type of audience watching or reading a media product.

Upmarket People who are comfortably off with a reasonable income.

Downmarket People who have smaller incomes and less money to spend on anything beyond the basic living requirements.

Red tops Tabloid newspapers with red mastheads.

Masthead The title of the newspaper which appears in large type at the top of the front page.

Targeting their audience

There are two main types of newspaper. They used to be divided into **broadsheets** and **tabloids.** Although this definition was based on the size of the paper they used, with broadsheets being much larger than tabloids, only a few papers still use the largest format. Most broadsheets are now a compact size. Nevertheless, the term has stuck.

There are also generalisations about the type of person who reads each sort of paper which are based on audience research. Broadsheets are associated with people in well-paid jobs who represent an **upmarket demograph**. Tabloids are associated with less well-off readers, or a **downmarket** demograph.

The five daily tabloids can be subdivided into two groups:

1. The *Sun*, *Mirror* and *Daily Star* are called the **red tops** because they have red **mastheads**. These papers report on politics and international news but generally include more gossip about celebrities from the pop or film world and sleaze or scandal of any sort. Stories are written simply and are quite short. Red tops tend to have more pictures than other papers, particularly the broadsheets. Their main aim is to be an easy read.

2. The *Daily Mail* and the *Daily Express* are often called the 'middle market' dailies. They target a readership somewhere between those of the red tops and the broadsheets. They print plenty of news and features for people wanting a paper that is not too gossipy or trivial, but they also have a variety of lightweight articles and pictures.

As well as entertaining, the tabloid papers line up behind one of the two major political parties. At one time only the *Daily Mirror* was a Labour-supporting tabloid. In 1992, the Labour Party was widely expected to win the General Election. But after John Major's surprise victory for the Tories, the *Sun*, which had supported the Conservatives, claimed that it had won the election for them. An important triumph for the Labour Party was to convince Rupert Murdoch, the owner of the *Sun* (as well as *The Times*, *The Sunday Times* and the *News of the World*) to change sides and back Labour. Five years later Labour romped home to a big victory – and the *Sun* could claim to have swung the election again.

THE TIMES

SATURDAY APRIL 11 1992

Women tipped for cabinet after Tories sweep back with 21 majority

Major plans reshuffle today

THE NOT THE ELECTION TIMES

THE OLD CURIOSITY SHOPS

GREAT EXPECTATIONS

NOT SO BLEAK HOUSE?

Beaten Kinnock will announce resignation

...oters let the pollsters down

ABBEY NATIONAL INVESTMENT ACCOUNT

THE Sun

FREE TODAY PLUS THE GREAT AMERICAN

IT'S THE SUN WOT WON IT

HERE'S HOW PAGE 3 WILL LOOK UNDER KINNOCK!

PHOTO FINISH

If Kinnock wins today will the last person to leave Britain please turn out the lights

Truth hailed by Tories

Broadsheets

The five quality papers have higher news content, usually higher prices for each copy and lower circulation figures than the tabloids.

- *The Times* is the oldest of all the dailies; it used to have the reputation for being rather stuffy and the 'voice of the ruling classes'. In 1979 it was bought by Rupert Murdoch's News International company and is now a genuinely modern paper, but still with more of an 'establishment' view than some others.
- The *Daily Telegraph* is the broadsheet with the highest circulation. It is a strong supporter of the Conservative Party. Still broadsheet in size.
- The *Guardian* is usually described as a liberal or left-wing paper.
- The *Independent* is the newest of the national dailies, set up in 1986 and intended to be independent of any one political party's viewpoint.
- The *Financial Times* is the only national daily to be printed on pink paper. It reports mainly on business and economic news, although it does have other news, including a sports section. Still broadsheet in size.

Ethnic newspapers

As Britain is home to an increasingly diverse number of cultures, there is a variety of newspapers to serve these audiences. The *New Nation* describes itself as 'Britain's number one black newspaper', while the *Asian Times* claims to be 'Britain's leading Asian newspaper'.

Look at the online versions of one tabloid and one broadsheet daily national newspaper.

Examine the content, layout and advertising on each site. To what extent do you think it is correct to say that the broadsheet is appealing to an upmarket audience while the tabloid targets a downmarket demograph?

Newspaper language

The 'language' of newspapers is not just the words that appear in them. As with other media languages, it includes the pictures that are used, different font styles and sizes in text and headings, and the way these things are put together in the layout of the page.

No aspect of the way newspapers are put together is an accident. At every stage of production people are making decisions which affect the way the paper looks, reads ... and sells!

The copy

Copy is written by journalists called reporters. Writing for newspapers is very different from the sort of writing done by, say, a novelist. News reporters need to get across the maximum amount of information in the shortest possible time. They also aim to get the 'bare bones' of the story established in the first sentence or two – if you are hooked into the story from the very start you will carry on reading.

Key terms

Copy Material for articles that appear in newspapers or magazines.

Here is an example from the *Daily Mail* on Monday, 21 July 2008:

Happy hours and 'supersize' wine glasses could be banned in an admission that the 24-hour drinking experiment has failed

Journalists are taught to KISS – Keep It Short and Simple. They used also to be taught to get the 'Five Ws' – Who? What? Where? When? Why? – into the first sentences of their story. Now styles of writing for newspapers have moved on. Trying to pack in all five Ws made for indigestible sentences and this rule is not always followed to the letter.

ACTIVITY 3

Find three different newspapers and look at the opening two sentences from the main front-page story in each. How many of the Five Ws has the reporter managed to get into the story?

The pictures

The first newspapers printed 300 years ago had few pictures – and those pictures were drawings because, of course, the camera had not been invented. Nowadays news photographs play an important part in the whole look of a newspaper, especially the front page.

Look at the image below to see how *The Times* set out its front page reporting on one of the biggest international news stories of recent times. The event was highly significant in the Western world. Almost anyone who was alive at the time remembers exactly what they were doing when they first heard the news of the terrorist attack on New York's twin towers.

No. 67242 WEDNESDAY SEPTEMBER 12 2001 40p www.thetimes.co.uk

When war came to America

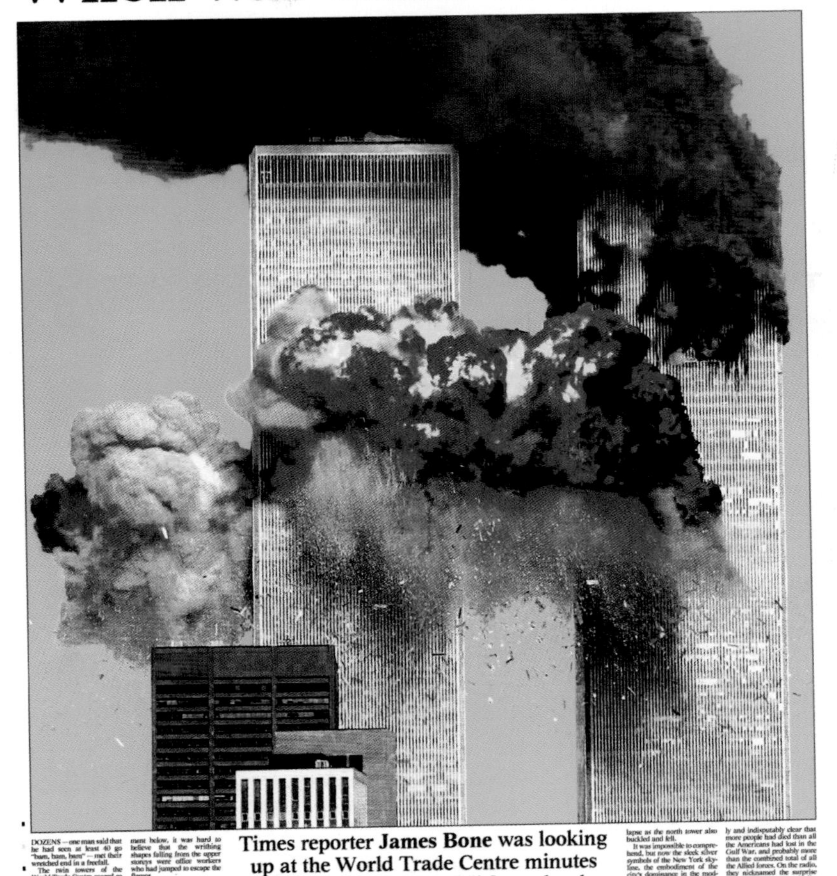

Photograph: SPENCER PLATT/Getty Images/Allsport

Times reporter James Bone was looking up at the World Trade Centre minutes before the twin towers fell from the sky

DOZENS — one man said that he had seen at least 40 go "bam, bam, bam" — met their wretched end in a freefall.

The twin towers of the World Trade Centre soared so majestically over the skyline of Manhattan that, from the pavement below, it was hard to believe that the writhing shapes falling from the upper storeys were office workers who had jumped to escape the flames.

What kind of desperation could drive these people to leap to a certain death when the streets below were lined with ambulances and help was clearly on its way?

From behind a police barricade several blocks north along the Hudson River, I could not see where they were landing. Then, in one almighty rumble, their dreadful reasoning became all too apparent. In excruciating slow-motion, the south tower crumbled, its middle billowed out and, before my eyes, one of the world's largest office buildings disappeared in a cloud of smoke that engulfed the rescuers below.

Even before the walls hit the ground, the onlookers around me turned and fled in panic through the canyons of Manhattan, screaming that the unthinkable had happened. A vast and silent dust-ball filled the surrounding streets, billowing inexorably towards me like a morning fog rolling over the normally vital neighbourhoods of Wall Street and Tribeca.

Those unfortunate to be closer to the collapse than I was vanished from view, submerged in the expanding balloon of debris. I felt a sudden pity for the scores, if not hundreds, of ambulance crews and firefighters who had just, I'm sure, lost their lives. Until then, the burning twin towers, holes gaping in their sides, seemed somehow familiar, even inevitable, a staple of our fevered imagination, something that a screenwriter might describe as Towering Inferno — times two. But even the most devilish imagination in all Hollywood had never concocted a scene so awesome in its devastation as the sight of first one and then another 110-storey skyscraper crashing to extinction.

It was at this point that many of the New Yorkers who had thronged the streets to watch this compelling spectacle — many of them refugees from wars in other parts of the world — decided that it was just safer to go home. Their judgment, too, was soon justified by another terrifying collapse as the north tower also buckled and fell.

It was impossible to comprehend, but now the sleek silver symbols of the New York skyline, the embodiment of the city's dominance in the modern world, were no more. New York, the self-proclaimed "capital of the world", had been irrevocably diminished.

We were all wrong, it turns out, to believe all those reassurances after the first bombing in 1993 that the twin towers were built to withstand the full force of a commercial airliner. We are told, only now, that the experts were referring merely to a Boeing 727.

It was said that 50,000 people, enough to populate a small city, worked in those two behemoths. It was immediately and indisputably clear that more people had died than all the Americans had lost in the Gulf War, and probably more than the combined total of all the Allied forces. On the radio, they nicknamed the surprise attack after a recent Hollywood blockbuster: Pearl Harbor II.

Minutes after the second building collapsed, I was amazed to find survivors — yes, some survived — wandering dazed and dusty and often lost among the retreating crowds. These were people who realised, even if they were still missing loved ones, that they had just lived the luckiest day of their lives.

The thriving often frantic island of Manhattan had been

Continued on page 3, col 1

TERROR IN AMERICA: News, pages 2-6; Target America: Times 2. PLUS: 24-page special supplement of news, comment and analysis

Front page of *The Times*, 12 September, 2001

ACTIVITY 4

Look at the front page on page 57, paying special attention to the photograph.

1. ***What is it about the photograph that helps to create an impact on the reader?***
2. ***Why do you think the picture editor chose this particular image? What does the photo tell us about the story?***

Captions

People say that 'a picture is worth a thousand words'. Certainly the photograph of New York after the attack on the twin towers on page 57 says a great deal about the event. The **caption** that goes with a photograph is also important because it can **anchor** a meaning – it tries to push the reader towards one **angle** by providing an interpretation for them.

Key terms

Picture editor The person responsible for choosing the photographs that go into a newspaper.

Caption Descriptive words next to a picture.

Anchor To pin down a particular meaning of a drawing or photograph, often by adding a caption.

Angle The particular point of view a newspaper wants its readers to take on a story.

Street scene in Khayelitsha, South Africa

Look at the photograph above. There could be a number of interpretations of this image. However, choosing suitable captions could alter the way people read it.

- *South Africa's government has managed to re-house many of its people from tin shacks into solid, brick-built houses*: this caption gives a positive slant on the picture.
- *Unemployment still blights South Africa's townships*: this caption gives a different, more negative meaning.

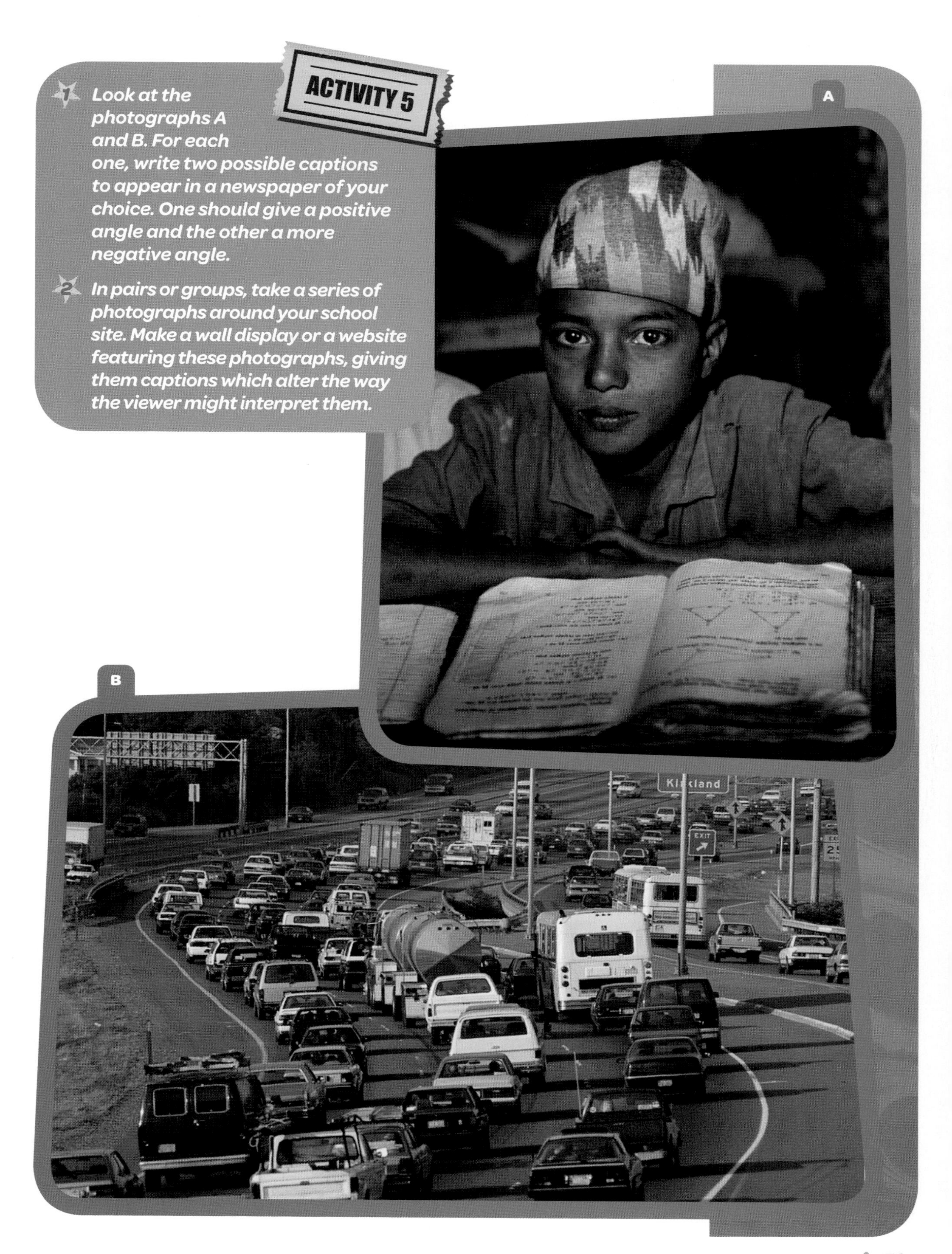

ACTIVITY 5

1. *Look at the photographs A and B. For each one, write two possible captions to appear in a newspaper of your choice. One should give a positive angle and the other a more negative angle.*

2. *In pairs or groups, take a series of photographs around your school site. Make a wall display or a website featuring these photographs, giving them captions which alter the way the viewer might interpret them.*

Headlines

Good headlines are crucial, especially on the front page. It's the headline which will draw a purchaser's attention to the paper when it is on the shelf among its competitors. Broadsheet editors will try to draw readers to their stories by using concise (brief) headlines which sometimes also give the newspaper's angle on the story, but tabloid headlines are large and catchy.

The *Sun* has become famous for its controversial headlines. Although these can be amusing, they sometimes cross the line from humour into bad taste. In 1989 the paper printed the headline 'THE TRUTH' above an article about the Hillsborough football disaster in which 95 Liverpool fans were killed. The *Sun*'s 'truth' was that the disaster was caused by drunken Liverpool fans behaving badly. Sales of the paper in Liverpool collapsed, with many newsagents refusing to stock it.

Some of the techniques headline writers use include:

- abbreviating names, for example, BECKS for David Beckham
- parodying well-known phrases, for example, BRAWL OVER BAR THE SHOUTING
- Incorrect or invented spelling, for example, GOTCHA
- puns (play on words), for example, BOOTIFUL – winning goal in a Cup Final
- rhyming, for example, FAME GAME TURNS VERY LAME.

Look at some back copies of tabloid front pages and try to find examples of each of the headline techniques listed above.

Layout

When all the copy is written and all the photographs have been chosen, the final choices concern how the page is to be laid out. Layout is a key part of the battle to grab the reader's attention and hang on to it.

The front page from the *Daily Mail* on page 61 has been marked up with the terms used by **sub-editors** to describe modern newspaper layout. The sub-editors of the paper set out the pages on a computer screen which breaks the page into a series of columns called a page grid. In the past, pages were almost always set out in columns, with nothing breaking the grid pattern. Modern page design often allows both photographs and text to spill outside rigid columns to create dramatic visual impact.

Newspapers are constantly researching the ways in which people *read* pages. They have found, for example, that:

- headlines near photographs are read more than those placed further away
- using colour does not make a story more likely to be read
- people reading a paper look at most of the photographs, artwork and headlines – but much less of the copy.

Above all, a newspaper wants to achieve an individual visual style. This is about individual preferences.

Masthead

Dateline

Daily Mail

MONDAY, JULY 21, 2008

www.dailymail.co.uk

DAILY NEWSPAPER OF THE YEAR 50p

NEW 18-DISC COLLECTION

Front cover flash

FREE DVD

BLEAK HOUSE

Another sensational FREE costume drama for you to collect

PICK UP FROM TESCO OR WHSMITH OR WE CAN POST YOU THE WHOLE SET DETAILS PAGE 30 P&P PAYABLE

Strapline

Three years after relaxing drink laws, ministers signal U-turn

Splash head full caps

TIME'S UP FOR HAPPY HOUR

By-line

By **Michael Lea**
Political Correspondent

Page lead

HAPPY hours and 'super-size' wine glasses could be banned in an admission that the 24-hour drinking experiment is failing.

Labour's hopes of creating a Continental-style cafe culture have not materialised since licensing laws were relaxed nearly three years ago.

Instead, booze-fuelled violence and alcohol-related deaths, injuries and illnesses have surged.

Now, having previously refused to heed warnings from police and doctors, ministers are preparing a climbdown by toughening up the laws on alcohol sales.

Key measures are likely to include:

- A ban on happy hours and cut-price promotions;
- Pubs and clubs ordered to serve smaller measures of wines and spirits as standard;
- Cigarette-style health warnings on cans and bottles, extending a voluntary scheme where containers show the units of alcohol;
- Loss-leading alcohol sales by supermarkets may also be targeted.

The moves will build on a review by the audit firm KPMG into the link between price promotions and alcohol abuse, which could be published this week. Ministers have been dismayed at the lack of voluntary action from the drinks industry. Some pubs have extended happy hours

Turn to Page 4

Kate McCann: The inquiry into her daughter's disappearance is to be closed

Support story

New agony for Kate as Maddie detective cashes in

Underscored

SEE PAGE FIVE

4 colour pic

Caption

Cross-reference

ACTIVITY 7

Below and opposite are two front pages designed by the Sun to show how their paper might have reported famous moments from history, using modern page design techniques.

Choose two other events from the list of historical events below and design your own tabloid front page.

- *The assassination of American President John F. Kennedy in 1963.*
- *The end of the Second World War in 1945.*
- *Neil Armstrong becomes the first man to walk on the moon in 1969.*
- *Elizabeth I becomes Queen of England in 1558.*
- *Nelson Mandela is released from jail in 1990 after 27 years.*

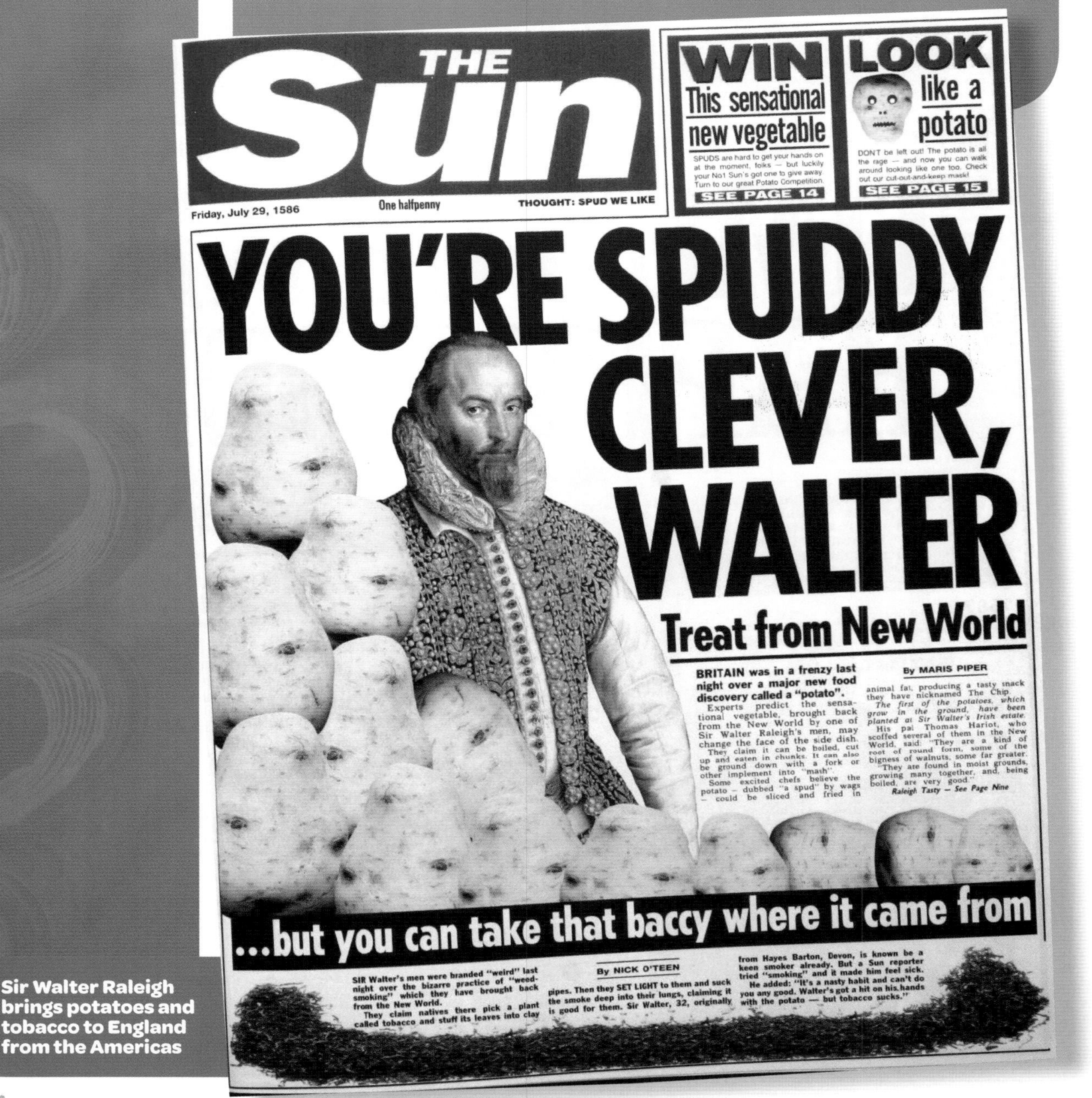

THE Sun

Friday, July 29, 1586 | One halfpenny | THOUGHT: SPUD WE LIKE

WIN This sensational new vegetable

SPUDS are hard to get your hands on at the moment, folks — but luckily your No1 Sun's got one to give away. Turn to our great Potato Competition.

SEE PAGE 14

LOOK like a potato

DON'T be left out! The potato is all the rage — and now you can walk around looking like one too. Check out our cut-out-and-keep mask!

SEE PAGE 15

YOU'RE SPUDDY CLEVER, WALTER

Treat from New World

By MARIS PIPER

BRITAIN was in a frenzy last night over a major new food discovery called a "potato".

Experts predict the sensational vegetable, brought back from the New World by one of Sir Walter Raleigh's men, may change the face of the side dish.

They claim it can be boiled, cut up and eaten in chunks. It can also be ground down with a fork or other implement into "mash".

Some excited chefs believe the potato – dubbed "a spud" by wags – could be sliced and fried in animal fat, producing a tasty snack they have nicknamed The Chip.

The first of the potatoes, which grow in the ground, have been planted at Sir Walter's Irish estate.

His pal Thomas Hariot, who scoffed sereral of them in the New World, said: "They are a kind of root of round form, some of the bigness of walnuts, some far greater.

"They are found in moist grounds, growing many together, and, being boiled, are very good."

Raleigh Tasty – See Page Nine

...but you can take that baccy where it came from

By NICK O'TEEN

SIR Walter's men were branded "weird" last night over the bizarre practice of "weed-smoking" which they have brought back from the New World.

They claim natives there pick a plant called tobacco and stuff its leaves into clay pipes. Then they SET LIGHT to them and suck the smoke deep into their lungs, claiming it is good for them. Sir Walter, 32, originally from Hayes Barton, Devon, is known be a keen smoker already. But a Sun reporter tried "smoking" and it made him feel sick.

He added: "It's a nasty habit and can't do you any good. Walter's got a hit on his hands with the potato — but tobacco sucks."

Sir Walter Raleigh brings potatoes and tobacco to England from the Americas

ARE YOU A CHIMP OFF THE OLD BLOCK?
SEE PAGES 4 AND 5

Friday, November 25, 1859 Penny farthing THOUGHT: SPEAK FOR YOURSELF

Monkey nutter

Barmy boffin Darwin reckons we are all descended from apes

MAD scientist Charles Darwin caused fury last night by claiming we're all descended from APES.

By JEAN POOLE

Darwin, 50, makes a string of outrageous allegations in his controversial book On The Origin Of Species, which sold out on its first day yesterday.

Darwin **SCOFFS** at the "Adam and Eve" theory of mankind's creation. He says the real answer lies in the **FOSSILS** he once studied on a sailing trip.

The barmy boffin, from Shrewsbury, reckons all animals "evolve" – becoming more and more refined and advanced over thousands of years. This is all thanks to "natural selection" which means only the fittest and best examples of a species survive to breed and pass on their successful characteristics.

Darwin avoids mentioning man in his book, concentrating on plants and animals. But experts say he **MUST** believe in mankind being merely advanced apes, or his theory doesn't hold water.

Furious scientists last night insisted Darwin did not have a shred of real evidence.

And Church chiefs said he was belittling the Bible and the importance of man over animals.

Buffoon as a baboon . . . how he'd look

Charles Darwin writes *On the Origin of the Species* in which he outlines his theory of human evolution

Having looked at the techniques used by newspapers, find two newspapers that cover the same story. Compare the way they reported it. You should think about:

- *the pictures they have used*
- *the type of language they have used*
- *what view they have taken about the story.*

REPRESENTATION IN NEWS

In this case study we will consider the convergent media nature of representation in news. The key concept of* representation *is an important one for all Media Studies students to understand. In studying the news, representation is about understanding that news stories are a representation of events, and the people and ideas who are part of those events. Someone has always made a choice about the pictures that represent the story and the words used to link with the pictures. If the choices made had been different, the representation would have taken on a different meaning.

Key terms

Representation How people, places, events or ideas are represented or portrayed to audiences in media texts. Sometimes this is simplistically through stereotypes so the audience can see immediately what is meant, and sometimes the meanings are less obvious.

Putting people, events or ideas into categories is a part of the way representation works. When we see repeated representations of famine-stricken children in Africa, those images can begin to affect the way we think about that continent. The generalisation that 'Africa equals Poverty' means we might be surprised to learn that, for example, there are many highly successful hi-tech businesses and entrepreneurs in Africa. It doesn't fit with our 'common sense' view of Africa – a view fuelled by endless repetitions of the same images in the media.

An example of the way the media can deal in negative representations has been the coverage of young people in 'hoodies'. Such people are not usually shown sympathetically; they are usually associated with stories of disturbances or petty crime, even though most young people who wear hoodies are normal, law-abiding citizens.

So it is important to explore news stories to judge the extent to which they contain a point of view. Television news broadcasters are required to ensure they show *fairness* and *balance* in their treatment of stories. A balance of opposing viewpoints should be included in contentious stories. Newspaper reporting is not always as balanced.

One group who are often targeted by media campaigns are so-called 'benefit scroungers'. Michael Philpott was an individual who found himself labelled in this way by the national newspapers.

SHAMELESS

£26,000 a year benefits but scrounger who has 14 children wants MORE of your cash and moans: Britain has let me down

BY JOHN CHAPMAN

A LAYABOUT with 14 children by five different women last night demanded a bigger council house for his family.

Unemployed Michael Philpott claimed that he has to sleep outside in a tent because of his 'overcrowded home'.

The 49-year-old, branded Britain's biggest scrounger, even accused the country of 'going down the pan' because his plight was being ignored.

Philpott, who pays £68 a week for his three-bedroom house, receives £26,500 a year in benefits. Now he wants a six-bedroom home for his children, wife and heavily pregnant lover.

But last night his antics met with outrage. Tory MP Ann Widdecombe said: 'This man beggars belief. It's the most preposterous thing I have ever heard of'.

CASE STUDY ACTIVITY

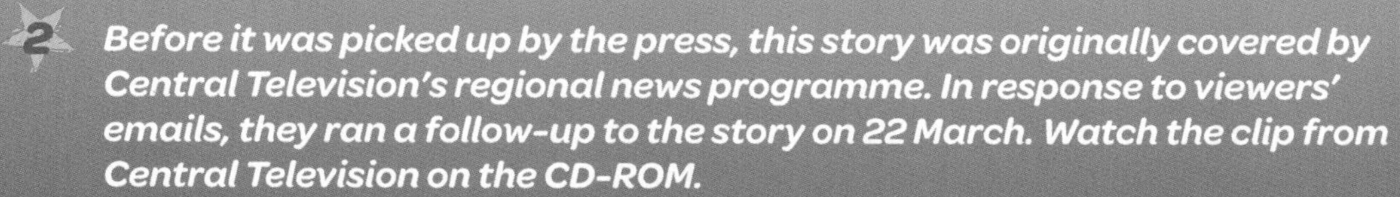

1. *Look at the newspaper piece about Mr Philpott.*
   - *What opinions are expressed about him?*
   - *What words are used to stir up the emotions of the readers?*

2. *Before it was picked up by the press, this story was originally covered by Central Television's regional news programme. In response to viewers' emails, they ran a follow-up to the story on 22 March. Watch the clip from Central Television on the CD-ROM.*
   - *What representation are we given of Mr Philpott in this news coverage?*
   - *From what you are told in the article, make a list of the facts we know about Mr Philpott.*
   - *Now list the way* opinions *about him have been used to make us think about him in a particular way.*
   - *Would you say it is a 'positive' representation or a 'negative' one? You should support what you say by giving detailed examples from the actual news story. This should not just include the words from the script which has been written for the piece, but also where the crew have placed Mr Philpott, what other things appear in the shots, the tone of voice and types of question asked.*
   - *To what extent do you think the piece on Mr Philpott succeeded in presenting all sides and leaving the audience to judge for itself?*

The selection process

Where do news stories come from?

Every story and item of news that you read in a paper or on a website, hear on the radio, or see on television, has a source. In an age with 24-hour rolling television news, it is easy to imagine that all news journalists rush around the globe, chasing action-packed stories about war, crime or other high-profile events. While this may be true for a few of the top reporters, most journalists, and particularly those working on local newspapers or local radio, will spend their whole time on their local patch.

Journalists get their stories from a variety of sources:

- *News agencies* – such as The Press Association and Reuters Association Press which supply news from all over the world.
- *Reporters* – the BBC has the biggest range of reporters based all over the globe. The smaller the organisation, the fewer reporters there are to cover events.
- *From each other* – foreign television, the national press and radio all provide stories. Stories from local television stations and newspapers sometimes appear on national television or radio news.
- *Freelance journalists* may approach a station with a story, or may be commissioned to research one.
- *Processed news* – this is gathered from items such as press releases, agendas for council meetings, and police, fire and rescue services voicebanks.

How are news items chosen?

With so many sources of news, there are far more stories than can be included in the papers for one day or a half-hour television news bulletin. The people who select the news have to consider the whole audience and provide news which has relevance to the mass audience in the case of something like the BBC's *Ten O'Clock News* or the local community for a local radio station.

ACTIVITY 9

It is your job to choose the story which will go 'at the top of the show' for tonight's BBC Ten O'Clock News, and a further three stories which will be the major news items of the day. Read through the possibilities below and choose your top story and the three stories that will follow it.

Story	Images available to support the story
The cost of living has risen for the fourth month in a row.	**Stock footage** of supermarket shelves, petrol stations, high street stores.
Prince William has a new girlfriend.	Twenty seconds of shaky footage from a camera held above the heads of a crowd as a girl rushes out of her house and into a car.
Fourteen people die in a mud slide in Colombia.	Aerial footage of the scenes of devastation. An interview with a woman who has lost her home.
Liverpool FC pay a record transfer fee to Barcelona for a striker.	Archive footage of striker playing for Barcelona. Press conference where manager introduces new player.
An important Tudor palace is on fire.	Mobile phone footage from a member of the public taken from some distance away from fire.
Fifteen soldiers are killed in an attack on their barracks in Afghanistan.	Video phone link to reporter at the scene. Still images of the barracks after the blast.
The Mayor of London is caught speeding on the M25.	Press conference where Mayor apologises.
Channel 4 announces a new reality TV show where contestants are isolated in a series of igloos in Greenland.	Stock footage of the Arctic Circle. Interview with Channel 4 Head of Programmes.

Key terms

Stock footage Material held in a library which shows something relevant to the news story but was not filmed specifically to go with it.

When you were deciding which of the stories to include in Activity 9, you probably asked yourself about the importance of the stories to the audience who watch the programme and balanced that with the visual material you had to support the story. Like news journalists anywhere, an important part of your decision will have been based on **news values**.

Most journalists will tell you that selecting the right stories for the day is a matter of experience and instinct. However, in a famous study in 1973, researchers Galtang and Ruge found that certain factors help a story to get into the news.

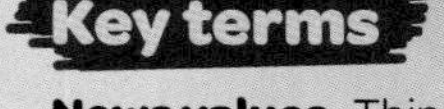

News values Things that help a story get into the news.

The text below outlines the factors that Galtang and Ruge identified that determine which stories get into the news.

Timescale – a murder is committed and discovered quickly, so it fits the timescale on which news organisations work. An increase in gun crime, which happens over a long period, will only get reported when there is a series of gun-related crimes.

The size of an event – a rail crash killing 25 people is big news; a train derailment with no injuries is not.

Surprise – was the event unexpected?

Predictability – if the news organisations expect something to happen, then it will. A big anti-capitalist demonstration planned for central London will get reported, even if it passes off peacefully, because the news organisations expect violence and send journalists to cover it.

Continuity – a running story, like a war, will continue to be covered.

How clear the event is – news need not be simple, but a very complicated story will probably be left out.

Reference to elite people or nations – news about the USA or the US president is more likely to get covered than similar news from Costa Rica.

Key terms

Gatekeeping Where reporters or editors block certain issues but allow others through into newspapers or news broadcasts.

This process of selecting and rejecting items for the news is called **gatekeeping**. The gatekeepers who make the decisions will be influenced by their own backgrounds and education.

Branding TV news

There are television channels which are entirely devoted to up-to-the-minute, round-the-clock news coverage. Like any part of the television industry, news is thus big business. It is important for each channel to develop its own distinctive **branding** so that viewers recognise it and – hopefully – identify with it enough to show *brand loyalty* by regularly tuning in to the station to watch its news programmes.

Key terms

Branding The distinctive features by which we recognise products.

In the early days, the news was usually read by a white male in a suit and tie, sitting at a desk. There were few additional pictures and hardly any on-screen graphics. Things are dramatically different today. Cameras shift position around news presenters who are often a male/female partnership. They sometimes come out from behind their desk and walk about the studio, talking to their audience in a conversational way.

Elaborate sets are designed to give a distinctive tone to the type of news coverage the station is providing. Printed information is often scrolled across the screen, giving facts about stories other than the one being focused on by the presenters.

Modern-day news on Channel 5

An important part of the Media Studies Key Concept of media language is the idea of *mise-en-scène*. This French expression literally means 'put in the scene'. It helps us to explore how scenes from film and television convey their meaning by looking carefully at the *connotations* brought into our minds by the sets, props, lighting, type of actors/presenters and costume. For television news, the visual look of the set and the presenters' clothing will match the expectations of the target audience and the tone the programme hopes to set.

ACTIVITY 10

You have been asked to plan the set for the launch of a news programme which will be shown at 6 o'clock on ITV 3. It is attempting to attract a younger audience in the 16–34 age range.

1. *Decide on the name you will give your news programme.*
2. *Draw up some ideas for what the set will look like, thinking very carefully about the furniture, the colours of the set and especially what will appear on the large plasma screens to be sited behind the presenters.*

What have you learned?

In this chapter you have learned about:

Texts

- How newspaper stories are constructed
- Investigating stories from different news media

Media language

Genre

- How the news media have changed across time
- How the style and content of different news media allow audiences to classify and engage with them
- The branding of television news

Narrative

- The construction of narratives in the news media

Representation

- How individuals, ideas and groups are represented in the news media

Audiences

- Who reads and watches which news media
- How the news media address specific audience demographs

Organisational issues

- Sources of news in the news media
- The news values that influence which stories get into the news

Convergent media

- How new technology is affecting the way news media operate

Magazines

Your learning

In this chapter you will learn about:

- categorising magazines
- investigating magazine covers and contents pages
- who reads magazines, when, where and why
- values and lifestyles
- describing audiences
- stars and celebrities
- magazines and advertising
- online magazines.

Categorising magazines

ACTIVITY 1

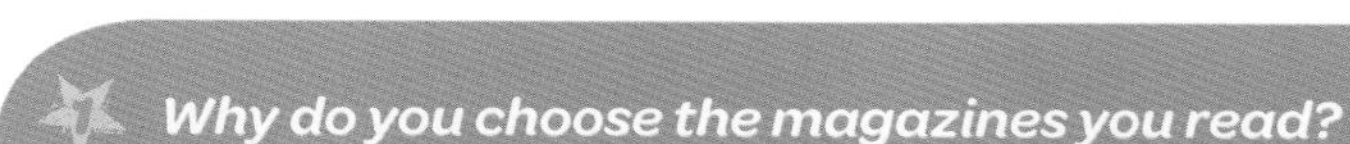

1. ***Why do you choose the magazines you read?***
2. ***Do you always read the same magazines or do you choose a different one each time?***
3. ***Where do you read them?***
4. ***Do you read magazines while you are doing something else, such as talking with friends?***

Magazines displayed in a store

Go into any supermarket, newsagent or garage. The choice of magazines is staggering. Looking at the way they are displayed will help you to understand what types of magazine there are.

TIP

Start a topic notebook to jot down your thoughts and ideas in response to the questions in activity 2. This could be used as evidence of production research or for a textual investigation. See the material in the chapter on Controlled Assessment at the end of this book.

Key terms

Categorising Ordering or grouping similar texts, for example, magazines, according to the features they have in common.

Lifestyle magazines Magazines dealing with many topics and issues to appeal to a wide audience.

Specialist magazines Magazines focusing on a particular area of interest to appeal to a narrow or niche audience.

Cover price The price charged for the magazine that is displayed on the front cover.

Target audience The specific group of people that a media text is aimed at.

Conduct some research into the magazines on sale by going into your local newsagent or supermarket. Stand back and look at the rows of magazines on the shelves.

 *What are your first impressions of the display?*

 *How have the magazines been arranged?*

 *Do any colours stand out strongly? Which ones?*

 *What features on the covers tell you what time of year it is?*

 *Do any faces appear on more than one magazine? Whose?*

 *Which subjects or themes are covered by more than one magazine?*

One obvious way to start **categorising** magazines is to split them into general interest or lifestyle, and specialist groups. General interest/**lifestyle magazines**, such as *Glamour*, have a broad range of subject matter, covering many topics and issues. **Specialist magazines**, such as *Digital Camera*, are tailored to a particular area of interest. Think about the magazines you read – which category do they belong to?

ACTIVITY 3

 *Work in a pair or small group and decide whether each of these magazine titles is in the general interest or the specialist category. The first two have been done for you.*

General interest magazines	Specialist magazines
OK	Empire

- OK
- Empire
- Good Food
- New Woman
- Rugby World
- PC Format
- Heat
- Radio Times
- Men's Health
- Match of the Day
- Angler's Mail
- Digital Camera
- Family Circle
- Bob the Builder
- Hair
- Stuff
- Inside Soap
- Mizz
- Glamour
- NGamer
- Woman's Own

Remember that there are also many other ways of categorising magazines, perhaps by **cover price**, **target audience**, *or in terms of the companies that publish them.*

 *Look again at the list of magazine titles. Choose another way of categorising them. You may need to go back to your supermarket or newsagent, speak to magazine readers or look up titles on the Internet – each title usually has its own website.*

Investigating magazine covers

Magazine publishing is a hugely profitable media industry. It is also very competitive. You will have realised from your research activities so far that a key technique used by magazines to attract and address their audiences involves capturing their interest on the shelf.

Now you are going to look closely at a magazine cover and investigate its features. This is an excellent way to find out what messages a magazine is conveying to its audience. To be successful, a magazine must establish a close, personal and almost friendly relationship with its readers. This is called the **mode of address**. On the cover on page 74, the central image is photographed looking straight out at the reader; this is known as a *direct* mode of address and suggests she is establishing a personal relationship with the reader with whom she is on friendly terms.

Before you look at the annotated magazine cover, make sure you understand some of the other terms used in the annotations. It is always important to use the correct terms when you investigate a media text:

- **seasonal theme**: when the colours and contents of a magazine relate to the time of year; for example, red hearts and features on love and romance in February for St Valentine's Day
- **mise-en-scène**: the way in which every element of the text is arranged to create meanings
- **anchorage text**: writing that fixes the meaning of an image (also known as a caption)
- **buzz word**: a word that stands out on the text, for example, 'Free'
- **key signifier**: the first thing on a cover that attracts the eye – it could be an image or words
- **puffs**: information on the front cover that is about the inside contents of the magazine (also known as 'coverlines')
- **superimposition**: when images and words are laid over each other. Often the title is partially covered by the central image – it is assumed the audience will recognise the title anyway.

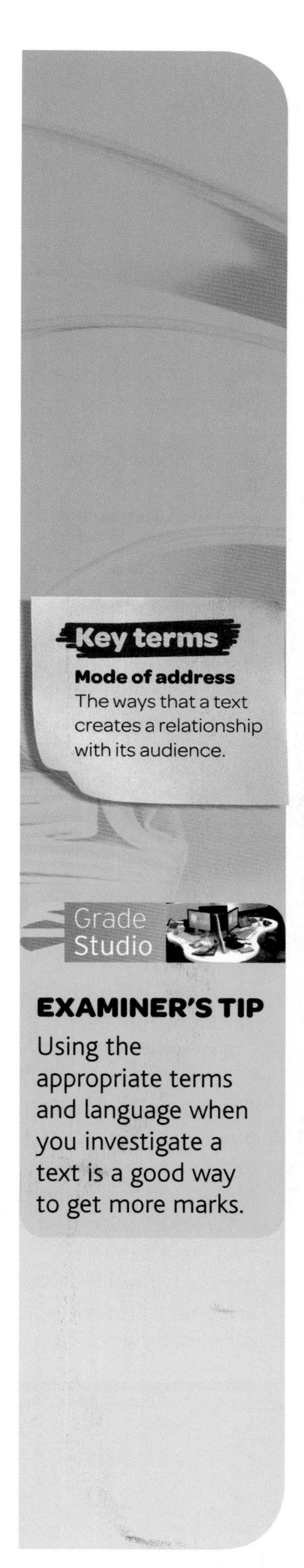

Key terms

Mode of address
The ways that a text creates a relationship with its audience.

Grade Studio

EXAMINER'S TIP

Using the appropriate terms and language when you investigate a text is a good way to get more marks.

The model, Courtney Love, is celebrity who uses DIRECT MODE OF ADDRESS and looks straight at the reader to establish a relationship with them.

The TITLE BLOCK is white SERIF font which suggests longstanding, high quality sophistication. The name *Elle* is the French word for 'she' and suggests high class, as well as a focus on fashion which is associated with France.

The magazine WEBSITE makes it possible for readers to go beyond the hard copy of this edition and read the online version too.

Words like 'rules' and 'great style' make the reader feel that the advice on fashion and accessories in this magazine is going to be valuable in their own lives.

The ANCHORAGE TEXT links the central image to the topics of the article on Courtney Love. It uses the RULE OF THREE for interest.

The main PUFF emphasises the need to follow and imitate the latest fashion trends closely.

Featuring stars and celebrities are very popular with female readers. It is an example of media industries using each other to increase their profits.

The advice to readers on style and wearing fashion is an example of the U and G theory, where audiences will choose a text that they can identify with and that will help them belong socially.

The free hair stylist is an INCENTIVE to encourage readers to buy the magazine.

It is rare for a central image to be seen in full length. Here, Courtney Love's 'look' is like a representation of what *Elle* magazine suggest the reader should be wearing.

ACTIVITY 4

Now have a go at investigating a magazine front cover yourself. PC Gamer is a specialist computer games magazine aimed at 16–35-year-old males. Try to identify how the cover has been designed to appeal to its audience.

- ***Remember to use the appropriate terms whenever you can.***
- ***Look back at how the cover on page 74 was investigated if you need help.***

PC Gamer's **readers are mostly male computer games fans aged 16–35**

Who reads magazines?

Considering the ways in which audiences read or watch different media texts is an important part of Media Studies. The best way to start is with YOU, since so many texts are aimed at people like you. You are part of the powerful 14–18-year-old audience, and media producers are keen to know what you like and what you want.

Can you think why your age group is so powerful? The main reason is that, even though you don't usually earn large sums of money, what you do earn is virtually all **disposable income** – there is only you to spend it on. After all, most young people do not have to pay for food or housing, so media producers want you to spend your money on their products. Producers also want readers with spending power to attract advertisers who **subsidise** the cost of production. The money that advertisers pay for space in print-based texts is used to reduce the selling price. Without subsidy, print-based media texts would cost over twice as much. We'll look more closely at the relationship between magazines and advertisers later in this chapter.

Why do people consume media texts?

Some media theorists have suggested that media audiences make *active* choices about what to consume in order to meet certain needs. This is sometimes called the Uses and Gratifications Theory, and it tries to show the different needs that audiences want to satisfy by consuming certain media texts.

Key terms

Disposable income The money someone has left to spend after they have paid for essentials such as housing and food.

Subsidise To reduce the cover price of a media text, such as a magazine or newspaper, by selling advertising space.

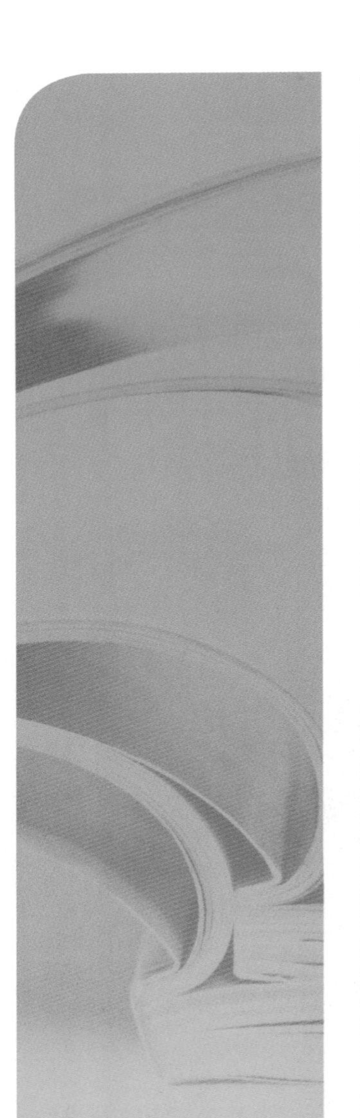

The Uses and Gratifications Theory

Media consumers choose texts that fulfil one or more of these needs:

- the need to be INFORMED and EDUCATED about the world in which they live
- the need to IDENTIFY personally with characters and situations in order to learn more about themselves
- the need to be ENTERTAINED by a range and variety of well constructed texts
- the need to use the media as a talking point for SOCIAL INTERACTION or DISCUSSION
- the need to ESCAPE from their 'daily grind' into other worlds and situations.

ACTIVITY 5

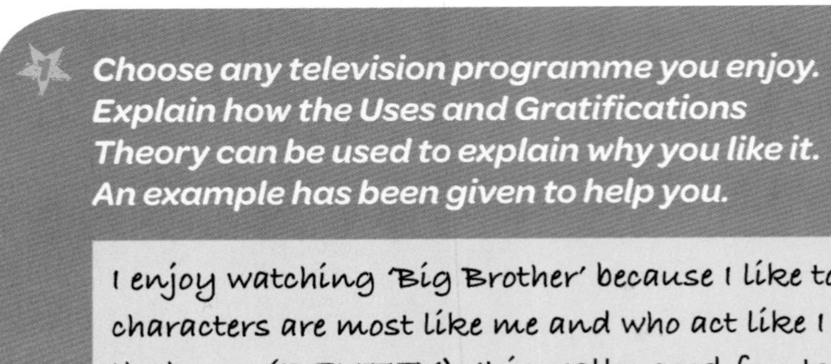

1. ***Choose any television programme you enjoy. Explain how the Uses and Gratifications Theory can be used to explain why you like it. An example has been given to help you.***

I enjoy watching 'Big Brother' because I like to choose which characters are most like me and who act like I would in the house (IDENTIFY). It is really good fun to watch the housemates make such fools of themselves (ENTERTAINED). My friends enjoy 'Big Brother' too, and sometimes we watch together on eviction night to see who is voted out (SOCIAL INTERACTION). I would never go on 'Big Brother' myself, but it takes my mind off my work (ESCAPE)!

2. ***Now apply the Uses and Gratifications Theory to a magazine you read regularly.***

Lifestyle magazines

Lifestyle magazines offer a sense of identity, companionship and reassurance, and include titles such as *Cosmopolitan*, *FHM*, *Heat*, *Nuts*, *OK* and *Closer*. They share with their readers the problems and issues of other similar people who also read the magazines. Lifestyle magazines offer guidance and instruction on how to live a particular lifestyle as well as entertainment and escapism. The magazines also challenge readers to respond to advice offered on such matters as relationships, careers and material possessions. It would be interesting to consider how realistic the lifestyle is that is being promoted.

When and how do people consume media texts?

Audiences consume – that is, watch, read or listen to – media products in a range of situations and places. Sometimes they give the text their full attention – primary consumption. At other times they may be watching, reading or listening while doing other things – secondary consumption. This is known as the pattern of **media consumption**. How are the girls in the photos below consuming their texts?

People consume media products in different ways

Key terms

Media consumption The media texts you watch, listen to or read.

EXAMINER'S TIP

This kind of in-depth research of audience consumption could be helpful for your Controlled Assessment package.

Key terms

Primary consumer Someone who is focused on watching, listening to or reading a media text.

Secondary consumer Someone watching, listening to or reading a media text while doing something else, such as talking or homework.

You are going to investigate the media products you consume in one week.

Keep a diary for one week of all the magazines, television and radio programmes, films, CDs, websites, interactive games, etc. that you consume. This will be your media consumption diary. Remember to:

- *note how long you spend on each text*
- *write down whether you were a **primary consumer** or a **secondary consumer**.*

A typical diary entry for one day might start like this:

Friday, 20 March 2009

- Listened to the radio while getting dressed. 45 minutes. Secondary
- Watched C4 while having breakfast. 45 minutes. Secondary
- Listened to Duffy album on my iPod on the way to school. 20 minutes. Primary

Add up your consumption of each type of media for the week. Choose a way to show your results, e.g. a bar graph, table or pie chart.

Write a few paragraphs about your media consumption during the week. You may wish to use these headings: Film, TV, Radio, Magazines and newspapers, Own music, The Internet, Gaming. *Remember to comment on:*

- *why you chose the texts you consumed*
- *what needs the texts met*
- *what your patterns of consumption are*
- *any media texts you deliberately chose not to consume. If so, why was this?*

Key terms

Ideology A system of values, beliefs or ideas that is common to a specific group of people.

Values and lifestyles

Values and lifestyle – sometimes called **ideology** – may at first glance seem like difficult concepts to grasp, but these are simply terms for the way people think about themselves, about others and about the world in which they live. The only difficult thing about ideology is that it is so instinctive and unspoken that it can be rather invisible. People tend not to know what their values and beliefs are unless they are challenged in some way.

ACTIVITY 7

Try this exercise to help you understand ideology and values. Imagine all the students in your class have been stranded on a desert island. No one else is there. Each of you must write down the names of the four students who would best fill these roles:

- ***A:** The leader of the group*
- ***B:** The most trustworthy emotional support for the group*
- ***C:** The person most likely to fall off the raft you have built into the shark-infested lagoon*
- ***D:** The person most likely to risk their life to dive in and rescue them.*

Count up the votes.

When you count up the votes, you may find a surprising level of agreement amongst your ideal choices for these roles. Since you have similar values or ideologies, you will have similar ideas of who best meets the requirements for each role. For example, the leader may well be the most outspoken, popular member of the group, while the emotional support person is likely to be a mature, cheerful person who happily speaks to everyone, and not just those in their friendship group. The class will have agreed on this because you all understand that, in order to take any of those roles, people need to have demonstrated certain values and standards of behaviour.

Ideology in magazines

Magazines reflect the values and ideologies of their readers because they want readers to feel they can identify with the magazine.

Here are two descriptions of the target readers of two lifestyle magazines as presented on the magazines' websites:

> *'The* Elle *reader is spirited, stylish, and intelligent; she expects to be successful at everything she does. She takes the lead and breaks the rules.'*
>
> *'The* Sight & Sound *reader is a true film buff who expects to be given intelligent information on all film releases, not just Hollywood mainstream movies.'*

Look at the following web pages showing the online versions of *Elle* and *Sight and Sound* magazines. Read the notes around one of the web pages – these will help you with the activity that follows.

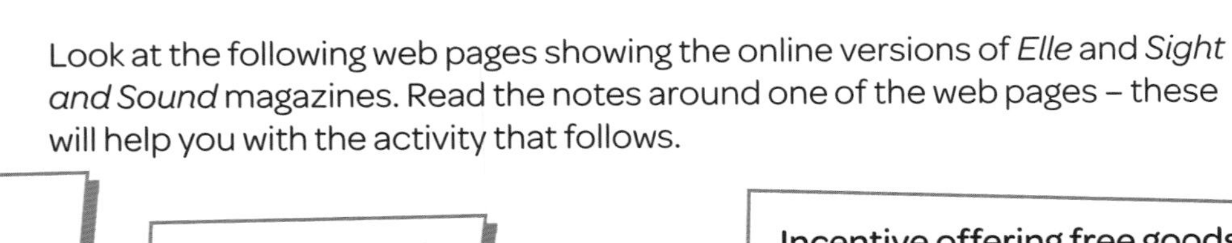

The title of the web page matches the title of the magazine itself

Links to the main areas of interest

Incentive offering free goods in exchange for subscribing

Main image from leading fashion designer catwalk

Links to main fashion items

Opportunity to subscribe to the magazine is built into the page

Feature on fashion 'must-have'

Web page editor gives advice about beauty focus of attention

CD-ROM Extra!

ElleUK.com

Open the CD in the back of this book and click on the icon below to open a link to the ElleUK.com website.

The magazine and website are produced by the British Film Institute – an organistion that takes film seriously

The website guide makes site navigation straightforward

The site finder makes it easy for a user to go straight to a specific area

→ SEE FILMS
→ SHOP FOR FILMS
→ LEARN ABOUT FILMS
→ RESEARCH FILMS
→ DOWNLOAD FILMS

about BFI
what's on
film & tv info
national archive
members' space
join the BFI

BECAUSE FILMS INSPIRE...

Home > Sight & Sound

- Sight & Sound
- December 2008 issue
- Archive
- Subscribe
- Advertise
- The Best Music in Film
- Top ten

Sight & Sound

- Discover the best world cinema
- In-depth interviews with leading directors
- Retrospective articles vividly bringing film history to life
- All the latest film news

In this issue

Our December issue features an interview with Oliver Stone about *W.* while Michael Atkinson considers the cinema of the Bush era. We also talk to the Dardenne brothers about their latest film *The Silence of Lorna*= and to Ari Folman about *Waltz with Bashir*, his animated documentary about Israel's 1982 Invasion of Lebanon. Meanwhile, we also pay tribute to two underrated directors, Abel Ferrara whose latest feature will not be distributed in the UK and also Manoel de Oliveira who turns 100 this month.

The DVDs of 2008

Our critics choose their personal favourite DVDs from 2008

Archive

Search our online database for full contents of back issues from 1999 to the present. A list of back issues to purchase is also available.

Subscribe to *Sight & Sound*

If you want grown-up comment on films this is the magazine for you.

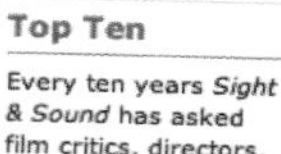

Top Ten

Every ten years *Sight & Sound* has asked film critics, directors, writers and academics to compile a list of the best films of all time. All these polls can be viewed online.

The Best Music in Film

In September 2004 *Sight & Sound* invited film-makers and musicians from across the world to reflect on the relationship between cinema and music.

Advertise in *Sight & Sound*

Advertise in the UK's original movie magazine.

Sight & Sound

December issue: The DVDs of 2008

BFI Members

Log in to the Members' Space

BFI Emails

Sign up for email bulletins or change your preferences

Contact or Visit the BFI

Telephone numbers and visitor information

Clear link made to the magazine itself

Contents of current magazine made clear

Interactive links for users with several opportunities to sign up to site

Key focus of magazine and website – the history and role of film critics

Poll-based judgements on best film music

Best films lists compiled by respected film personnel

Invitation to advertisers to buy space in *Sight & Sound* magazine

Now that you have looked at the two web pages, can you see how the magazine sites reflect the values, interests and ideologies of their readers? Make some notes under the following headings:

- ***typography (choice of font style, colour, placement)***
- ***use of images***
- ***how the page is laid out to attract the eye***
- ***the use of language – look out for 'specialist' words that the reader will understand, use of informal address 'you'***
- ***promises connected to values, ideology and/or pleasure.***

CD-ROM Extra!

BFI

Open the CD in the back of this book and click on the icon below to open a link to the BFI website.

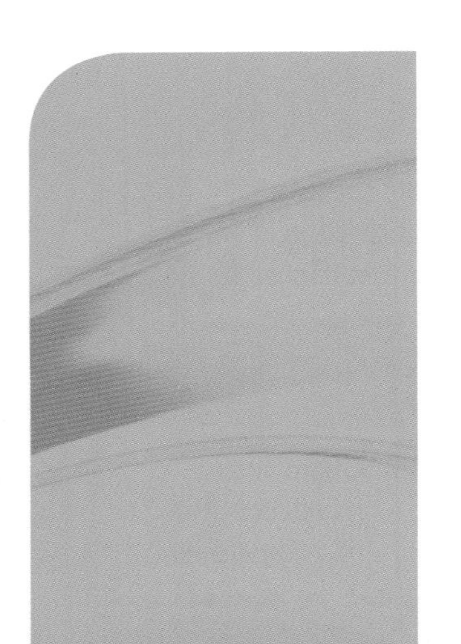

Ideologies can be seen on many different levels. Countries have *national ideologies*: if you go on holiday abroad, you will notice patterns of behaviour that would be unusual in the UK. In Japan, for example, people are always extremely polite to each other, and it is considered rude to show anger. Can you think of any things that visitors to the UK might notice about our patterns of behaviour? For example, people often say that the British value patience and love queuing!

Understanding ideology is helpful when it comes to investigating the ways in which magazines and other media texts are constructed to appeal to their target audiences, by offering them material that they will enjoy, understand, value and aspire to.

TIP

Knowing how to define target audiences is useful in many other Media Studies areas and when investigating media texts.

You will need to be able to describe and pinpoint target audiences throughout your Media Studies course and final External Assessment, so it is worth considering a few ways of defining the audiences for magazines.

Grade Studio

EXAMINER'S TIP

Sweeping statements are best avoided as they are not specific and are unlikely to receive high marks in your Controlled or External Assessments.

Describing magazines' audiences

Gender

Some texts have an obvious gender bias. *Action Man* and *Girl Talk* are examples of magazines with a clear male/female bias. Sometimes you can identify if gender is a relevant issue by considering the themes or values at the heart of a text. Look again at the front cover of *Elle* magazine on page 74. A focus on appearance and image is often associated with female audiences. Some people think that magazines can be harmful by reinforcing female stereotypes – for example, girls and women can make themselves ill trying to look like the models in the pictures. What do you think?

Age

Try to avoid making sweeping statements about the age of a target audience, such as: 'this text is aimed at teenagers' or 'the target audience for this magazine is middle-aged people'. You might find the following breakdown helpful because it considers age bands in a more specific way:

Under 5	6–8	9–12	13–15	16–18
19–25	26–40	41–60	Over 60	

Imagine you are a media producer considering the target audience for your new magazine. What do you know about people of different ages?

1. ***List and discuss the probable lifestyle, likes and dislikes of people in these age groups: 6–8; 16–18; 25–40; over 60.***
2. ***Ask yourself about their hobbies, their favourite night out, the television programmes they watch, etc.***

People over 60 are <u>likely</u> to: have low disposable incomes; have similar, non-active lifestyles; not enjoy violence; enjoy films and programmes from the past.

When target audiences are described by their age and probable lifestyle, it is possible that groups can be **stereotyped**. The description of over-60s in Activity 9 may be true of some people, but it is important to remember that many over-60s earn high salaries, run marathons, enjoy thrillers and go to pop concerts!

Ethnicity

Although ethnicity is not always relevant when considering target audience – a text may be aimed at all ethnicities – the racial or religious background of an audience can sometimes be a factor that will influence what a text contains and what messages it will send out. For example, *Asiana* is a magazine that targets Asian women.

Key terms

Stereotyping Grouping people together according to simple shared characteristics, without allowing for any individual uniqueness.

1. ***What clues are there on this magazine cover to suggest that the ethnicity of the target audience is important? You might like to consider the words chosen and the epresentation of the model, for example.***
2. ***Working in groups, find out what magazines are most popular with people in your school. Try to ask students who represent a mix of ages, genders and ethnic backgrounds. What links can you see between these factors and the magazines people enjoy?***
3. ***Present your findings in the form of a chart, graph or table and discuss in class.***

Ethnicity is a major factor in the audience targeting of *Asiana*

Lifestyle

Being able to discuss the possible lifestyle habits of an audience is important. Try to consider the audience **values and aspirations** (ideology) for the text you are investigating. Media producers research their audiences to find out what kinds of thing are important to them, so that the messages in their texts will appeal to them and make them respond positively. Ask yourself how the text highlights and perhaps reinforces those values.

Key terms

Values and aspirations The ideas and goals that are important to people.

Look at the front cover of *Shout* magazine below.

- It suggests that the audience might be anxious about their appearance based on the clothes, hair and make-up of the models.
- The audience are obviously very interested in stories about stars and celebrities, and probably use pictures of them to provide role models of beauty, fame and success.
- The magazine assumes that readers will want to know as much about the personal life of celebrities as possible.

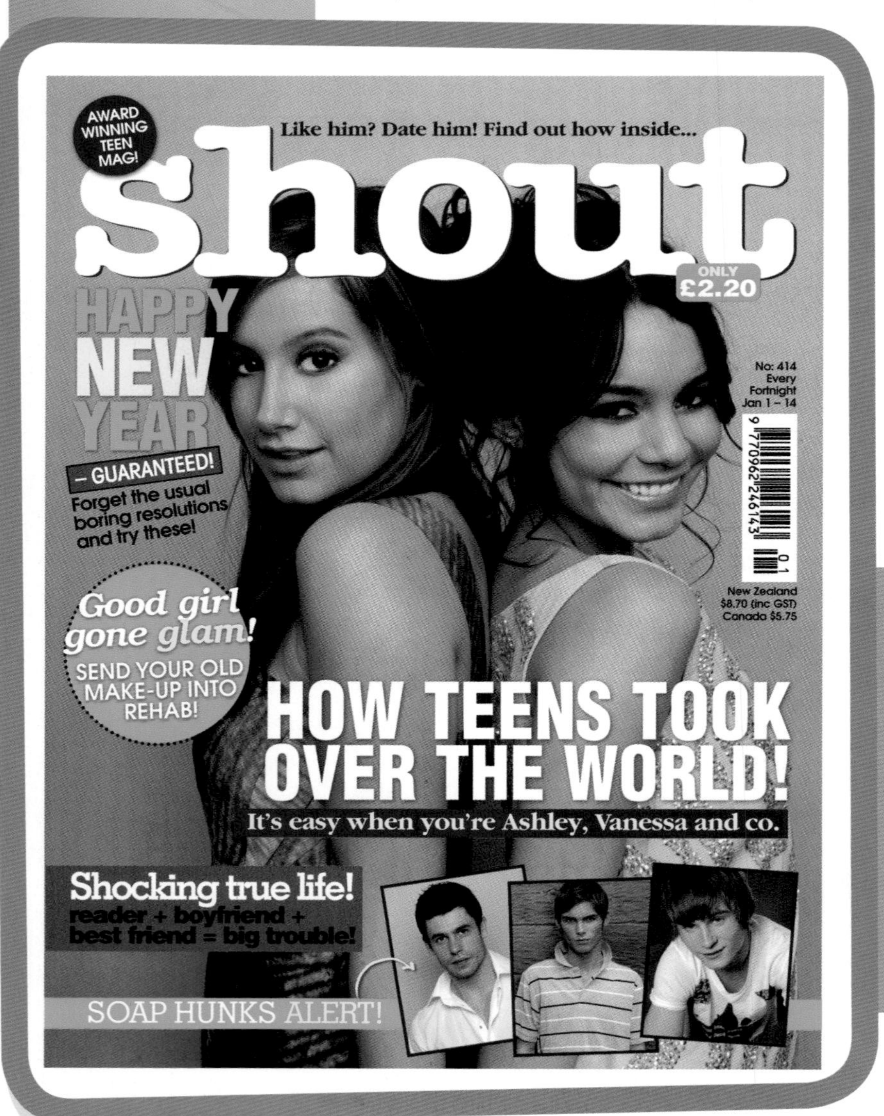

In many ways this magazine is a forerunner to magazines aimed at older girls that feature stories about celebrities and their partners.

ACTIVITY 11

Look closely at the front cover of Shout.
Write bullet-point answers on the following:

- *the likely audience of the magazine*
- *the kinds of feature that might be appealing to this audience.*

ACTIVITY 12

In Activity 3 on page 72, you categorised magazines into general interest and specialist groups. Now that you understand how magazine targeting works, and have learned about describing audiences, describe the target audiences of the following magazines:

Sugar Radio Times Rugby World Good Housekeeping FHM

Lifestyle magazine ideologies

Lifestyle, or general interest, magazines literally offer their readers a 'life style'; or in other words, a model on which to base their lives at this particular moment and advice on what might be needed to get the life they want. To do this successfully, magazines need to be able to make their readers identify with the lifestyle on offer, but at the same time offer them slightly more than they already have. The magazines offer both guidance and **aspiration**: 'You, too, can be like this, if only you do this/buy that, etc.' Successful magazines need to have a clear sense of their target audience and to adopt an appropriate mode of address. The audience for lifestyle magazines is likely to be:

- commercially successful
- aspirational females
- concerned with appearance and image
- the highest spenders on toiletries/cosmetics
- in control of their own lives and living for themselves
- interested in 'ideal' representations of self, home, family, career, relationships and lifestyle
- enjoying their freedom and independence.

Key terms

Aspiration When an audience sees fashion, accessories, a lifestyle, etc. in a magazine that they wish they could have for themselves.

Specialist magazine ideologies

Specialist magazines have smaller audiences than lifestyle magazines, as they focus on specific areas of interest, but they are popular with their audiences. Titles include *Total Film*, *NME*, *Angler's Mail* and *Nintendo*. What are your favourite specialist magazines? Why do you like them? It may be because they are more individual in their contents and mode of address than general interest or lifestyle magazines, which can be very 'samey' with an emphasis on fashion, celebrities and health. The following are some of the values of specialist magazines:

- They aim to celebrate the passion and interest of smaller, more individual audiences.
- They are published by and for specialist interest groups.
- They are often written by people with a personal interest in the subject.
- They exist so that people with shared interests can meet and say, 'Hey, I'm into that too!'
- They encourage relationships to form between readers who share the same interests. (See the section on page 93 on online magazines.)

- They will never sell as many copies as the general interest or lifestyle magazines, but they will always be appreciated by audiences who enjoy the 'alternative' or individual feel of a magazine which does not try to cover too many areas. It is interesting to note that this also applies to other media areas, such as film, when independent, low-budget films appeal to an audience who like quality acting and scripts, and reject big-budget Hollywood films.

Stars and celebrities

Key terms

Celebrity Someone who is popular in one country for appearing in one media field, such as a soap opera.

Star A performer who is famous internationally.

Magazine producers often feature a **celebrity** or **star** on a front cover in order to increase sales, and therefore profit. Which of these famous people would you classify as stars and which as celebrities?

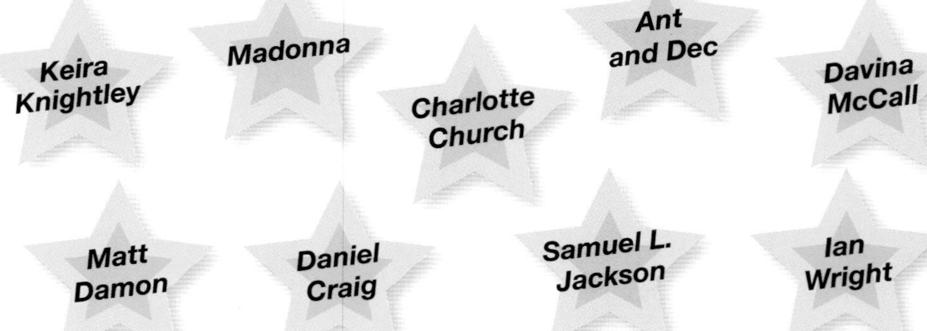

As a nation, people in the UK are fascinated by the lives of the famous, but how much of this enthusiasm is caused in the first place by the wide coverage of celebrities in the UK media?

Look at the list of stars and celebrities on the previous page. Choose one example of a star and one of a celebrity. Write a factfile on each one, indicating:

- *what you know about them already*
- *what they are most famous for*
- *which media areas might represent (or cover) them in some form.*

Example factfile: Charlotte Church

- *First became famous as a child star singing classical music and was referred to as having the 'Voice of an Angel'.*
- *Released her first pop song, 'Crazy Chick' in 2005 and was given a new pop image.*
- *Hosted her first television chat show –* The Charlotte Church Show *– in 2006 on Channel 4.*
- *Is well known for her marriage to Welsh rugby star Gavin Henson, and has appeared in many lifestyle magazines with him.*

Media producers create texts featuring stars partly to generate audience interest, for example, in a film trailer, and partly to satisfy audience demand for information on stars, for example, magazine spreads showing stars without their make-up. Consider the following:

- Producers make texts which audiences consume and respond to.
- These responses to texts are taken into account by producers when they make more texts.
- Popular formats are repeated so that audiences are given the sorts of text they 'ask for'.

Look at the media triangle diagram, which shows how media producers, texts and audiences are related to each other.

Charlotte Church: Celebrity or star?

TIP

It is useful to understand just how much influence the media has in 'making' a star. Consider the range of programmes that do this.

The media triangle

Take a few moments to discuss this triangle and the complex relationship between the maker of a magazine, the magazine itself and its target audience. Who has the most power in this process – the producers who make texts, the texts themselves or the audiences who consume and respond to them?

The media are often criticised for constantly representing stars and celebrities, and possibly even intruding into their private lives. However, famous people need the media to maintain their 'stardom', and we, the audience, are greedy for more information about them. Can you name any people who have become famous very quickly because of constant media attention? Can you think of anyone who has received negative media attention? You might like to think about the star image of Jade Goody, for example. Jade became 'famous' after being in the Big Brother house in 2002, and went on to feature in a series of reality TV shows such as *Celebrity Driving School* in 2003, *Jade's Salon* in 2005 and *Jade's PA* in 2006. She entered the celebrity Big Brother house in 2007 and received overwhelmingly negative media attention when she was seen making racist comments against another housemate, Shilpa Shetty. Since then, Jade has had to work hard to win back media favour.

ACTIVITY 14

Talk with a partner about stars and celebrities and their coverage in the media. Try to decide how far you agree with this statement:

Magazines feature too many stories about stars and celebrities.

How stars are represented

The **representation** of stars and celebrities is worth considering in any media form you are studying. Much has been written about film and television stars, and there are many theories about how and why they achieve fame. Consider this statement:

Stars are people who have become famous in one specialist area of activity and then also often achieve fame in other areas.

The Beckhams have been famous for some time but what are they most famous for *now*? Think about each family member in turn. How has this changed over time?

Key terms

Representation
How people, places, events or ideas are represented or portrayed to audiences in media texts. Sometimes this is simplistically through stereotypes so the audience can see immediately what is meant, and sometimes the meanings are less obvious.

Another way of looking at stars is to say that they are *'complex representations of real people'*. In other words, they are not completely real, but they are based on someone who *is* real. They are people who have been given some kind of image treatment that will affect how audiences see and respond to them. Even though you may feel you know a lot about David Beckham, could you say that you actually know him?

Catherine Zeta Jones, for example, grew up in Swansea, Wales, and was a little-known television and stage actress until she won roles in Hollywood films in the late 1990s. When she moved to Hollywood and married Michael Douglas, her 'girl next door' image was changed to a more 'A list' look that made her seem more glamorous and unobtainable.

ACTIVITY 15

'Stars are people who have become famous in one specialist area of activity and then also often achieve fame in other areas.'

1. ***Discuss this quotation with a partner, then feed back and discuss it as a class. Is this quote helpful when considering star/celebrity coverage in magazines? You may find it useful to have a range of magazines to look at.***
2. ***Investigate the representation of one of your favourite stars or celebrities in at least two different magazines. Make a list of similarities and differences. How can the same person be shown differently? You may find it helpful to look at the two images on the right.***

The representation of stars is often linked to 'star image'

Mise-en-scène

The creation of every image, whether still or moving, involves planning and setting up. The careful arrangement of every element in an image to create a particular message or meaning is called the **mise-en-scène**.

Key terms

Mise-en-scène
A French phrase which literally means 'put in shot'.

This mise-en-scène makes the subjects look studious

Exactly the same elements are used here to create a different meaning!

The best way to understand how mise-en-scène works is to try it out yourself. Imagine you are the producer of a magazine called School Leaver. *You want the magazine to communicate to its teenage readers that it is cool to be studious and to care about the future, as well as to be popular and trendy. You want to take a picture of a 16-year-old for the front cover. How would you create the mise-en-scène ?*

- *Choose a suitable setting, for example, a classroom with good displays. Place a desk and a chair in the shot.*
- *Choose a subject from your class who you think has the right image for the shot.*
- *Wearing school uniform – how will you make sure the subject looks the part?*
- *Ask the subject to sit at a desk. How will they position their legs?*
- *What expression will they adopt?*
- *Which items of stationery, books, etc. will be on the desk? Why?*
- *What kind of bag will the subject have?*
- *Just before you take the shot, how will you ask the subject to pose?*

If possible, take the shot!

When you have taken the photo, try something else. This time you are the producer of Bliss *magazine for teenage girls aged 11–14. A photo story needs a shot of a two-timing, school-hating, football-mad teenage boy who is bored in his lesson and desperate for the bell to go. Using only the elements you used in the first mise-en-scène, change their arrangement to create a different meaning.*

- *What changes might you make to the subject's uniform and general appearance?*
- *What might happen to the books and pens?*
- *What pose will you ask for this time?*

Grade Studio

EXAMINER'S TIP

Your photograph could be used as part of a production piece of Controlled Assessment.

ACTIVITY 17

Using everything you have learned about texts, audiences and producers, as well as about representation and mise-en-scène, you are now going to transform yourself or a friend into a media star.
You are going to create a profile of yourself as a star and then take a photograph of yourself as a star to go in a magazine of your choice.
Think carefully about the following:

Choose an area of specialism, for example, a television celebrity who presents children's programmes.

List five bullet points connected to your representation. You could include: a zany sense of humour, a love of animals which is built into your shows, a famous mother.

Now create a 'look' for yourself that matches your profile. Think carefully about the mise-en-scène of the magazine page, so that the background is as appropriate as your costume and make-up. Set the shot up and ask someone to take the photograph. Make sure that your facial expression creates an impression of your star personality.

Investigating magazine contents pages

You have already seen that you can find out a lot about what a magazine has to offer by looking at its cover. The next step is to look at the contents page. This will give you an overview of what is inside the magazine you are studying. You can also see how it has been laid out to catch the reader's attention.

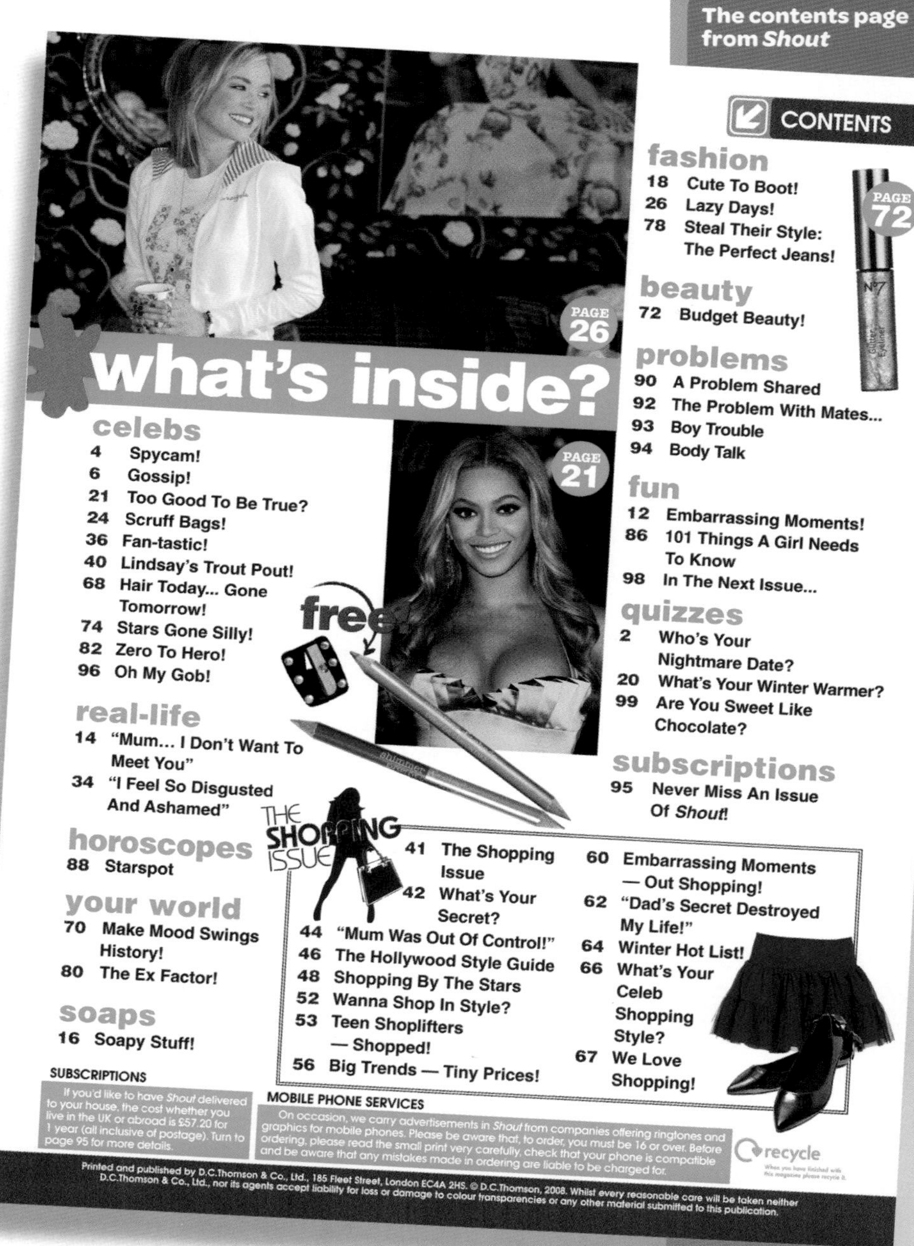

CONTENTS

what's inside?

PAGE 26

PAGE 21

PAGE 72

free

celebs
4 Spycam!
6 Gossip!
21 Too Good To Be True?
24 Scruff Bags!
36 Fan-tastic!
40 Lindsay's Trout Pout!
68 Hair Today... Gone Tomorrow!
74 Stars Gone Silly!
82 Zero To Hero!
96 Oh My Gob!

real-life
14 "Mum... I Don't Want To Meet You"
34 "I Feel So Disgusted And Ashamed"

horoscopes
88 Starspot

your world
70 Make Mood Swings History!
80 The Ex Factor!

soaps
16 Soapy Stuff!

fashion
18 Cute To Boot!
26 Lazy Days!
78 Steal Their Style: The Perfect Jeans!

beauty
72 Budget Beauty!

problems
90 A Problem Shared
92 The Problem With Mates...
93 Boy Trouble
94 Body Talk

fun
12 Embarrassing Moments!
86 101 Things A Girl Needs To Know
98 In The Next Issue...

quizzes
2 Who's Your Nightmare Date?
20 What's Your Winter Warmer?
99 Are You Sweet Like Chocolate?

subscriptions
95 Never Miss An Issue Of *Shout*!

THE SHOPPING ISSUE
41 The Shopping Issue
42 What's Your Secret?
44 "Mum Was Out Of Control!"
46 The Hollywood Style Guide
48 Shopping By The Stars
52 Wanna Shop In Style?
53 Teen Shoplifters — Shopped!
56 Big Trends — Tiny Prices!
60 Embarrassing Moments — Out Shopping!
62 "Dad's Secret Destroyed My Life!"
64 Winter Hot List!
66 What's Your Celeb Shopping Style?
67 We Love Shopping!

SUBSCRIPTIONS

If you'd like to have *Shout* delivered to your house, the cost whether you live in the UK or abroad is £57.20 for 1 year (all inclusive of postage). Turn to page 95 for more details.

MOBILE PHONE SERVICES

On occasion, we carry advertisements in *Shout* from companies offering ringtones and graphics for mobile phones. Please be aware that, to order, you must be 16 or over. Before ordering, please read the small print very carefully, check that your phone is compatible and be aware that any mistakes made in ordering are liable to be charged for.

recycle

Printed and published by D.C.Thomson & Co., Ltd., 185 Fleet Street, London EC4A 2HS. © D.C.Thomson, 2008. Whilst every reasonable care will be taken neither D.C.Thomson & Co., Ltd., nor its agents accept liability for loss or damage to colour transparencies or any other material submitted to this publication.

The contents page from *Shout*

Look for:

- the main areas of interest that the magazine covers, for example fashion, celebrities
- the kinds of feature in each area, for example, real life stories and problem solving
- how the reader's attention is drawn to special features, for example, through large-coloured font in eye-catching boxes
- how images and words are combined, for example, the free make-up in the contents page above.

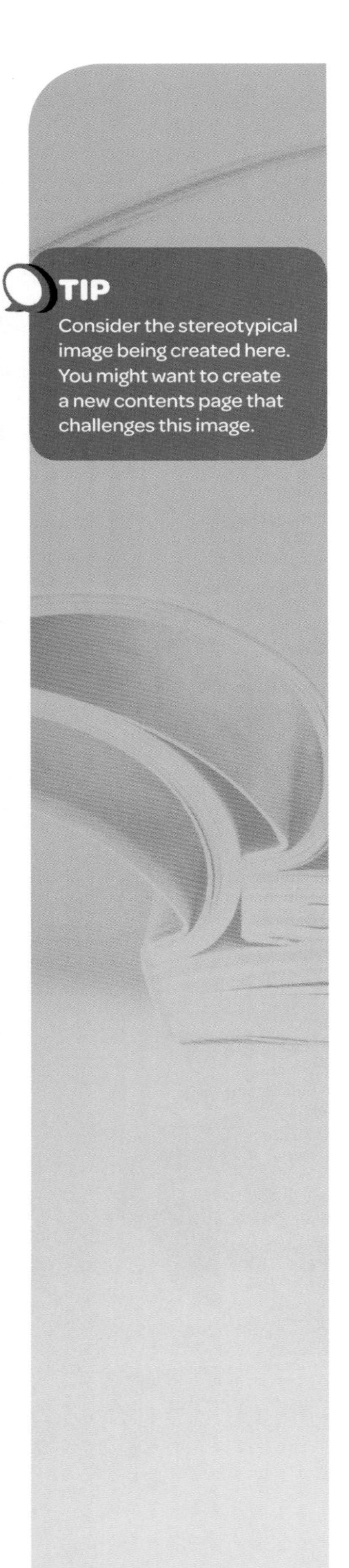

TIP

Consider the stereotypical image being created here. You might want to create a new contents page that challenges this image.

Although every magazine is different, each type of magazine has its own typical features. As an example, look at the typical features of a magazine aimed at teenage girls – *Shout*.

Some of the key features to look out for include:

- **Contents** – (see page 91) tells the reader how to find their way around the magazine. What first impressions do you get about what this magazine considers to be important?
- **Articles on cooking, crafts and make-up** – these encourage girls to take an interest in caring for others and making themselves look beautiful.
- **The 'true story'** – an immediate hook into the reader's own life as she tries to make links between the story and her real-life experiences.
- **The quiz** – a fictional but realistic scenario aims to test readers' potential responses in the real world. Quizzes often promote an 'average' response as the best one. If the girl scores the right number of points, she knows she will not stand out as being too different from her peers. This can directly influence the way that teenage girls see themselves. They are encouraged to conform to certain stereotypes of looks and behaviour, and discouraged from breaking 'out of the mould'.
- **Features about celebrities** – stories about pop, film and television stars help readers to feel they have a relationship with the 'great' and famous. Everyone is interested in the private lives of public figures!
- **Problem pages** – these give a genuine point of contact between the magazine and the reader. Reading about familiar situations or fears is reassuring and removes feelings of abnormality and separation. Look back at the Uses and Gratifications Theory on page 76 – what needs do problem pages satisfy?
- **Advertising for fashion and beauty products** – stereotypical representations of beautiful 'perfect' peers reinforce image and identity and give pre-teenagers a range of products which they can be sure will be acceptable to others.

Why are some magazines blamed for having a bad influence on teenagers? You may like to refer to two or three examples in your explanation.

Magazines and convergent media

All media areas have relationships with other media areas – in some cases they even depend on each other. Magazines, for example, depend on selling advertising space to keep the cover price cost down for readers.

Advertising

Have you ever noticed how many pages in a magazine are devoted to advertisements? If you carry out a survey of lifestyle or general interest magazines, you may be shocked to find that possibly over half the pages are filled with advertisements. It is estimated that women spend £230 million a year on monthly '**glossies**' and that the magazines themselves then earn another £190 million from advertising.

ACTIVITY 19

Watch the 'Making a profit' clip on the CD.

Discuss with a partner what you have learned about how magazines make money.

Investigate advertising in magazines. Choose two contrasting magazines. Then:

- *see how many pages are in each magazine*
- *decide what the main ideologies/values of each magazine are*
- *count how many pages are used for advertisements*
- *decide what kinds of advertisement appear most often.*

In your opinion, what is the relationship between your chosen magazine titles and the adverts they contain?

The **revenue** that lifestyle magazines get from selling advertising space is far more important than the income they receive from the cover price and individual sales. The amount that they can charge for their advertising space is based on **circulation**. This is why magazines try so hard to be appealing, entertaining and interesting – in order to keep their circulation figures up and charge advertisers more!

Lifestyle magazines are all trying to create an ideology or lifestyle that will end up delivering particular audiences to advertisers, and advertisers in return try to reflect the main interests of the magazine. Advertisers for health, beauty and fashion products will try to buy space in these magazines as they know their target audiences will already be reading the magazine.

Online magazines

With improvements in technology over the last ten years, many media areas such as film and television are crossing over into others. You will notice in the chapter on film, for example, that there is a convergence between film and magazines, the Internet and advertising. In much the same way, magazines have been converging with the Internet.

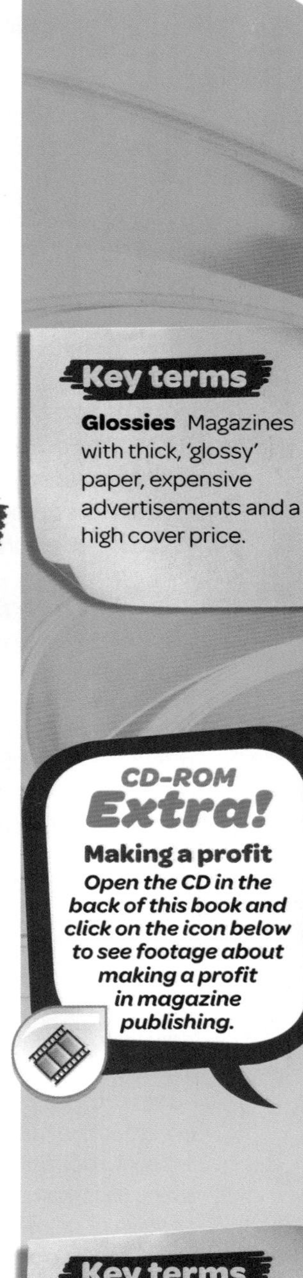

Key terms

Glossies Magazines with thick, 'glossy' paper, expensive advertisements and a high cover price.

CD-ROM Extra!

Making a profit

Open the CD in the back of this book and click on the icon below to see footage about making a profit in magazine publishing.

Key terms

Revenue The money generated by selling advertising space in a magazine or newspaper, on television, websites etc.

Circulation The number of copies of a newspaper or magazine which are sold.

Here we will consider the convergent media nature of film magazines. Many magazines now have equivalent online versions.

Empire *magazine is the most popular specialist film magazine in the UK. In 2004, the online version of the magazine, called empireonline.co.uk was first posted on the web. It is a successful and popular site, and there is a free subscription for anyone who wants to have the online magazine sent to them each week.*

This is what a regular reader of the print version of* Empire *magazine said about the online version:

> *'Having read the magazine for a while now, I saw the advert for the site and was amazed. I was shocked to see that there was actually a magazine out there that had a running website that was updated in real time as soon as they had the news. The main features are available to all users with links to the news and reviews section. Their witty reviews and sarcastic news segments live up to the magazine's legend. Your first view of a site is the most important section of any website and* Empire *doesn't disappoint!'*

What the site offers

CD-ROM
Extra!
Empireonline
Open the CD in the back of this book and click on the icon below to open a link to the Empireonline website.
HTML

The site offers:

- trailers and film stills of forthcoming films
- reviews of newly released films
- user polls, voting on favourite categories of films already released
- interviews with actors, directors, producers, etc.
- daily quiz and competitions with prizes
- blogs
- updates on newly released DVDs
- readers' views and opinions and relevant film fan information, for example, National Film Week.

Convergent media aspects

The convergent nature of the site is important too, and is a good example of how media areas work together. There are links, for example, to:

- advertisements for recording television programmes to PS3 consoles and Play TV
- information on films released to DVD
- links to television sites
- links to magazine offers.

★CASE STUDY★
ACTIVITY

1. ***Visit the empireonline.co.uk site. Navigate through the news, features, articles and gallery shots. Why do you think the site has proved so popular with users?***

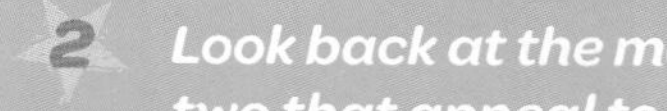

2. ***Look back at the magazine titles mentioned in this chapter. Choose one or two that appeal to you and explore their online version.***
   - ***How are the web pages laid out?***
   - ***Can you see any similarities or differences between the print and online versions?***
   - ***What are the most interesting links that the site allows you to explore?***
   - ***What does the site offer that the print version does not?***

Publishing houses

Magazine publishers are often part of huge, international media companies that also own newspapers, radio and television stations. This is a good example of convergent media. Below is some background information on some of the magazine publishing houses:

IPC has nearly 100 titles, including NME, and sells on average one magazine every 11 seconds throughout the year in the UK.

BAUER (which used to be called EMAP) publishes *Empire* magazine and sells 150 titles in the UK, France and around the world. It is also involved in the marketing of radio, television and music.

FUTURE is a smaller company based in Bath, specialising in film, computing and sports magazines including *Total Film* and *PC Gamer*.

BBC WORLDWIDE is the third largest consumer magazine publisher in the UK. Titles include *The Radio Times* and *Good Food* magazine.

EGMONT publishes 12 titles in the UK aimed at children. Although they refer to their publications as magazines, it is clear that some, such as *Thomas and Friends* would be referred to by many as comics.

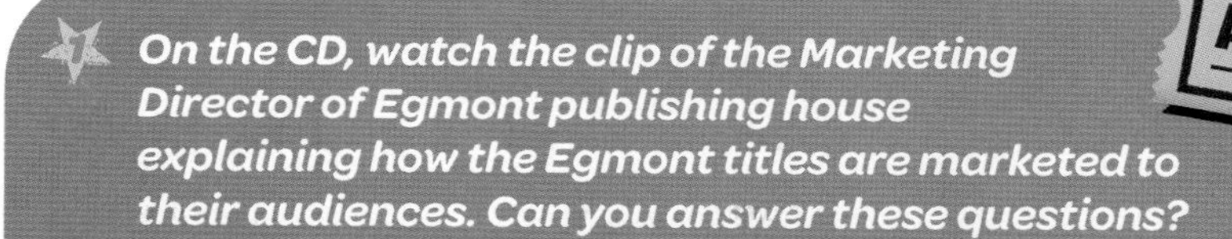

ACTIVITY 20

1. On the CD, watch the clip of the Marketing Director of Egmont publishing house explaining how the Egmont titles are marketed to their audiences. Can you answer these questions?
   - How do new titles come about?
   - What have you learned about the relationship between magazines and films and television programmes?
   - How are audiences encouraged to become loyal readers of titles?
2. Look again at the list of magazines in Activity 3. Choose ten titles. Create a chart like the one below and fill it in. The first title has been completed for you.

Magazine	Publisher	Circulation	Target audience
Empire	EMAP	2,000 per month	Mostly male, aged 18–35

CD-ROM Extra!

Marketing magazines

Open the CD in the back of this book and click on the icon below to see the Marketing Director of Egmont publishing house explain how the Egmont titles are marketed to their audiences.

ACTIVITY 22

Having read the section on publishing houses, discuss the following issues and questions:

- A recent online survey suggested that there has been a drop in the circulation of music and film magazines. Can you think of any reasons for this?
- What would happen to the choice of magazines available if there were fewer publishing houses?
- How do magazine titles compete with each other? Refer to specific titles if you can.

What have you learned?

In this chapter you have learned about:

Texts

- New terms in relation to investigating magazines
- Conducting a contents investigation to see what is inside any magazine, how it is laid out and the elements on which the magazine places importance
- The values and ideologies of specific magazines
- Creating star profiles for magazine pages

Media language

Genre

- Categorising magazines in a variety of ways
- How to analyse the different features of print and online magazines

Narrative

- The features of magazines that relate to readers' lives
- Telling the stories of stars and celebrities

Representation

- How and why a mise-en-scène is set up
- How to create a mise-en-scène in order to see how many elements in a shot are combined to create meaning
- Representing stars and celebrities

Audiences

- Thinking about and reaching target audiences
- Identifying and describing target audience of specific magazines
- How audiences use magazines and what they get out of them
- Different audiences having different values and beliefs, thus affecting the way they respond to magazines

Organisational issues

- How design and marketing are directly linked to consumers
- The relationship between producers, texts and audiences
- The profile of some publishing houses
- Generating advertising revenue

Convergent media

- The convergent media nature of magazines, including their important relationship with advertisers and the development of online magazines

Comics, cartoons and animation

Your learning

In this chapter you will learn about:

- comic and cartoon characters, including superheroes
- the codes and conventions of comics, cartoons and animations that are used to communicate meanings for audiences
- attracting target audiences
- types of animation and their effects on audiences
- comics and convergence.

The popularity of comics, cartoons and animations

Comics, cartoons and **animations** are popular with a huge range of audiences. Comics, for example, are not only enjoyed by young children but (like science fiction) also by older people. This is because they are often used to explore big concepts like human nature, good and evil, and social issues and concerns such as the protection of the environment.

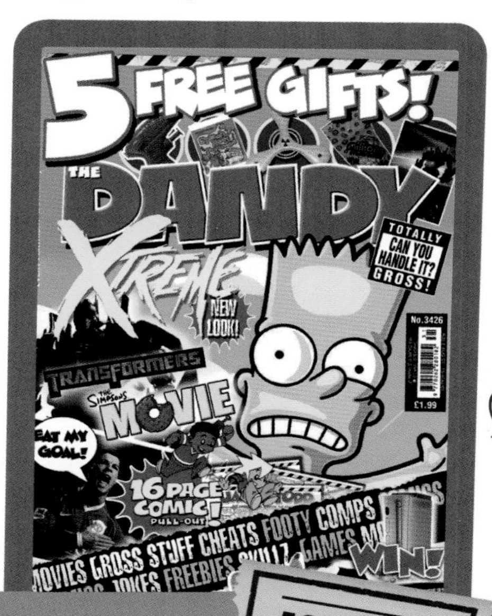

Key terms

Animations Audio-visual versions of comics that are used in a variety of media forms such as films and adverts.

TIP

The concept of representation can be clearly illustrated in this section by looking at how you identify the good and evil characters.

ACTIVITY 1

Name the first example that comes into your head of each of the following. Why did you think of them?

- ***Comic***
- ***Cartoon***
- ***Animation***

Comic and cartoon characters – old favourites

TIP
Use information from family and friends, old comics and videos and the Internet to help you.

People become passionate about the media texts they enjoyed when they were young, partly because they were so involved when they read or watched them. Young children look forward eagerly to their favourite characters coming on television, or to watching the video again and again and joining in with the words and actions. Your childhood favourites become part of your identity. Try talking about your favourite – you may be surprised how much you still care!

ACTIVITY 2

1. ***Complete a table like the one below to find out as much as you can about each of the characters listed. Try to discover:***
   - ***when and where they first appeared***
   - ***who created them***
   - ***if they were used in more than one media genre, for example, a comic strip that became a television series***
   - ***whether they are still featured in comics or television stories today.***

Character name	When and where did they first appear?	Who created them?	Are they used in more than one media genre?	Are they still featured in comics or TV stories today?
Scooby Doo	1969 on CBS television, America	Hanna-Barbera productions	Many series on different television channels, plus comics, video games and films	Marvel produce the comic today and there are still re-runs of the TV show in the UK
Desperate Dan				
Care Bears				
Mickey Mouse				
Batman				
Tintin				
Zebedee				

2. ***Try to build up an information sheet on one of the characters. If you can, include drawings of your chosen character. Discuss your findings with the rest of the class.***

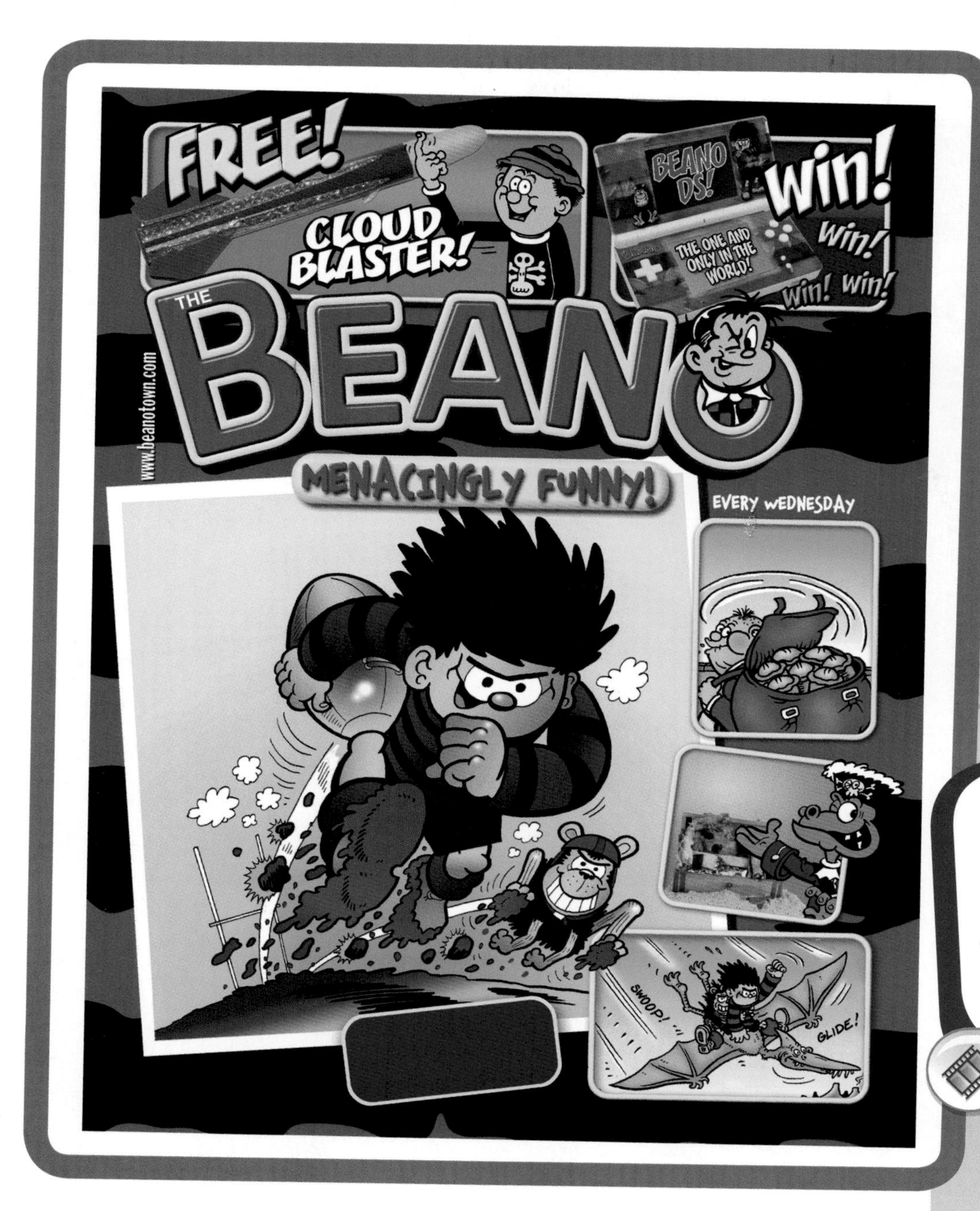

CD-ROM Extra!

Comic characters

Open the CD in the back of this book and click on the icon below to find out about designing characters in comics

Comic and cartoon characters are created deliberately for children to identify with and remember. Many comics and cartoons use 'licensed' characters that readers and viewers are already familiar with. These characters enable comic and cartoon producers to establish business relationships with the creators of the characters. Film studios will sell the rights to popular characters to related media industries.

Winnie the Pooh

Though Disney didn't create Winnie the Pooh, it has the right to license it to be used in a range of media texts as well as Disney films, including a comic, a cartoon series, CD soundtracks and computer games, and also allows Marks and Spencer to sell Winnie the Pooh clothing. This is a good example of the *convergent* nature of the media, when one media text uses **tie-ins** and **spin-offs** that involve other media industries.

Key terms

Tie-in A media text that uses the characters, and possibly storyline, of a text in another form.

Spin-off Merchandise that uses characters from a media text.

Thomas the Tank Engine

The Reverend W. Awdry first created Thomas the Tank Engine out of a piece of broomstick for his son Christopher. This character ended up being licensed in a series of books, an ITV television series, a film called *Thomas and the Magic Railroad* (2000) and the comic *Thomas and Friends* (published by Egmont Magazines).

1. *Can you think of any other characters that appear in so many forms as Thomas the Tank Engine?*
2. *Discuss the ways that comic producers create characters and use licensed characters.*

Grade Studio

EXAMINER'S TIP

These kinds of activity could form part of your research for Controlled Assessment, or form part of a textual investigation. See pages 215–218 for suggestions on comic-related coursework.

1. *Choose a character that was important to you as a child. How did you discover the character and why did you enjoy them?*
2. *If possible, undertake some research with young children about the characters they enjoy in comic/magazine form. You will need to create a survey to ask them questions about their favourite comics and characters. Questions could include:*
   - *What comics/magazines do you like to read?*
   - *What do you like best about comics/magazines?*
   - *Can you make a list of your favourite characters from films, comics and television programmes?*
   - *Can you draw one of your favourite characters?*
   - *Design a new character. What do you like best about your character? The face? Dress? Actions? (You may need to give some help here.)*
3. *Using your knowledge of the kinds of character which are popular with children, create a brand new character for a new comic or cartoon series. Draw the character and label him/her with the main features of interest.*

Character type and function

Vladimir Propp suggested in 1928 that in any story there are only a limited number of character types, each of which have their own purpose in the narrative. Some of these are shown below.

Propp's main character types

Hero

The **central protagonist** of the narrative who drives it forward and has some kind of quest or mission to undertake in return for a reward. Traditionally male, for example, Thomas the Tank Engine, but can be female in modern narratives, for example, Dora the Explorer.

Heroine or Princess

Acts as a reward for the hero for succeeding in the quest. In older, more stereotypical narratives the heroine is a **passive** princess and female, for example, Minnie Mouse. In modern narratives, the heroine can be more active and feisty, for example, Leela in *Futurama*.

Villain

Seeks riches, glory and/or power, and also seeks to stop the hero from succeeding in the quest or mission, while presenting a genuine threat. They sometimes want the heroine for themselves too! They can be male, for example, Mr Burns in *The Simpsons* or female, for example, Mystique in the *X-Men* comics.

Donor or Mentor

Gives the hero important information or equipment to help him or her in the quest. They are often represented as wise or as having special powers, but are not able to do the quest without the hero, for example, Shredder in *Teenage Mutant Hero Turtles*.

Helper

Accompanies the hero for some or most of the journey of the quest, and can even help the hero to succeed, but cannot themselves complete the quest, for example, Jess the cat in *Postman Pat*.

TIP

These character types are relevant in other media areas, such as film and television.

Key terms

Central protagonist Character around whom the text and narrative are centred.

Passive Not helping the narrative to move forward or not helping the hero.

You have to be flexible when you classify characters into these types. Some characters fulfil two, or even more, functions. For example, the heroine could also be the helper – April is the heroine in *Teenage Mutant Hero Turtles*, but she also comes to the aid of the turtles on numerous occasions.

Hero, villain, heroine – but who's who?

1. ***Think up more examples of Propp's character types from stories you know. Create your own chart showing typical characteristics of those types. Were any characters hard to classify? Why?***

2. ***Create a character design for a new character, using your chart from the previous part of Activity 5. Label your character to show what type he/she is.***

Helper: Yuna

Hero: Myke

A student created these characters

Comic front covers

ACTIVITY 6

1. *Look at a range of comic front covers. How have they been designed to attract the attention of potential readers? The front cover below has been investigated for you.*

Logo shows quality and authenticity.

Mysterious figure adds reason for the reader to buy the comic and find out more.

Indexical sign of the Eiffel Tower gives sense of place.

Images of heroes using their powers shows action and makes heroes instantly recognisable to the reader.

Villains shown as well as heroes to indicate danger and excitement.

Added feature in the comic is advertised boldly under the main title in an attempt to persuade readers to buy the comic.

Villains fighting heroes shows action and gives the reader a sense of what's to come.

Large image of hero as well as smaller images of other heroes are iconic to the reader and draws the reader to the heroes.

Small amounts of open space so that important figures occupy the most space and make the cover more exciting and attractive.

2. *Choose a different comic and investigate the main features that you think will appeal to its target audience.*

3. *Create the front cover of a brand-new comic that you think will appeal to either boys or girls. Think carefully about your target audience here – look again at the CD-ROM.*

Comic conventions

Key terms

Storyboard The key moments of a story shown using images and notes – see the example on page 107.

Key terms

Oppositional character A character who will play opposite the key central character, either in a relationship (for example, the hero/heroine) or in conflict (for example, the hero/villain).

The main conventions of comics are understood by their audiences and are an important part of the way that comics are read. Although comic strips are not audio-visual texts, they follow many of the same rules of narrative as film or television. They are constructed to be like the frozen frames of moving texts. They are like dynamic **storyboards** which combine words and pictures to create the impression of sound, movement and tension. They rely most of all on complex reading skills on the part of the comic reader – reading comics is far from a waste of time!

Key moments

When you are making a storyboard for a comic strip, it is useful to remember Todorov's Narrative Theory. This suggests five stages in any story:

1. Equilibrium: establish setting, characters and storyline.
2. Disruption of the equilibrium, perhaps by an **oppositional character.**
3. Recognition of the disruption (often the longest part).
4. An attempt to repair the disruption.
5. Reinstatement of the equilibrium.

Your comic storyboard will need at least one frame or panel for each stage.

Richard's skateboard disaster

Richard was fed up with school. One evening, before school the next day, he went to his friend Yousaf's house to watch scary movies. Before they knew it, time had moved on and it was after midnight.

Richard rushed home on his skateboard and fell into bed exhausted.

The next morning, Richard was woken by his Mum shouting to him that he had overslept and his breakfast was ready. He jumped out of bed and hurriedly dressed for school.

Unfortunately, he forgot that he had left his skateboard at the top of the stairs the night before. As he tried to rush downstairs, he trod on the skateboard,which shot out from under him.

Poor Richard fell down the stairs and he ended up at the bottom with a nasty fracture to his leg. His Mum called an ambulance and he was rushed to casualty.

Richard ended up with his leg in traction, and could not go to school for six weeks. Yousaf visited him regularly and Richard was heard to confess to his friend that he actually missed school!

ACTIVITY 7

You are going to work in pairs to make a storyboard for Richard's story. You can see an example of a comic storyboard below. You may like to look at the illustrations of comic techniques on page 108 to help you.

1. *Decide on the most important details of the story – make a list first. You are going to tell the story in six to eight frames, but you must also remember that the story should control* ***pace*** *and* ***tension*** *while making sense.*
2. *Now make a comic storyboard to tell the story. Try to make sure that the meaning is clear. Vary your camera framing so that some frames/panels will be close-ups and some will be from further away.*
3. *Think about the information you want to add underneath each frame/panel – this should give an idea about the effect of each image.*
4. *Pass the storyboards around the class so that everyone can see them. Discuss the similarities and differences between the storyboards. Did any pairs use techniques in addition to drawing the key moments? How did these help to improve the impact of the story?*

Key terms

Pace The speed at which something happens or a story develops.

Tension The build-up of suspense or anticipation as a story develops.

Example of a comic storyboard written by a student.

Establishment Shot - Castle
Pan wide shot 4 seconds
Harp playing

Full Length shot - princess's window
2 seconds
Harp continues playing
(weeping sound)

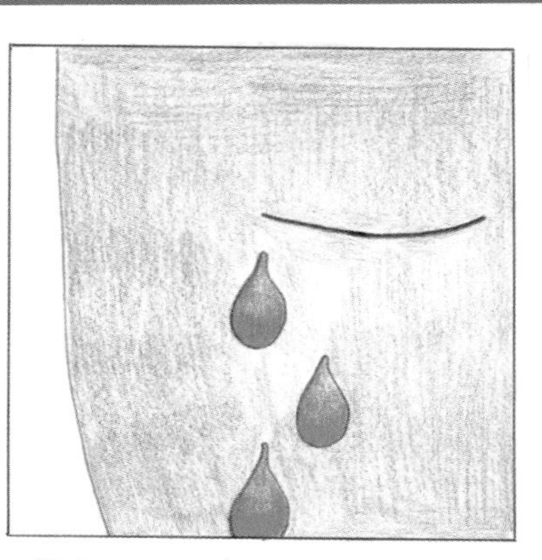

Extreme close up
3 seconds
Harp continues playing
(v/o: 'The Mouse princess was very sad')

You will have seen how important it is to choose moments which are rich with meaning and convey a lot of information to the audience. Remember that comic readers are good at reading not only the information in each frame, but also the information implied between frames. For example, if a character is shown in place A in one frame and place B in the next, the audience will understand that the character has travelled there and time has passed between the frames.

CD-ROM
Extra!

Comic stories

Open the CD in the back of this book and click on the icon below to find out more about making comic stories.

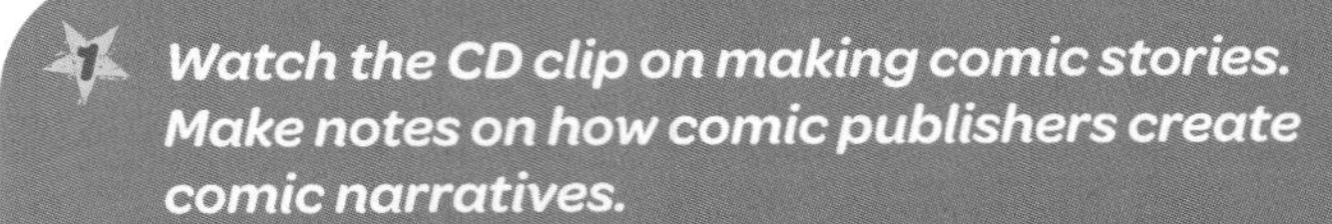

1. ***Watch the CD clip on making comic stories. Make notes on how comic publishers create comic narratives.***
2. ***Practise creating frames/panels that would show the key moments from fairy tales and well-known stories that you enjoyed as a child.***

Examples of comic techniques

The following techniques are often used in comic strips:

IT WAS GETTING LATE, AND DAVID STILL HADN'T FINISHED HIS HISTORY ESSAY...

Text boxes – small boxes of text which give details that would be hard to show in pictures alone. They are placed at the top or bottom of a frame, or underneath a frame (common in comics aimed at young children).

Thought bubbles – like speech bubbles, but the words are placed in cloud-shaped bubbles to show what the character is thinking.

LATER, AT LIZ'S HOUSE...

Speech bubbles – words of speech placed in a bubble pointing towards the mouth of the character who is speaking. Sometimes speech bubbles can point out of a frame to show that a character we can't see is speaking.

Frame links – copy placed between frames to help the reader understand events which may have happened after the last frame and before the next.

ACTIVITY 9

Split into teams of three or four people. Look at a range of comics aimed at different target audiences, for example, **The Beano** ***is targeted at 9–13 year olds, predominantly boys, who enjoy funny stories. Try to find an example of every one of the comic techniques listed opposite and below. The team to do this in the quickest time wins.***

Sound words – comics give the impression of sounds by using inventive onomatopoeic words like 'POW!' and 'ZAPP!!'.

Emotion words – like sound words, comics also use words to show exactly how a character is feeling, for example, 'BOOOOOOOOOOOOORED!!!!'

Facial expressions – simple alterations to a character's face to show emotion.

Movement lines – comic frames give the impression of movement by adding small lines around the edges of characters' bodies and moving objects.

The best way to appreciate how sophisticated comic techniques are is to use them yourself. Follow the steps in the activity below to create a four-to-six-frame photo-comic based on a fairy tale or childhood story you know well. Your aim is to create a text which is eye-catching and easy to understand.

ACTIVITY 10

1. ***Start by sketching the frames as a simple storyboard (see page 107). Decide together how to take the shots.***
2. ***Take the shots. Elaborate settings or costumes are not necessary, since you can alter the photos using gel pens or correcting pen, by sticking things onto them or by cutting parts of them out. If you use a digital camera you can use a photo-editing package.***
3. ***When your photos are ready, create your photo comic. You will need:***
   - a large sheet of sugar paper
   - mounting paper for each photo
   - plain paper for writing or typing out text boxes and speech bubbles
   - an assortment of coloured pens, etc. for decoration.
4. ***Give a group presentation to the rest of the class: show your photo-comic and explain how you created it and why. Alternatively, make a wall display: label your photo-comic to show how and why you made it as you did.***

Discuss the process of creating comics. For example, choosing the key moments of a narrative and varying, as much as possible, the size and shape of the frames in which these key moments will be shown.

Superheroes

Many stories in comics, cartoons and animated films are centred on heroic deeds. Yet there is a difference between a hero – who we simply follow throughout the narrative – and a **superhero**, who often has special powers to help him or her save the world! Why do you think that animation is a particularly good media genre for portraying superheroes?

Key terms

Superhero A heroic character with special powers and a lifelong mission.

ACTIVITY 12

1. *If you were a superhero, what superpowers would you choose? Why?*
2. *Make notes on, or draw, the superhero you would be.*
3. *Explain how your superhero got their powers.*
4. *If you have time, make notes or draw the **arch-villain** who opposes your superhero.*

Key terms

Arch-villain The character who opposes the superhero and often has special powers too, that are used only for evil. The most memorable arch-villains are those who have a reason for turning to evil, for example, Doctor Octopus in *Spiderman*.

Audiences love superheroes because, through them, they are able to:

- explore beyond the boundaries of human possibility, for example, imagine what it is like to fly like Superman
- engage with the conflict between good and evil, for example, sympathise with Spiderman as he fights against the Sandman
- enjoy exploring the 'dark side' that so many superheroes have, for example, wonder what it is like to give up popularity like Batman.

In recent years, films that are based on comic or cartoon superhero characters have become very popular. This demonstrates the convergent nature of comics, cartoons and animations.

It is interesting to investigate what has influenced the creation or development of superheroes. For instance, the spread of nuclear weapons or changes presented by radiation are real historical developments that have influenced superheroes.

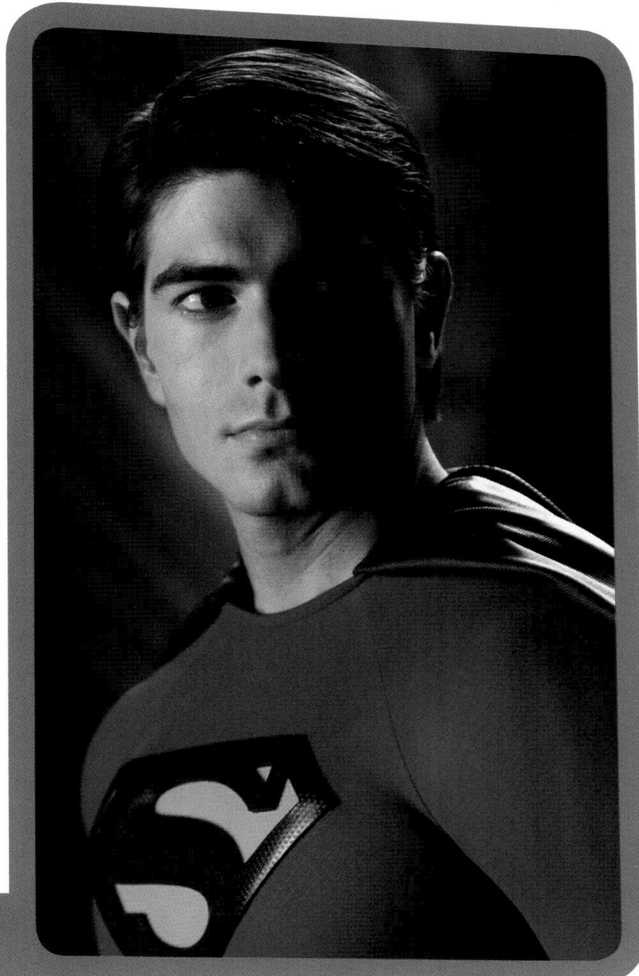

Superman: comic and film superhero

CASE STUDY

MARVEL COMICS

This case study considers some of the convergent aspects of Marvel comics. Your favourite film superheroes will probably come from the gallery created by Marvel comics. Marvel is well known for its colourful and dramatic superheroes, which include Spiderman, The Incredible Hulk, the Fantastic Four and The Silver Surfer.

The first Marvel comic was published in the USA in 1939, introducing the Submariner. Many of the best known Marvel characters were created in the 1960s, starting with the Fantastic Four in 1961. The Incredible Hulk (1962) – influenced by characters from the books *Frankenstein* and *Dr Jekyll and Mr Hyde* – and Spiderman (1963) soon followed. Already Marvel were using **intertextual reference** to create the Marvel universe – characters would guest star in each other's comic strips.

> **Key terms**
>
> **Intertextual reference**
> When one media text mimics or refers to another media text in a way that many consumers will recognise.

By 1966 Marvel characters had their own animated series on television, showing five different stories featuring Captain America, Iron Man, The Incredible Hulk, Thor and Submariner. In the 1970s not only did Marvel heroes feature in full-length films, but Marvel were asked to create comics based on popular films such as *Star Wars*.

Marvel Enterprises today owns the rights to over 4000 characters, used in comic books, films, television programmes and video games. The success of several blockbuster superhero films in recent years has led to spin-offs such as a Marvel Superhero Top Trumps game.

Iron Man

A helpful research activity could be to choose one of your favourite superhero characters and find out about their history and development. Iron Man, for example, was first introduced in 1963 by Marvel's designer, Stan Lee: he wanted to make a hero out of a businessman, Tony Stark, who would be 'a rich, glamorous ladies' man but one with a secret that would plague and torment him as well'. Iron Man was a comic character who was first used to explore the fears behind the Cold War, but later to raise awareness of heart problems and alcoholism.

Iron Man was adapted for film in 2008 with Robert Downey Jr playing Tony Stark.

Marvel superheroes

Marvel superheroes often show certain characteristics:

- some kind of tragedy in their past for which they want revenge, for example, The Incredible Hulk
- double identity, for example, Superman
- some kind of change to their genetic make-up that gave them their superpowers, for example, Spiderman.

CASE STUDY ACTIVITY A

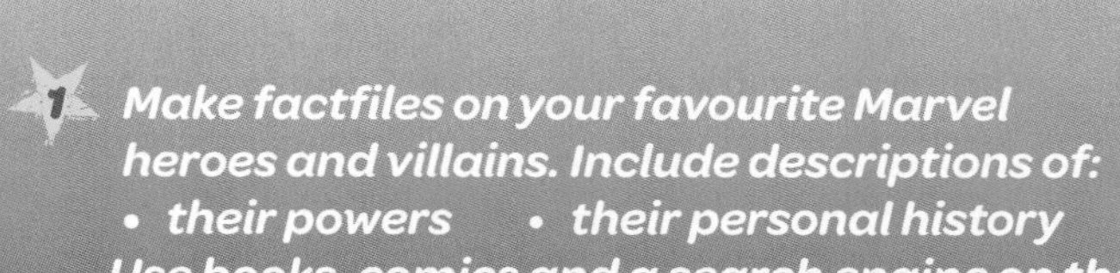

1. Make factfiles on your favourite Marvel heroes and villains. Include descriptions of:
   - their powers
   - their personal history
   - their greatest adventures.

   Use books, comics and a search engine on the Internet. You could also talk to comic fans, or visit a comic supplier such as Forbidden Planet.
2. Now compare the comic and film versions of some well-known superheroes, such as Superman, X-Men and The Incredible Hulk. List and discuss the main similarities and differences between the two treatments. You may find it helpful to read through the information on investigating openings below before you complete this activity.

Investigating openings

The way a cartoon or animation begins is important in setting up its narrative, characters, setting, main themes and general mood. Marvel comics are the basis for many film adaptations. These films usually begin with an *ident* in the form of a comic strip of famous superheroes to show the audience the roots of the film's storyline. The opening sequence that follows may show some of these features:

- establishing shots to set location
- first appearance of the superhero (who may not appear in their superhero form)
- a soundtrack that establishes mood
- graphics that establish the style of the film
- codes and symbols that suggest plot.

CASE STUDY ACTIVITY B

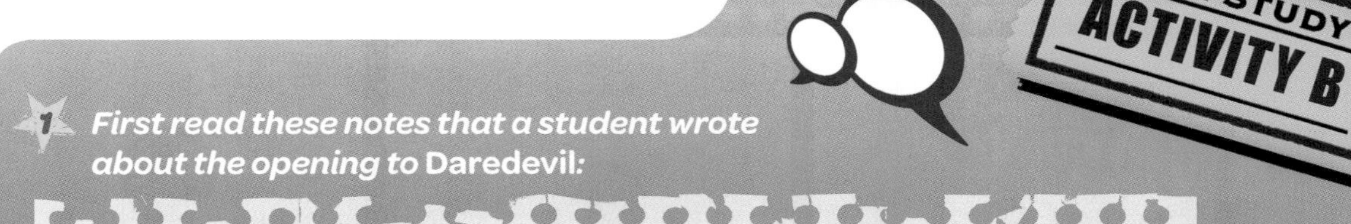

1. First read these notes that a student wrote about the opening to Daredevil:

   - Opening panning shot of skyscrapers zooms into individual 'braille' style lights which are then 'translated' into title credits. Could the hero be blind?
   - The hero wears a dark red lycra outfit with his face hidden. His mask is removed and we are shocked that he is 'revealed'.
   - A flashback helps us to understand that he suffered tragedy as a child, but that he also received supersonic sonar hearing as a result of the accident.

2. Watch two or three more openings to films based on Marvel superheroes. Write down the most important points in notes like those above.
3. Share your ideas about the openings you have seen with the class. Make a class list of the important features of openings.

Animation convergence

The Sony Bravia's animated rabbit campaign has been very successful

We tend to think of animation as being used for cartoon programmes and films, but animation techniques are used right across media areas. Animation is often used in:

- advertising, for example, the Sony Bravia advert with animated plasticine rabbits using stop-frame animation (see image). This advertisement has been used in both print and audio-visual form
- non-animated films as a special effect, for example, the scenes in *The Lord of the Rings* showing Gollum and the Orcs using computer-generated imagery
- openings of non-animated films and television programmes, for example, the award-winning opening film sequence of *Juno* (2008) that cleverly uses a combination of live action and line animation.

Animation techniques

Different techniques can be used to 'animate' still images, each bringing its own unique style to the animation.

Line or cel drawing

This technique was used by the first animators. They drew a figure, framed in a background, many times, each time making tiny adjustments, and filmed each picture for just a frame or two. When the film was shown at normal speed, the figure appeared to move.

These six frames form a simple animation when played continuously

ACTIVITY 13

Try creating your own line animation. Think of a simple figure that you can draw, and choose a simple action, for example, raising a hand to wave. You could even copy out the illustrated six-frame animation above and animate it as shown below.

1. *Draw the figure on the first page of a small notebook in the top right-hand corner.*
2. *On the second page, draw the same figure with a slight change to show the beginning of the action.*
3. *On the next page, move the figure further, and so on until the action is completed.*
4. *Holding the notebook firmly in one hand, flick quickly through the pages with the other thumb so that you can see your drawings in rapid succession. Your character will appear to move.*

Model animation or stop-motion

Another successful and easy-to-recognise animation technique is **model animation**. A scale model of a character is moved and filmed in very small stages. This obviously takes a great deal of patience and time, and software that allows the camera to film single frames to create the effect of start–stop motion.

This technique became popular in the 1960s and 1970s, when Ray Harryhausen made model animation his speciality. He created characters such as the skeleton army in *Jason and the Argonauts* (1963), the goddess Kali in *The Golden Voyage of Sinbad* (1974) and Pegasus in *Clash of the Titans* (1980). The latter was his last film and it took Harryhausen a year to create the effects, which used 202 specially constructed shots.

CD-ROM
Extra!
Ray Harryhausen
Open the CD in the back of this book and click on the icon below to visit Ray Harryhausen's official website.

Key terms

Model animation
An animation technique using posable scale models.

The skeleton army in *Jason and the Argonauts*

CD-ROM
Extra!
Curse of the Were Rabbit website
Open the CD in the back of this book and click on the icon below to open a link to the official site.

HTML

In 1985, Nick Park joined Aardman Animations in Bristol and a few years later they introduced the world to Wallace and Gromit. Three short films and two full-length films have proved hugely popular with young and old alike. (2000) featured the voices of Mel Gibson and Julia Sawalha, while (2005) featured Ralph Fiennes and Helena Bonham Carter. The popularity of Aardman's unique style of model animation is set to last!

Grade Studio

EXAMINER'S TIP

The research you carry out here could be used in a textual investigation or as part of a production.

ACTIVITY 14

1. ***Watch one or two scenes from Nick Park's animations. Try to spot how the animators have made the characters and settings as realistic and true to life as possible, for example, Gromit raises an eyebrow to show his feelings; the wallpaper and pictures on the wall.***
2. ***Explore the official*** **Curse of the Were Rabbit** ***website. It is lively, informative ... and animated! Look at the 'behind the scenes' material and discuss what you have discovered about creating model animation characters.***

ACTIVITY 15

If you have access to the right technology, you could create your own simple model animation as a piece of coursework. You can use almost anything for this: Plasticine, yoghurt pots, dolls, Lego, plastic bags ... anything you can imagine coming to life.

1. *Make or draw a simple character.*
2. *Work out a simple series of movements for the character to perform, and film each stage for 1–2 seconds.*
3. *You only need to record about 2 minutes of footage. Ideally you should use animation software such as istopmotion.*

Computer-generated imagery (CGI)

It was obviously very time-consuming to draw so many frames. It took three years, for example, for the animators on Walt Disney's *Snow White* (1937) to complete their drawings. As early as the 1960s, people were working on ways to use computers to make the small adjustments to the original frame.

Since the 1970s, computers have been used in more and more sophisticated ways in animation. The first film to use 3D **computer-generated imagery** (**CGI**) techniques in a significant way was Disney's *Tron* (1983). The film was about a computer programmer (played by Jeff Bridges) who is sucked into his computer and turned into a 'virtual person' who must fight the main programme in order to survive. If you are able to see this film for yourself, you will notice immediately how simple the technology is compared to that of today.

Key terms

Computer-generated imagery (CGI) Using computer graphics, especially 3D computer graphics, in special effects.

Tron (1983)

TIP

You might like to explore how ***Shrek*** uses role reversal and subversion of traditional narratives.

Today CGI allows whole worlds to be created and inhabited – sometimes without any human actors at all. Films entirely animated by computer include *Toy Story* (1995) and the *Shrek* trilogy (2001–2007), while *Beowulf* (2007) uses video-gaming motion-capture computer technology.

What are your own favourite examples of film moments using CGI? Can you think of any moments when the technology works less well?

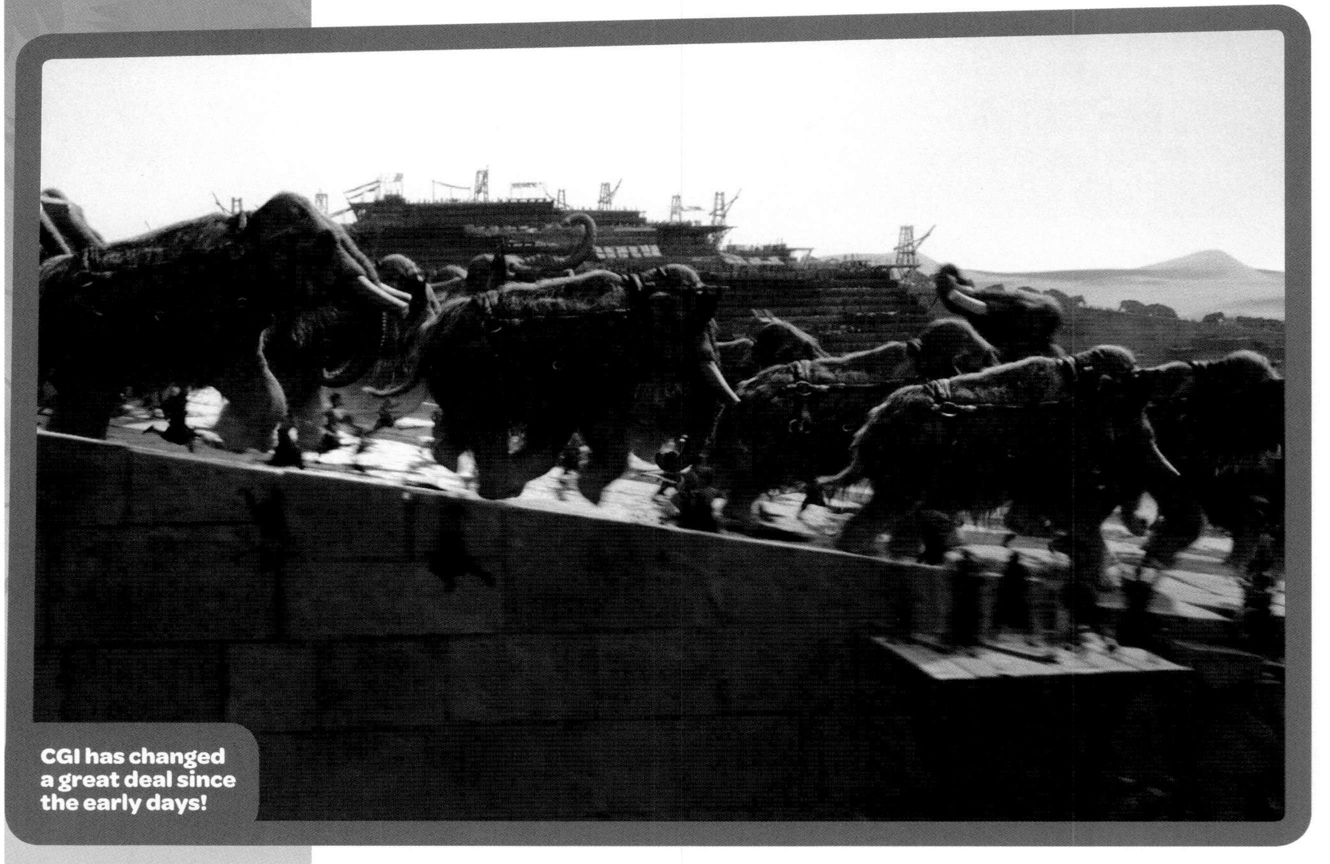

CGI has changed a great deal since the early days!

ACTIVITY 16

1 ***Can you think of any issues that using CGI may raise? Think about CGI being used in celebrity photo-shoots, music videos and advertisements as well as films and cartoons.***

Grade Studio

EXAMINER'S TIP

This is an ideal activity to use for a textual investigation on representation. See the chapter on Controlled Assessments at the back of this book for further help.

ACTIVITY 17

Watch the film Simone (2002) directed by Andrew Niccol. It explores the whole notion of using computer technology to create perfect computerised people or actors. It also raises some interesting points in relation to audiences and their adoration of stars.

Having watched the film, discuss with your classmates whether 'virtual actors' would work in reality. Support your arguments by referring to moments from the film.

Anime

Anime is a Japanese animation form which combines film-making with Manga comic form. **Manga** comics have been made in Japan for many years, calling on the longstanding tradition of line art and Buddhist scrolls which had to be unrolled to reveal a message. They also used the Western tradition of telling stories in sequence, and the traditions of American comic books.

Key terms

Anime A Japanese animation form that combines camera movements with still frames.

Manga Popular Japanese comics that have influenced anime films.

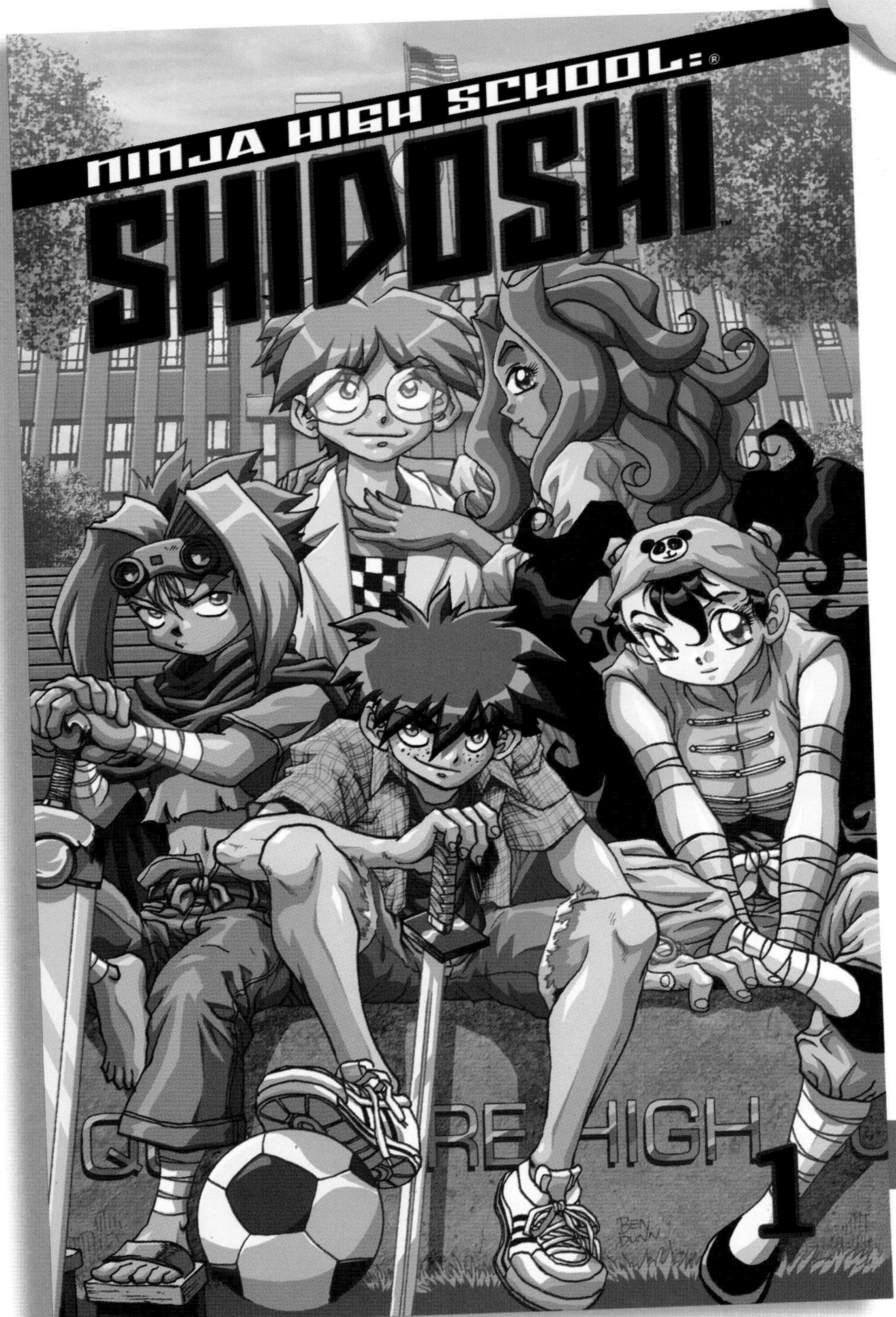

A manga graphic novel

Anime directors are interested in the effects of technology on society. The link to comics can be seen easily, since the intention of anime is to control the ways in which the viewer's eye looks at the screen. Many of the characters in anime are westernised, and some even look like early Disney characters.

Early anime animation leaned heavily on the idea of big comic frames (which were still) with large painted cels, but gave the impression of movement because the camera panned across them as it would in a film. The result was a semi-frozen animation, which emphasised angles and facial expressions, used tilt-ups and tilt-downs to give the impression of seeing more of a scene, and zoom-ins to draw attention to dramatic detail.

Hayao Miyazaki directed Japanese animation *Spirited Away* (2001)

ACTIVITY 18

1. ***Working in a small group or on your own, try using anime techniques. Draw some large comic frames or put together a sequence of photographs to tell a simple story – even the story of your holiday.***
2. ***Film the frames or images in close up, then experiment with zooming in on certain details.***
3. ***Play the footage back to see how effective this simple animation is.***
4. ***You could develop your anime-style work by writing a voice-over commentary to accompany the footage, or adding text boxes, speech bubbles, etc.***

Japanese animation is concerned with meaning and symbolism. It draws attention to important details – since the frozen scene allows more time to look at everything – and gives clues about characters by their appearance. For example, large eyes suggest that characters are heroes or heroines, with good hearts and intentions. Small eyes suggest evil intent and usually belong to characters who are villains or villain's helpers.

Some good examples of anime are *Akira* (1988), *Ghost in the Shell* (1995) and *Howl's Moving Castle* (2004). If you have the chance to see them, or any other anime films or cartoons, you will also notice how music and sound effects are used to create mood and atmosphere.

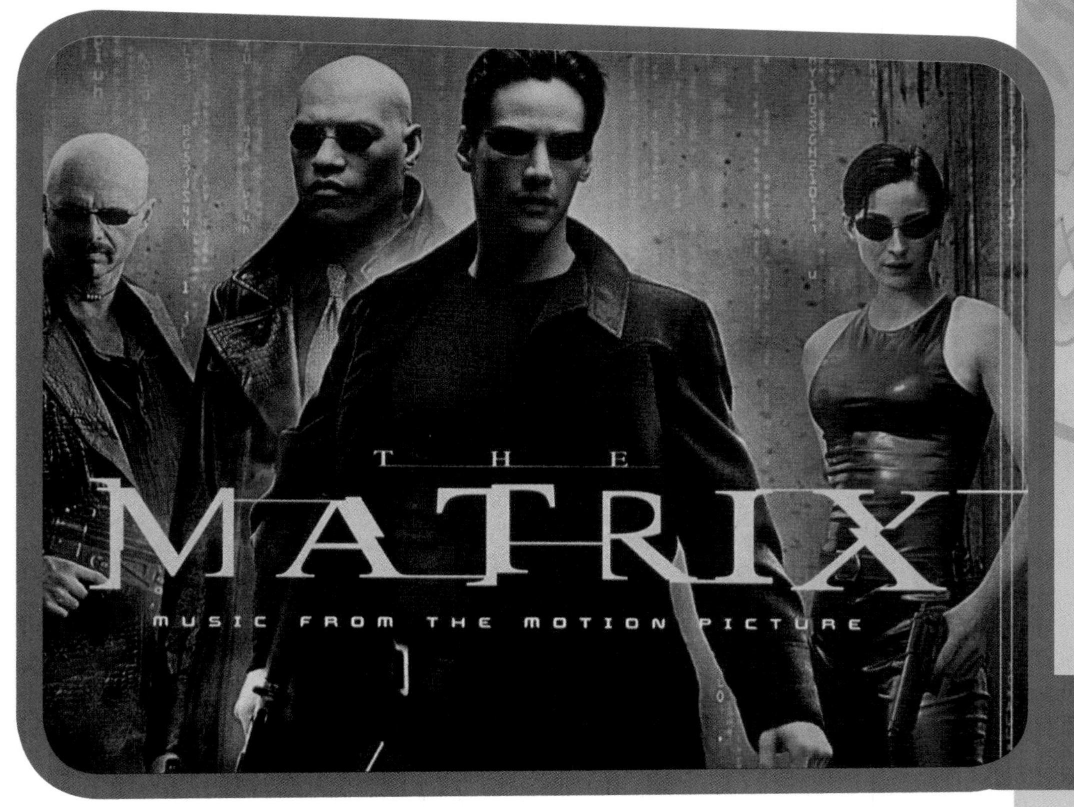

The *Matrix* trilogy was influenced by manga and anime

Many of you will have seen one or more of the *Matrix* trilogy, directed by the Wachowski brothers, who have admitted to the strong influence of manga and anime on their film-making. They also produced the *Animatrix* series of anime cartoons to accompany the films. This is another good example of media convergence.

ACTIVITY 19

1. ***Watch an episode from* Animatrix*.***
2. ***Write about the techniques it uses to create mood and tension. Focus on characters' expressions and reactions, music, camera techniques (especially framing, point-of-view shots and panning from one place to another) and sound effects.***
3. ***Try to explore the possible meanings and messages in the text.***

What have you learned?

In this chapter you have learned about:

Texts

- Investigating comics and the openings of cartoons and animations
- Looking at the construction of comic front covers
- Storyboarding and focusing on frames and panels

Media language

Genre

- How comics, cartoons and animations use clear characteristics to allow audiences to engage with, and enjoy, them
- How comic and animation techniques exist in a wide range of genres
- How to include an understanding of comic/animations in coursework

Narrative

- The importance of character types and their function in narratives
- Telling a simple story in key moments
- Codes of realism in comic and animated narratives

Representation

- Representations of the human and non-human
- Ways in which character types are represented
- Superheroes
- How representations are used in anime

Audiences

- Thinking about and attracting target audiences
- Creating surveys and questionnaires
- Exploring audience responses
- Discussing the effect of licensed characters on audiences

Organisational issues

- How design is directly linked to consumers
- Potentially negative effects of computer-generated imagery
- The history of some publishers
- Use of animated characters as a signature for an animation company

Convergent media

- The convergent nature of comics, cartoons and animations including their use in advertising, websites, films and television
- Animated websites

6 Pop music

Your learning

In this chapter you will learn about:

- how the music industry is changing in the face of new technology, for example, the Internet
- who decides what music we listen to
- the importance of genre in the music industry
- the importance of the music video in selling music
- what changes are occurring in the way the music press covers the music scene.

Wild things: a brief history of pop music and youth culture

In the decade after the Second World War, teenagers wanted to see themselves as being very different from their parents. Boys dressed in drape suits and ripped up cinema seats when the film *Rock Around the Clock* was shown. Girls combed their hair into 'beehives' and wore high stiletto heels.

EXAMINER'S TIP

You must consider the convergent media aspects of pop music whenever you complete a task on it.

Teenagers were often presented by the media as unruly and violent. When Mods fought Rockers on the beach at the seaside town of Margate during the Easter weekend of 1964, many newspapers treated the incident as if war had broken out. The magistrate who tried 44 young people for various offences described them as 'miserable specimens', 'strutting hooligans', 'louts', 'dregs' and 'long-haired, mentally unstable, petty hoodlums'.

But while the press presented a negative view of teenagers, the music and fashion industry soon realised that there was a lot of money to be made from them. They were a new, young audience who had money to spend on enjoying themselves. In 1960 there were 5 million teenagers in the UK, spending £800 million on clothes and entertainment – a tenth of the total of all leisure spending. When it came to records and record players, teenagers made up half the market.

Key terms

Genre This means 'type'. In music, different genres might include heavy metal, RnB, soul, punk, etc.

In 1955, British listeners bought just 4 million singles (on record). By 1960 they were buying 52 million singles a year and by 1963, 61 million. This wasn't just due to the popularity of pop stars like Elvis Presley – radio was now broadcasting music and was becoming hugely popular.

Genre became an important part of the record industry. To keep the sales soaring, it was good to have new teenage crazes – different genres – appearing regularly. And if different fashion styles could be linked to music genres, even more money would go through the tills.

This activity will help you investigate the importance of pop music to different generations.

1. ***Interview someone at least 20 years older than you about their memories of the music they listened to when they were young and how important it was to them. You could use some of the following questions to start you off:***

Questions to ask	Response
In which decade were you a teenager (1950s, 1960s, 1970s, 1980s, 1990s)?	
What kind of music did you like when you were a teenager?	
What sort of fashions or style did you dress in? Was this linked with the music?	
How did you buy music – on vinyl? On tape? On CD? Do you have a preference for any of these formats and why?	
What technical equipment did you use to listen to music?	
Which music TV programmes did you watch?	
Which radio stations or programmes did you listen to?	
Did you read music magazines? Which ones?	
What did you like about the music magazines back then?	
Do you think music was better back then?	

2. ***Now ask yourself the following questions about your own music consumption:***

Questions to ask	Response
How do you access or purchase the music you like?	
How much does this cost?	
What format is most of your music in?	
What technology is available to you to listen to music?	
How do you hear new music?	
How do you find out information about music or bands?	
Which music websites are you aware of?	
Which music magazines do you read? Why do you like them?	
Which music websites do you visit? Why do you like them?	
What kind of clothing style is associated with the kind of music you like?	

Key terms

Re-issuing When a record company releases songs recorded some time before and which have probably already sold well.

Back-catalogue All the previous work recorded by artists or bands.

Music across time

Listening to the same old-school music your parents liked would have been deeply uncool in the 1960s. But some people argue that the constant **re-issuing** and marketing of **back-catalogue** material by the record companies means there is no past, only a continuous present. With an iPod shuffle, the flow of music leaps backwards and forwards across time with every track change.

In no more than 300 words, compare your experience of music with that of the older person you interviewed in Activity 1.

1. ***Do you agree that young people today are listening to a much wider range of music genres? You should give examples of the different genres you and your friends listen to.***
2. ***How have technology and the digital revolution altered the way we access and enjoy music? You need to think about the restrictions that affected older people when they only had a vinyl disc and a record player. How do things like the Internet and the MP3 player make a difference for you?***

Genres in pop music

Look back at the interview you carried out in Activity 1 with an older person about their music listening habits. They will certainly have mentioned individual artists or bands by name. But did they say they listened to a particular genre or type of music? If they were teenagers in the early 1960s, they may have been fans of folk music, listening to artists like Bob Dylan or Joan Baez. If their listening habits developed ten years later, they might have been rock fans devoted to Led Zeppelin or reggae enthusiasts hooked on Bob Marley.

Star power!

You might be asking why genres are important in music. They are important for the same reasons they are important in any other part of the media:

- They help audiences to recognise things which they think they might like.
- They help the music industry organise the things they want to sell to the audience.

The most obvious way to see this in action is to press the genre link on an iPod – iTunes will have given everything a genre. If you want to sample your indie tunes without rock music bursting in, you can listen by genre.

Another way of exploring how the music industry uses genres is to go into any music retail store. The products on sale are arranged into categories. Some of the categories used in big music stores actually cover a variety of different types of music. Jazz is a good example of this. Shops only have limited display space, so it's easier to group Kid Ory (a New Orleans trombonist from the 1920s) with Weather Report (a 70s jazz rock band) in a section labelled 'Jazz'. This leaves much more space for the genres which make the retailers the most money. These are, by definition, 'popular' music – music that sells in large amounts.

Go into your nearest large music retailer and note down the categories they are using to organise their products.

1. ***Does breaking the store down into these sections make the music you want easier or harder to find?***
2. ***How often do you now go and buy a CD (or maybe even a vinyl) from a music store?***
3. ***Imagine that you are a new artist with your first album to sell. How do you think you could most effectively get your product out to a wide audience? Would you approach a major record label with a demo version of your songs? Would you place an advertisement in the local paper? Or would you use YouTube?***

GARY BROLSMA: SUPERSTAR

This case study discusses some of the convergent media aspects of pop music today. It focuses on Gary Brolsma, who became famous through the Internet for his version of a previously-recorded single. At the end you'll be asked in the Activity to discuss the issues that come out of this case study.

Gary Brolsma and the Internet

Have you heard of Gary Brolsma? He could claim to be one of the most successful artists in the history of pop music. His cover version of the song titled *Dragostea din tei*, by the Romanian band O-Zone, was released as *Numa Numa* on 14 August 2006. By March 2008, his song had reached a staggering 700 million people.

Let's put that into perspective. In 1964, The Beatles had the fastest selling vinyl single of all time with *I Want to Hold Your Hand*. The song sold 250,000 copies within three days in the USA and 1 million in two weeks. By October 1972, ten years after they issued their first record, The Beatles' worldwide sales total – that's everything they ever recorded – stood at 545 million units. In other words, Gary's version of *Numa Numa* outstripped the most successful pop band of all time!

Gary Brolsma: global success

Like the Beatles, Gary's success has turned global. Ana Peñalosa is a Mexican Brolsma fan. She first became aware of their global appeal when she arrived in a small village hours from any major city:

'I worked for six months in Bachajón, a town in the state of Chiapas, about 16 hours by bus from Mexico City. The day I arrived in Bachajón there was a market next to the ancient church that spilled over to straddle the one street. Some vendors sold fruit and vegetables, some sold shirts and jeans, others sold music and movie CDs and DVDs. People were sitting and standing in small groups, some were talking, others laughing. A sound system blared music to the crowd. The song was Numa, Numa.'

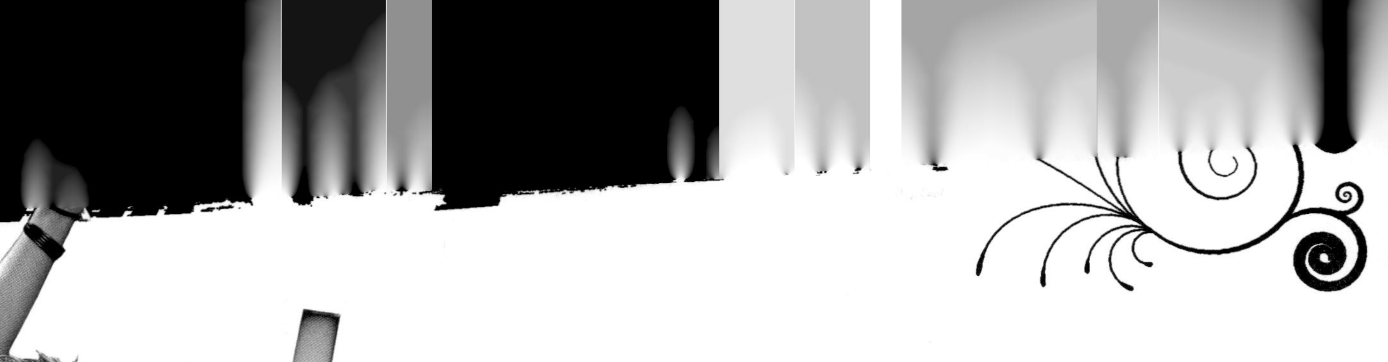

So where is Gary now? Sipping champagne in a huge villa on a palm-fringed beach? Flying to gigs in his private jet? Preparing to save the planet by dedicating a percentage of the earnings from his next release to combat global warming?

No. Gary never made a cent from *Numa Numa*. He filmed himself **lip-synching** the words of the song on a webcam in his bedroom and uploaded it onto YouTube. He never marketed it. He was never interviewed in the music press. And he certainly never paid O-Zone any royalty for ripping off their song. He just sat down and mimed his cover version, flicked the upload and millions of people saw it for free.

Key terms

Lip-synching Where a person in a video mimes so that their lip movement matches the words being heard on a soundtrack.

In case you missed out on the *Numa Numa* craze, you should be able to source it on the Internet.

Once you have watched Gary's effort, you can explore the new genre which he created. You'll find a whole galaxy of spin-off music videos dedicated to *Numa Numa*, including one featuring an Osama Bin Laden look-alike, and also Gary's follow-up single *New Numa*.

CD-ROM Extra!

Numa Numa

Open the CD in the back of this book and click on the icon below to open a link to see **Numa Numa.**

HTML

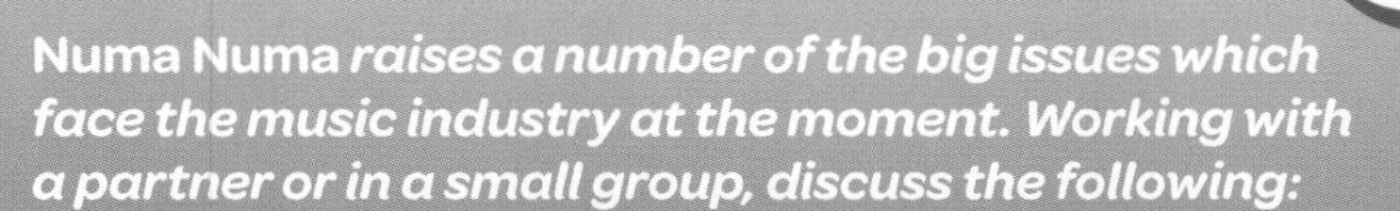

CASE STUDY ACTIVITY

Numa Numa raises a number of the big issues which face the music industry at the moment. Working with a partner or in a small group, discuss the following:

1. ***Would you say from what you have heard about him that Gary Brolsma is famous and successful? What difference is there between these two things?***
2. ***Why should Gary have offered to pay O-Zone before uploading his version of their track? Or shouldn't he? If not, why not?***
3. ***How might O-Zone have benefited from Gary using their tune?***
4. ***Audiences in 1964 had to go into shops and pay money to hold a Beatles record in their hand. Now anyone can get music free from downloads. Do you think it matters that artists and their record companies don't get paid for their work?***

The impact of the Internet

Key terms

Distribution method The way the music industry distributes music tracks to its audience.

Producer The person who makes a product.

Consumers The people who buy, read, watch or listen to media products.

Network An interconnected group or system.

Numa Numa is just one more indication of the phenomenal change the Internet has brought to our lives. It enables an obscure Central European pop song to spread at an extraordinary rate, eventually even making it to a small town in Mexico, without any help from 'big business'.

For the music industry, the *Numa Numa* case study pinpoints the dramatic shift in power. Before the Internet, record companies decided who got to make records, how much we had to pay for them and where we could buy them. Once the Internet was in place, music fans could share their own collections with each other and bands could upload their new albums for free.

This is what the music industry calls its **distribution method**. Put simply, this means how they get things into the hands of people who are prepared, not only to listen, but to pay for the privilege. The Internet has suddenly provided a whole new – and free – distribution method. Like a rabbit in the headlights of the Internet, the music industry has reacted very slowly indeed to the implications of downloads and uploads. As a result, it is in danger of being blown off the road by the juggernaut of Internet technology.

The crisis in the music industry is just a part of the wider impact that the digital revolution has had on the mass media industries. If the music industry is running scared, then so are big film producers, television companies and newspaper magnates.

The following simple communications model can help you to describe how the shift from **producer** to **consumer** works. We need to think of three types of **network**:

Broadcast network This is where there are one or two big producers (like the BBC or ITV) who transmit things like television programmes which an unknown audience can receive individually. They can't respond and they don't know how many others are receiving the same communication.

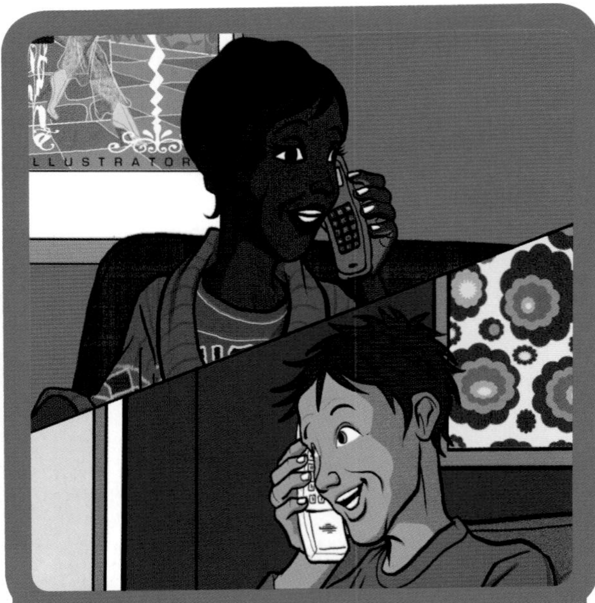

Metcalfe network The telephone system is the best example of this type of network. There is a greater opportunity to interact with other members of the network as any one individual can call any other individual in the network who has a phone.

Reed network The Internet is an example of a Reed network. It means that not only can any individual communicate with any other, they can also form groups. The number of possible connections is infinite. *Numa Numa* spread around the world because the Internet Reed network meant individuals could send it, in one click, to everyone in their address book. YouTube and Facebook are classic ways in which groups can use a Reed network.

Pre-Internet revolutions

The Internet isn't the first example of a sudden shift in the power balance between those who produce the messages and those who receive them. A much earlier example would be the invention of the printing press in 1450 by Johannes Gutenberg. In those days, the Church was the equivalent of the big media companies. It was the only organisation that could provide information: it was the Broadcast Network of its time. Monks laboriously copied out the gospels by hand, so there were hardly any books in existence at all.

Once Gutenburg had invented the printing press, the genie was out of the bottle. Other people could publish their ideas about religion and a lot of other things. And because books became much more widely available, many more people could be taught to read. People could challenge what we would call the **hegemony** of the Church.

TIP

Consider how you would promote yourself if you were building a website.

Key terms

Hegemony The way people are influenced into accepting the dominance of a power group who impose their views on the rest of the population.

Johannes Gutenberg: inventor of the printing press'

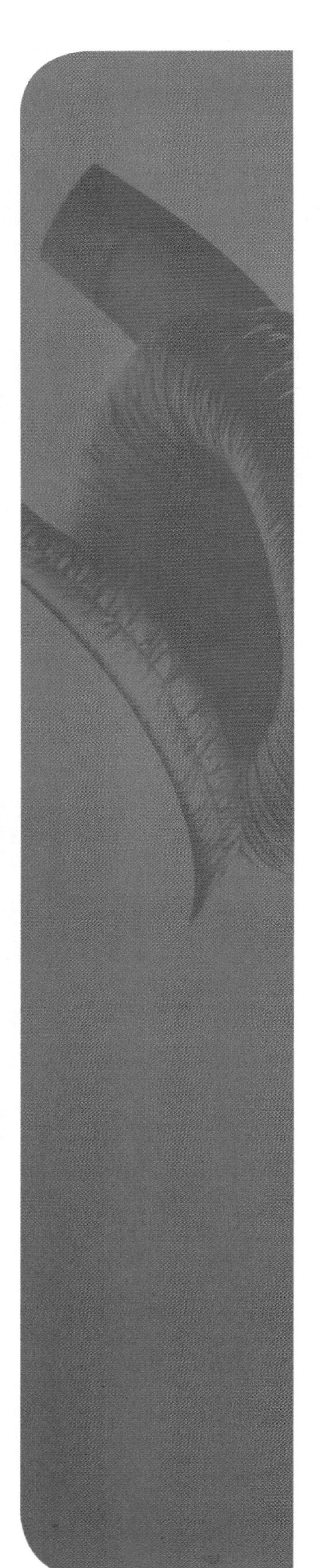

Working in a pair or small group, discuss the way that the digital revolution is affecting the following media.

1. **The film industry** – *in the past the only way people could see a film was to pay to go into a cinema. You should think about the many different ways that are now available for you to watch the latest blockbuster, including legally produced DVDs released at the same time as the film print, pirated DVD versions of films and web-streamed versions of films.*
2. **The newspaper industry** – *most newspapers now have an Internet edition. What does this add to a reader's experience?*
3. **The music industry** – *digital downloads are now a common way of buying music (or getting tracks for free). Recording equipment is now widely available. The advantages all seem to be to the consumer of music rather than the producer. Do you agree?*

In each case you should consider the ways in which they started as Broadcast networks and the extent to which they could now be described as Reed networks. What are the effects of this shift on each industry?

Music from the Internet: illegal downloading

The *Numa Numa* case study highlighted the issues of uploading, downloading and file sharing. But why were the record companies so afraid of this new development?

Copyright

The big issue is copyright. Copyright brings in about a third of a record company's profits, so companies are obviously keen to enforce laws that stop people illegally downloading or copying songs.

The battle against copyright infringement goes back as far as the 1980s, when companies became worried about people copying recorded tracks onto blank cassettes. But it has only really begun to hit the industry in the pocket in the last decade.

1968–1998

Record companies earned most of their money from albums in this period. Albums turn 'bands into brands', with the power of spin-offs allowing cash to be made from T-shirts and calendars. Money can also be generated from tie-ins, such as tours or TV shows.

1970s

Copyright infringement issues first arose when people began to record songs onto blank cassettes.

1999

Industry sales have fallen steadily since 1999 because of single file sharing. File sharing has also meant that, for the first time since the 1960s, single tracks have come back into fashion.

2000

The Recording Industry Association of America (RIAA) took the Internet site Napster to court in 2000, over their music file sharing system.

2001

Napster was found guilty, forced to shut down and to invent a new pay-for-download system. Their new site contains the Visa and Mastercard logos! The **media conglomerates**, who had controlled distribution of music before file sharing, kept up their battle to stop it by continuing to use the law. The companies also waged guerrilla warfare on the file sharers. They hired computer experts to dump corrupted files onto sites, so that users had to search around for hours to find the track they were looking for.

2003

Madonna even circulated fake tracks from her 2003 album *American Life*. Fans who tried to download songs were met with silence and an angry message from 'Madge' herself, asking what they thought they were doing!

Key terms

Media conglomerates
Large corporations who own more than one different media company and sometimes a large number of companies.

2004

The RIAA sued 914 Americans for millions of dollars for sharing songs. These people were using software packages KaZaA and BearShare to file-share songs. One of the accused was a 12-year-old girl. Her mother settled out of court by paying the RIAA $2000, and thousands of American families banned their children from using file-sharing sites. (No one knows if the ban worked!) Was the threat killed off? No. Figures from research companies in 2004 suggested that at any given time there were up to 5 million people illegally sharing songs worldwide.

July 2008

The industry claimed they were set to lose £1 billion over the following five years because of illegal downloads.

Record companies are waking up to the fact that digital music is the future and that they must adapt to modern technology or die. In 2007, EMI (one of the biggest record companies in the UK) was bought by a company called Terra Firma. The new owners got rid of people like the former vice-chairman, David Munns, who had likened file sharing to going into a music store and shoplifting CDs. The new owners say they are interested in getting music talent out to as many people as possible using multiple delivery methods and all the digital channels they think their customers might use. They recognise that the future is digital – not selling CDs and suing downloaders.

Marketing in the digital age

Michael Stipe: lead singer of REM

If they hadn't been so alarmed, the record companies might have realised more quickly that the Internet provided them with huge possibilities for marketing their products.

A recent trend has been the use of the Internet to launch new albums. Warner launched the new REM record, *Supernatural Superserious*, on Facebook. Radiohead took the unusual step of announcing that their *Rainbow* album was available to download from the Internet and asked fans to pay as much or as little for it as they thought it was worth. The publicity generated meant that it was soon selling in large quantities and it became a big hit. Prince sold 3 million copies of one of his albums through a deal with *The Mail on Sunday*, which gave it away with the paper. Lily Allen, Arctic Monkeys and countless others have launched themselves via email or social networking sites such as Myspace.

TIP

You might like to make a list of all the ways pop music is consumed. Then, briefly describe the organisation behind each of these consumption methods.

ACTIVITY 5

Working with two or three other people, imagine you are an advertising agency who have been employed by EMI's new owners, Terra Firma. They have asked you to prepare a short report on ways in which you think they should use the Internet to market the material in their catalogue. They are particularly interested in the 12–24-year-old audience.

Think about the way in which you use the Internet to find music, band information and gigs. Which bands have you recently discovered? How did you hear about them? If you heard about an exciting new band from a friend, where would you go to find out more about their music?

Write your report and try to include at least four suggestions for ways in which Terra Firma could market the material of the artists they have in their catalogue.

The rise of the pop music video

A lot of people claim that Queen invented the music video in 1975. But the first use of short clips of film to promote music goes back a lot further.

1940

1940s Films called 'Soundies', made by musicians like Big Joe Turner and Nat 'King' Cole, were shown in bars in the USA.

1950

1956 Films like *Rock Around the Clock* cashed in on the new teenage market for pop music.

1960

1964 The Beatles film *A Hard Day's Night* was released. It became a template for many of the music videos which followed.

1970

1975 Queen made the first music video as we know the genre now.

1980

1981 MTV was launched as a channel, showing only music videos.

1982 Michael Jackson's *Thriller* was launched.

1990

2000

2005 YouTube was founded and quickly became a major site for both amateur and professional musicians to launch their own music videos.

2010

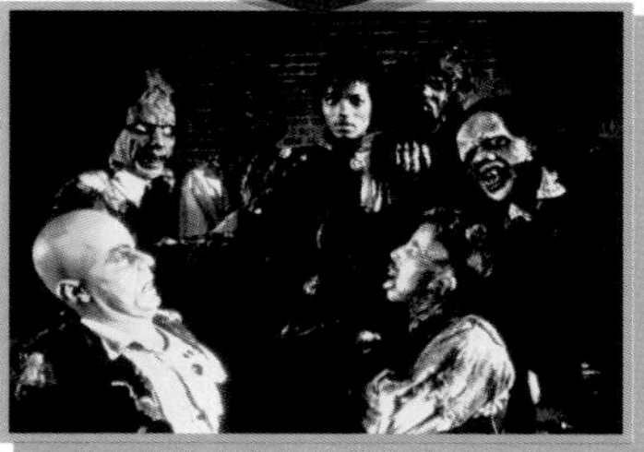

Key events during the rise of the pop music video

The beginning of rock and roll in the 1950s was the spur for a lot of films which featured the new style of music. These films were made cheaply and quickly to cash in on the latest fashion and so most of them were forgettable. *Rock Around the Clock* (1956) featured Bill Haley's music and swiftly captured the imagination of the new 'teenagers' in Europe and the USA.

By the mid 1960s, The Beatles and The Rolling Stones were major international stars touring all over the world. They began to make promotional films (promos) which could be screened on television while they were touring. Most of these promos were basically filmed performances of a song shot in a simple studio backdrop with the group miming to the record. But The Beatles could lay claim to producing the first music videos as we know them today. *A Hard Day's Night* was a fictional documentary film of the life of the band, directed by Richard Lester in 1964. The film is a mix of songs and comedy, including chases and sequences featuring **jump-cut** editing. It was a **template** for many of the music videos which followed.

Jump-cut Where the join between two shots is felt to be abrupt because what follows is something we don't expect to see.

Template A pattern which helps to shape the products that follow.

The big turning point for the music promo came in 1975 when EMI released a 6-minute single by Queen called 'Bohemian Rhapsody'. Releasing a single of this length was quite a risk as many radio stations felt this was too long to fit their type of programming. To help promote the song, the record company commissioned director Bruce Gowers to make a video to accompany the single. This video used trailing images of the band's disembodied heads together with live performance footage. The music press hailed it as a masterpiece and it made a lasting impression on the viewers who saw it on *Top of the Pops*. The video is thought to be one reason why the record stayed at number one in the charts for nine weeks.

In 1981, MTV was launched. It was by no means seen as a surefire success in its early stages – especially since it had less than 200 videos to play out. However, the company commissioned research which seemed to show that the appearance of videos on MTV increased sales of the record. The music industry was convinced, so more videos were made, which in turn improved sales and the connection between music and video was firmly cemented.

In 1982, Michael Jackson's video for 'Thriller' took the genre another step forward. Hiring Hollywood film director Jon Landis, who had made *American Werewolf in London*, Jackson acted out a variety of roles as the video engaged in a parody of the 'horror' genre. It had a lengthy live action sequence before the song actually started, taking the whole production beyond the established conventions and limitations of the music promo of the time, making it almost a short film – with a huge production budget to match. Its uniqueness helped the album to reach sales of over 35 million copies – still one of the biggest selling records of all time.

The importance of the music promo video has continued right through to today. The main change has been the distribution method: you are as likely to view videos on the Internet as on a music TV channel. In November 2005, YouTube was launched and immediately became a main site for musicians of all ages and levels of competence to share their music videos. It has become so successful that major recording artists now use it to launch their own videos.

Michael Jackson's 'Thriller' video

ACTIVITY 6

1. *Discuss the following points with a partner:*
   - *Are promotional videos for songs still important to help sell music?*
   - *Are sites like YouTube becoming the place where you watch music video promos, or do you still watch MTV as well? What would be lost if there were no MTV channels?*
2. *Now write a 200-word article to go in a music magazine of your choice, answering the following question:*
   - *Is the music video an endangered species?*

Investigating music video

Regardless of where you view them, the main purpose of music videos is to promote a song. For those who remember it, it is impossible to hear 'Bohemian Rhapsody' without also recalling the disembodied heads of the Queen band members floating rather awkwardly around the screen. The videos create a 'buzz' around the band and the song which helps to get it noticed and, with luck, purchased.

But some critics, like Andrew Goodwin, have argued that the importance of the music video – and MTV which ensured it was broadcast to a wide audience – goes beyond just selling music. It has altered the way we 'read' moving images. One of the main things about music video is the way in which it moves away from classic linear Hollywood narratives (see Chapter 1: Film, page 9). So, if you try to analyse them as if they used the same 'rules' as film or television, it won't work.

TIP

Studying music videos is exciting because they subvert the normal codes and conventions. You might like to deconstruct some music videos and identify how the subversion takes place.

Editing

The biggest difference between most film or television genres and the music video is the way in which they are edited. Some of the technical manuals for people who are training to be film or television editors now talk about 'MTV-style editing'. They point to the ways in which a music video is edited and show how it broke away from the dominant Hollywood style – which is called **continuity editing**.

Key terms

Continuity editing Editing which is designed to make one event follow on naturally from another. Nothing unusual happens to make the viewer notice the fact that an edit has been made.

Continuity editing is based on a number of rules which ensure that when hundreds (or in the case of Hollywood blockbusters, thousands) of separate shots are edited together, they appear to flow naturally. The aim is that the viewer doesn't notice the joins but concentrates on the story being told by the images.

MTV-style editing shouts out at the viewer, drawing attention to the whole process of joining the shots together. In particular, the jump-cut is used a lot in music video. This is where the join between two shots is felt to be abrupt because one shot is followed by something we would not expect to see. It makes the viewer 'jump' and wonder where the narrative storyline has been taken to. The pace of cutting between shots is also much more rapid in MTV-style editing than it is in continuity edits.

CD-ROM

Extra!

Illustration in video

Open the CD in the back of this book and click on the icon below to open a link to the video for The Jam's track 'That's Entertainment'.

HTML

Andrew Goodwin is Associate Professor of Communication Arts at the University of San Francisco. He is the author of a book on music video called *Dancing in the Distraction Factory* which breaks music videos down into three main categories. These may help you when you are trying to write about them:

- *Illustration* – in this type of video, everything we see in the finished version derives directly from the lyrics of the song. This could be just the artist or band performing the song. If there are other shots, these are easily linked to what is being sung. Goodwin gives the example from The Jam's track, 'That's Entertainment', where the video shows the band performing the song in the studio.

TIP

There are essentially two main types of music video – performance and narrative. However, clearly there are videos that combine the two (hybrids).

The Jam

CD-ROM

Extra!

Amplification in video

Open the CD in the back of this book and click on the icon below to open a link to the video for Garbage's track 'I'm Only Happy When It Rains'.

HTML

CD-ROM

Extra!

Disjuncture in video

Open the CD in the back of this book and click on the icon below to open a link to the video for 'There Goes the Fear' by Doves.

HTML

- *Amplification* – this type of video has sequences which add extra meanings that aren't necessarily in the lyrics themselves. An example would be the video for Garbage's song 'I'm Only Happy When It Rains'. As well as a lot of shots of vocalist Shirley Manson lip-synching the lyrics, there are shots of the other band members drilling holes in their instruments and wearing bizarre costumes and masks.
- *Disjuncture* – this is where the images on the video have no apparent link to the song's lyrics. Often a film-maker has been commissioned to produce what is almost a short film, the soundtrack being the song. An example would be 'There Goes the Fear' by Doves.

Videos which show either amplification or disjuncture are much more interesting to write about than those that just illustrate. The aim of the director will be to take the mood or tone of the song and then develop it in some way. Goodwin suggests that bands who use these approaches want to be seen as more 'arty' and serious about their music.

ACTIVITY 7

This activity will help you to focus on the media language of music videos.

1. ***Select an example of a music video which is either an amplification or a disjuncture.***
2. ***Write a 300-word investigation into the way the visuals capture the mood or tone of the original song. You should concentrate on:***
   - ***shots which are particularly effective for you – what do they make you think of?***
   - ***the editing style and how it affects the way the 'story' is told***
   - ***the narrative, which probably won't have a conventional 'beginning-middle-end' structure, but what 'story' has been told by the video?***

This case study discusses some of the convergent media aspects of pop music today. At the end you'll be asked in the activity to discuss the issues that arise.

All of us find out about our favourite bands from somewhere. Often friends point us in the direction of new things – 'word of mouth', or 'wom' as the music industry calls it. With the rise of the MP3 file, it is now more than just wom – you can send the actual track directly to your friend.

You might think that all this digital activity would have put print-based music magazines out of business. But you'd be wrong. Titles like *Kerrang!* and *Mojo* are selling just as well as ever – although of course they have websites related to their print magazines too.

Thirty years ago, the music press would probably have claimed they were largely responsible for making audiences aware of different bands . So are they still powerful opinion formers?

Here are three different viewpoints from music press 'insiders' on the importance of the music press.

CD-ROM Extra!

The rise and fall of Smash Hits

Open the CD in the back of this book and click on the icon below to open a link to an interview with an editor of* Smash Hits*.

CD-ROM Extra!

Kerrang!

Open the CD in the back of this book and click on the icon below to open a link to an interview with an editor of* Kerrang!*.

David Hepworth, former editor of* Smash Hits *and now publishing director of* Word *and* Mixmag*:

'The music press don't make bands successful. They're not big enough to do it. People always like to think that there's a plot and that somewhere in a record company boardroom, they're going to force people to like something that people don't like. Well it doesn't work like that.

If you're successful you are lucky, possibly talented, but people like you.

But of course there are bands that the music press like. They tend to be the ones who are groovy, who take good pictures, are a bit sexy and give good copy. But Keane were none of those things, they didn't fulfil any of those criteria at all but Keane found their way out to a huge great fan base.'

Paul Brannigan, editor of Kerrang!:
'The music press is still hugely important. Particularly now in the age of the Internet, there is so much choice out there.

But you still need someone to filter that stuff down. No one has all the time in the world to go checking out every band website, so you look to the music press to tell you where the good stuff is. That's the role of a music magazine.'

Karis Ferguson, founding editor of www.thisisfakediy.co.uk:
'When we first set up thisisfakediy I interviewed a band called Parva from Leeds. We published the interview, but nothing really happened. A few months later I got an email from them. They said they'd changed their name and had a few new MP3s. I downloaded some and it was Kaiser Chiefs.

We had to tell people about them. We uploaded a story instantly: "check out these MP3s!" People got interested. Another indie website, drownedinsound, released their first single. We reviewed it. It was really good underground, everybody talking about it. They signed to Be Unique and now they're touring the world. But they always thank us because we helped them out when nobody else was listening.'

influence
Open the CD in the back of this book and click on the icon below to open a link to some footage on the influence of the press.

CASE STUDY ACTIVITY

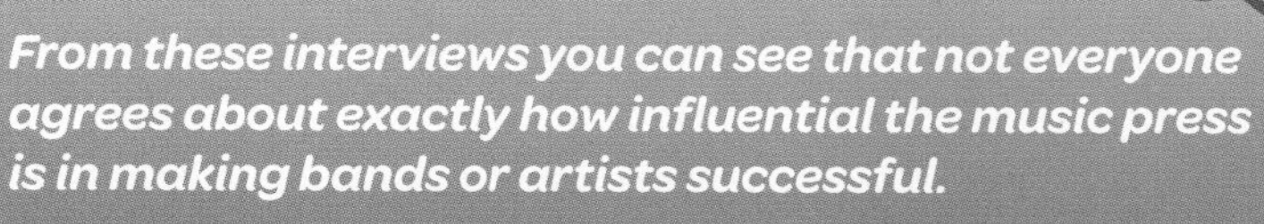

From these interviews you can see that not everyone agrees about exactly how influential the music press is in making bands or artists successful.

1. *In a small group, discuss how influential you think the music press is today.*

2. *As a group, write three or four paragraphs setting out your views, giving examples from the actual experience of group members.*

3. *Share your views with other groups and see if you can come to a whole-class decision about the influence of the music press today.*

Representations in the music press

> **Key terms**
>
> **Representation**
> How people, places, events or ideas are represented or portrayed to audiences in media texts. Sometimes this is simplistically through stereotypes so the audience can see immediately what is meant, and sometimes the meanings are less obvious.

> **Key terms**
>
> **Stereotypes**
> People grouped together according to simple shared characteristics, without allowing for any individual uniqueness.

Representation is an important Key Concept in Media Studies. It is about the way the media *represent* people, events or ideas to us. This representation will always involve choices. Any story could have been presented from a different angle or with a different picture.

A part of studying representation involves looking at the use of **stereotypes**. Are media images used so often and so powerfully that they suggest to audiences watching them that whole groups of people or ideas should be viewed in a certain way? Like any other media, the music industry will constantly represent people, places and ideas to its audience in particular ways. For example, look at the cover of *Mixmag* below. Are there any stereotypical features of the way the two men are represented on the cover of this magazine?

In the example below, taken from a 1980s *Smash Hits*, the singer Toyah was presented as someone who might be 'fancied' rather than being discussed as someone having an interesting voice or being an intelligent writer of lyrics. The males 'rate' her in terms of looks rather than musical talent.

Excuse me, my mate fancies you...

What do most people want to know about their favourite pop stars?

Toyah

Curt Smith on... ▶ 'When she's got all her make-up on she looks good. Not a very good actress though.'

Nick Heyward on... ▶ 'I wouldn't go out with her. She looks quite headstrong and she's ambitious, which is good. She's good-looking but I've never seen her without any make-up on.'

ACTIVITY 8

1. *What does the representation seem to imply that* Smash Hits *readers are interested in?*
2. *Look at one or two current music magazines. Has the way female stars are presented changed since* Smash Hits *was produced?*

Open the link on the CD-ROM where Kerrang! *staff talk about representation.*

1. *How does* Kerrang! *magazine seem to represent the issue of drug abuse?*
2. *How does Nichola Browne say that news in* Kerrang! *is different from news in the tabloid press? Why do you think music magazines might take a different approach to their presentation of news about the music industry and its stars?*
3. *From what is said by the* Kerrang! *team, what sorts of band are likely to be represented in their magazine and why?*

CD-ROM Extra!

Representations

Open the CD in the back of this book and click on the icon below to open a link to some footage on representations.

What have you learned?

In this chapter you have learned about:

Texts

- How the music video has grown in importance
- How the music press has changed to meet new technological developments like the Internet

Media language

Genre

- How music genres are used to classify and sell pop music

Narrative

- The way in which music videos use non-linear narrative to sell songs

Representation

- How the music press represents artists and issues

Audiences

- How audiences consume pop music genres
- How new technologies have altered the way we listen to music

Organisational issues

- How the Internet has transformed the way the music industry operates
- How the music industry is responding to the threat posed by downloading

Convergent media

- Case study: the strange case of Gary Brolsma 'Superstar' and how the Internet made him famous
- How the music press has responded to new technology and the Internet

Advertising and marketing

Your learning

In this chapter you will learn about:

- the three main marketing strategies for selling products, services or ideas:
  - promotional campaigns
  - advertising
  - public relations (PR)
- how patterns of advertising and marketing are changing due to the Internet
- how advertisements communicate their meaning
- how advertisers target particular audience groups
- how stereotyping is used by advertisers.

Key terms

Marketing The process of making customers aware of products, services and ideas in the hope that they will buy into them.

Marketing

Marketing products and services is big business. The purpose is to encourage us to buy things or to think about things in particular ways. The marketing industry spends billions of pounds every year and employs hundreds of thousands of people.

Researchers believe that we have over 1500 messages aimed at us every day. These messages appear on Internet pages, television screens, the radio, through your letter box, on the pages of magazines and newspapers, on billboards in the streets, on buses and trains, in the supermarket ... to name but a few. The fact that there is so much advertising around means that the marketing industry has to come up with ever more sophisticated ways of grabbing our attention.

ACTIVITY 1

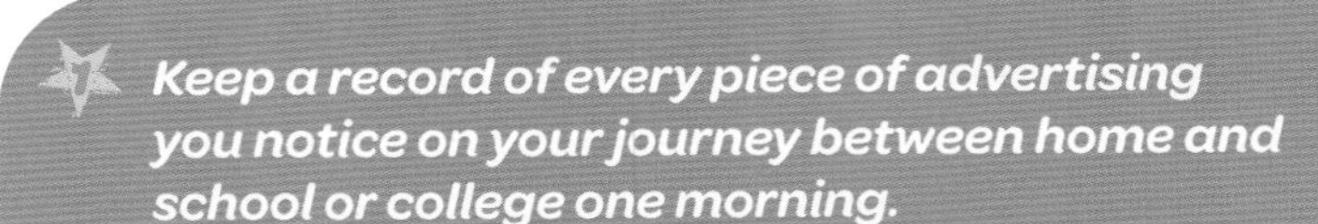

1. *Keep a record of every piece of advertising you notice on your journey between home and school or college one morning.*

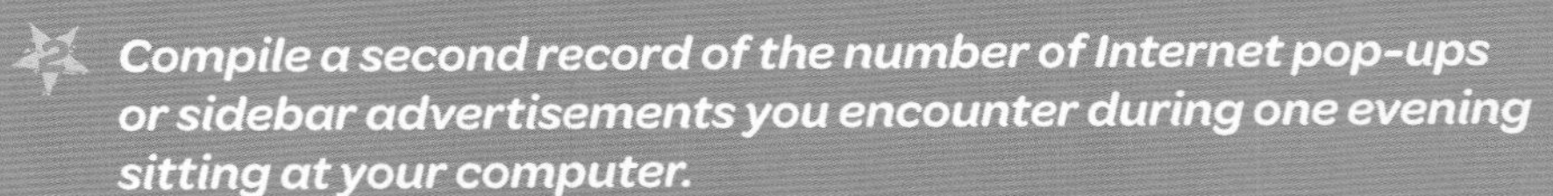

2. *Compile a second record of the number of Internet pop-ups or sidebar advertisements you encounter during one evening sitting at your computer.*
3. *Compare your notes with a partner. Were you surprised at the number of advertisements you saw? Which of them do you think were most effectively targeting you and therefore likely to make you follow them up in some way?*

Three ways to market your product

If a business wants to communicate with its customers, or **consumers**, it can choose to do this in three main ways:

1. **Sales promotion** – this has the most direct impact on a **brand**'s success because the technique directly affects sales. You will see promotions everywhere every day. Supermarket shelves will have 'buy one get one free' promotions; music magazines will have a free cover-mounted CD; cereal packets will contain a free gift.
2. **Advertising** – this reaches consumers through the creation of a message in a variety of possible forms: a 30-second television advertisement, a page in a magazine, a poster, etc. This is the glamorous part of the marketing industry because it is where all the big money is spent. But for a company or brand, it is also the most expensive way of getting the message out to consumers. Not only will a 30-second television advertisement cost hundreds of thousands of pounds to make, you then have to buy the **media space** to show it.
3. **Public relations (PR)** – by holding an event like a press conference or a launch party, public relations agencies can get a lot of media coverage for a product through articles written in magazines or newspapers, or stories on television or radio news. This isn't 'free' because you will have to pay the PR agent to get the coverage. But it can be a great deal cheaper than advertising.

We will now look in more detail at how these three approaches work.

Key terms

Consumers The people who buy, read, watch or listen to media products.

Brand A particular type of product, for example, Levi jeans.

Media space Any space in newspapers, magazines, on the radio or television where advertising can be placed.

Mail

SATURDAY, JULY 12, 2008

www.dailymail.co.uk

DAILY NEWSPAPER OF THE YEAR 70p

NEW 18-DISC COLLECTION

FREE DVD INSIDE

PRIDE AND PREJUDICE

STARRING COLIN FIRTH

THEN EVERY DAY PICK UP ANOTHER FREE CLASSIC COSTUME DRAMA ON DVD

DETAILS PAGES 38-39

A newspaper sales promotion

Sienna Miller, Matthew Williamson and Brooke Shields attending the Fragrance Launch party for Williamson's new fragrance

This case study discusses some of the convergent media aspects of sales promotion.

Print with CD/DVD promotions

A common strategy in newspaper and magazine publishing is to link with CD or DVD producers in joint sales promotion. Some of your music collection may well have come from the front of music magazines which frequently cover mount special edition CDs. David Hepworth, an editor of *MixMag*, says that this practice has now become so common that although magazines with a cover mount don't sell more copies, if you take the CD off, sales drop!

Daily Mirror *example*

In 2004, the Brand Communications Agency, Exposure, brought together two of its clients, the *Daily Mirror* and *Buena Vista Home Entertainment* in the biggest ever DVD promotion in a national newspaper. The campaign ran for a month and readers were offered 'the ultimate movie collection'. It was also supported by a national television and radio campaign.

In one month of continuous coverage, the total space which the *Daily Mirror* devoted to the promotion came to:

- 6 full pages, 3 three-quarter pages, 10 half pages, 16 third pages
- 6 front cover flashes

715,000 DVDs were claimed, meaning there was significant revenue generated for Buena Vista. The *Daily Mirror's* circulation per day increased by 30,000. All in all, Exposure, the marketing agency who devised the campaign, estimated that the equivalent of £1,300,000 editorial value was delivered to their two clients by the joint promotion.

★CASE STUDY★ ACTIVITY

You have been employed to promote a new men's deodorant. The product is in direct competition to the Lynx brand.

Choose at least two media spaces from the list below and explain how you would select them as a place to promote the brand.

- ***Newspapers***
- ***The music press***
- ***The Internet***
- ***Men's special interest sports magazines***
- ***The radio***

Advertising

Advertising is about persuading you to behave in a particular way: buy this chocolate bar; go to watch a new movie; give money to a charity, etc.

In the early days of advertising, there was often a simple presentation of the product. The advertisement for the Kodak Bulls-eye camera is a good example of what the industry call the simple **product (or pack) shot**.

Key terms

Product (or pack) shot A picture of the actual product, for example, a packet of Corn Flakes.

But just showing people things did not persuade them to change their behaviour. Soon advertisers were getting more sophisticated. The Westminster cigarette advertisement shows the beginning of a move towards modern techniques: the cigarette is being smoked by a glamorous woman. The implication is that the cigarette will link those who smoke it to a lifestyle.

Maslow and our needs

Some research in the 1970s by Abraham Maslow is one way of exploring how advertising works. Maslow suggested that human behaviour is focused on satisfying basic human needs. So the most successful advertisements may be the ones which appeal to a combination of the following needs.

Maslow's needs

- **Need to survive**: used by advertisements for food, drink, housing, etc.
- **Need to feel safe**: advertisements for insurance, loans and banks promise security and freedom from threats.
- **Need for affiliation or friendship**: advertisements that focus on lifestyle choices like diet and fashion use people's desire to be popular. They may also threaten them with the failure to be liked or to fit in.
- **Need to nurture or care for something**: advertising which shows cute animals and small children brings this out in the viewer.
- **Need to achieve**: advertisements that are linked with winning, often promoted by sports personalities, tap into the need to succeed at difficult tasks.
- **Need for attention**: advertisements for beauty products often play on the need to be noticed and admired.
- **Need for prominence**: advertisements for expensive furniture and jewellery may use people's need to be respected and to have high social status.
- **Need to dominate**: advertisements for products like fast cars offer the possibility of being in control through the product.
- **Need to find meaning in life**: advertisements for travel or music may appeal to people's need for fulfilment.

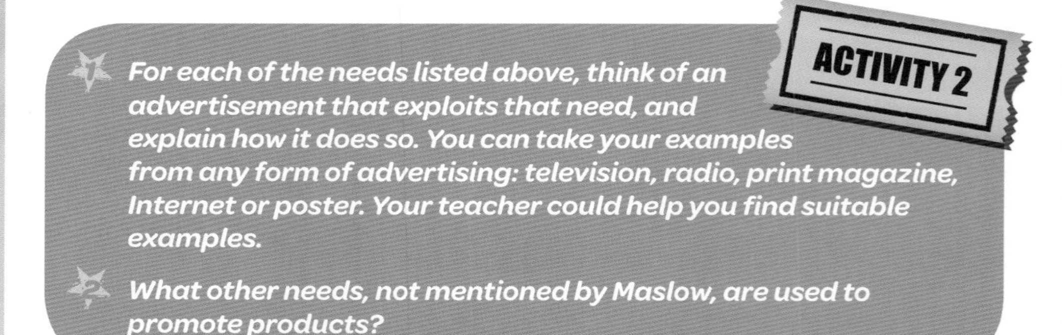

ACTIVITY 2

For each of the needs listed above, think of an advertisement that exploits that need, and explain how it does so. You can take your examples from any form of advertising: television, radio, print magazine, Internet or poster. Your teacher could help you find suitable examples.

What other needs, not mentioned by Maslow, are used to promote products?

Audience

When Steven Spielberg was asked who he thought was the core audience for his films, he said, 'At this point, it's pretty much everybody...'. Advertising agencies are not so lucky. They have to think hard about how the advertisement will be received by the target audience they are aiming to persuade.

Social class categories

The advertising industry has done a great deal of research into typical lifestyles of various groups in society. In the past, a lot of advertising tried to target people simply on the basis of social class. Six categories were used to parcel people up into particular audience types:

Social class categories

A	High-ranking managers in industry or the professions like law or medicine
B	Middle managers in companies or public services like health or education
C1	Junior managers or supervisors in industry or public services
C2	Skilled manual workers – like carpenters or electricians
D	Unskilled manual workers
E	The unemployed or others on very low incomes from casual work

Advertisers soon found that these broad social class categories were not sophisticated enough to distinguish between the various **niche markets** they needed to target to sell their products.

Key terms

Niche markets
Small groups who are targeted because they share the same interests, income, etc.

ITV Sales categories

The next set of categories shown below are those which have been used by ITV Sales to identify potential target audiences, which they call demographics. (The codes in the left-hand column are used by the sales team when they put their data onto computer analysis sheets.)

ITV Sales categories

Code	Explanation
HW	Housewives (these can be men as well as women. A *housewife* is defined as the person who does the major shopping for the household)
HC	Housewives with children
HA	Housewives in the ABC1 socio-economic groups, i.e. those who are more wealthy (as explained in the social class categories list above)
AD	Adults
A3	Adults aged between 16–34
AA	Adults in the ABC1 socio-economic groups
ME	Men
M3	Men aged between 16–34
MA	Men in the ABC1 socio-economic groups
WO	Women
W3	Women aged between 16–34
WA	Women in the ABC1 socio-economic groups
CH	Children

As you can see, the ITV Sales categories are more sharply defined than the much broader social class categories. This helps the ITV Sales team to target potential consumers in a more sophisticated way.

ACTIVITY 3

1. ***Choose two programmes on a commercial television channel, such as ITV, that you think would be watched by different types of audience.***
2. ***Watch the advertising breaks in the middle of two programmes.***
3. ***For each advertisement in the break, identify the category (or categories) the sales team would have identified as the target audience, using the codes from the ITV Sales table on page 151.***

Lifestyle categories

As consumers have become more sophisticated, advertisers have continued to develop the ways of trying to 'pigeon hole' audiences. The table below shows categories which are sometimes used to define the 16–34 age audience's outlook on life. The industry thinks they are useful where advertisements sell a lifestyle associated with a product.

Lifestyle categories	
Cowboys	People who want to make money quickly and easily.
Cynics	People who always have something to complain about.
Drifters	People who aren't at all sure what they want.
Drop-outs	People who do not want to get committed in any way.
Egoists	People who are mainly concerned to get the most pleasure for themselves out of life.
Groupies	People who want to be accepted by those around them.
Innovators	People who want to make their mark on the world.
Puritans	People who want to feel they have done their duty.
Rebels	People who want the world to fit in with their idea of how it should be.
Traditionalists	People who want everything to remain the same.
Trendies	People who are desperate to have the admiration of their peer group.
Utopians	People who want to make the world a better place.

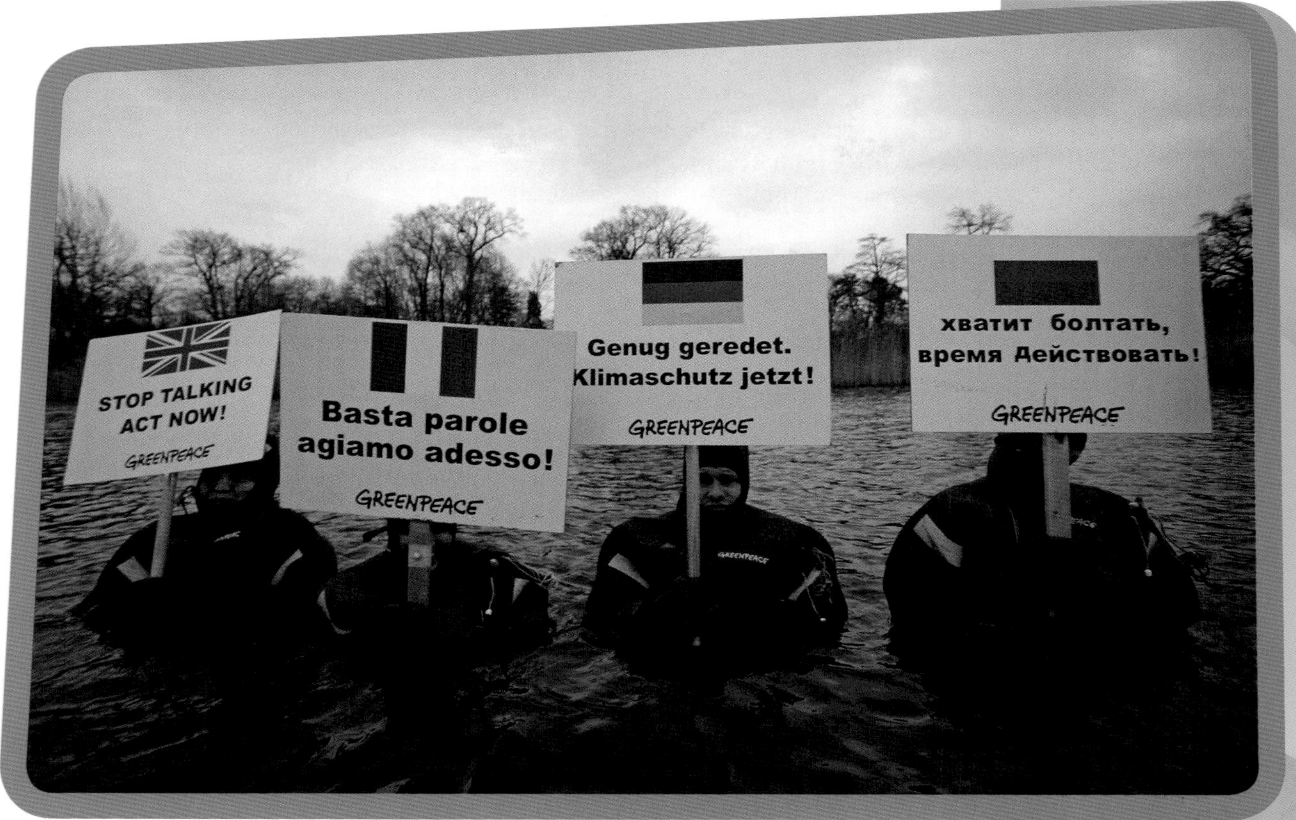

Some 'utopian' environmental campaigners

Advertisers are sharp enough to know that few of us fit only one box. People can change and can also fit more than one category. For example, someone who is an environmental campaigner could be described as a 'Rebel' and also a 'Utopian'. The categories are just helpful to advertisers when they are making distinctions between the various target audiences who might buy the product.

ACTIVITY 4

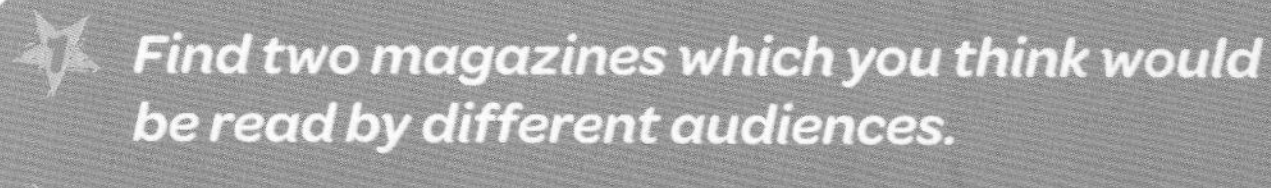
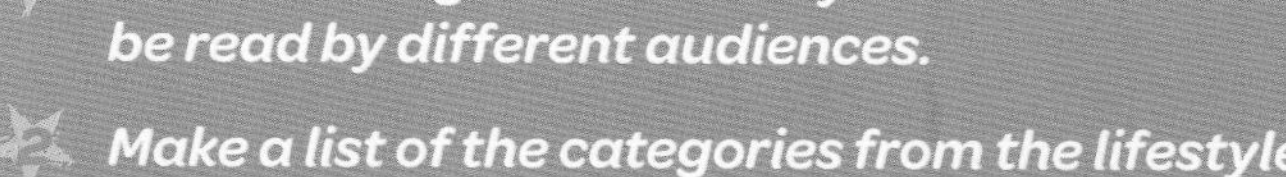

1. ***Find two magazines which you think would be read by different audiences.***
2. ***Make a list of the categories from the lifestyle list on page 152 which you think could apply to five advertisements from each magazine.***
3. ***What patterns are there in your two lists which might suggest that the magazines themselves are aimed at particular lifestyle categories?***

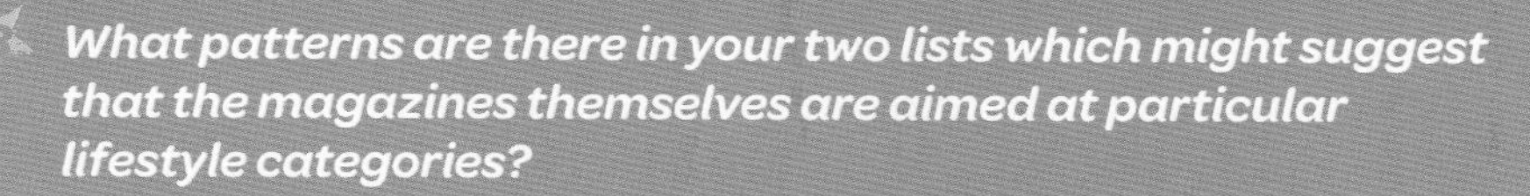

How magazine and newspaper advertisements create desires

As you saw earlier, Maslow suggests that advertising works by satisfying the consumer's needs. However, these needs are not always apparent to the consumer until the advertisement has created a desire.

One way this is done is by offering you an image of yourself, made to look more glamorous, powerful or popular as a result of using the product. This image is designed to make you see yourself transformed by the product.

Denotation and connotation

In trying to unpick how the advertisement is working, it is useful to look at two levels.

1. We can talk about what is *actually there* in the photograph. This is about *fact*. It is straight description which everyone can agree on. We call this level the **denotation** in the photograph.
2. We can move on to consider what the things we can see suggest to us. This might be different from one person to the next. We are moving into the realm of *opinion*. We call this level the **connotation** of the photograph.

> **Key terms**
>
> **Denotation** This is the understanding of media artefacts – what they look and sound like.
>
> **Connotation** The hidden meaning behind an image, word or sound that gives it depth.
>
> **Deconstruction** Looking carefully at how an advertisement communicates its meaning by analysing the connotations of the various parts of the image.

Media language and advertising

In the **deconstruction** of any printed advertisement you should think about each of the points in the chart on page 155. They will help you to explore the way media language works in advertising images.

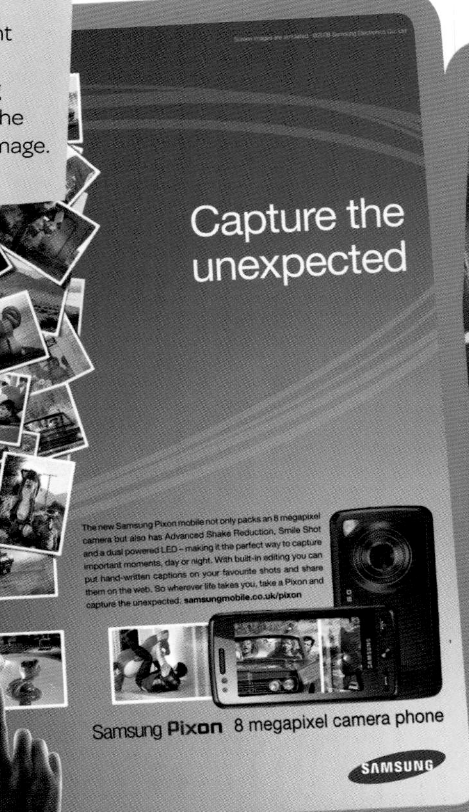

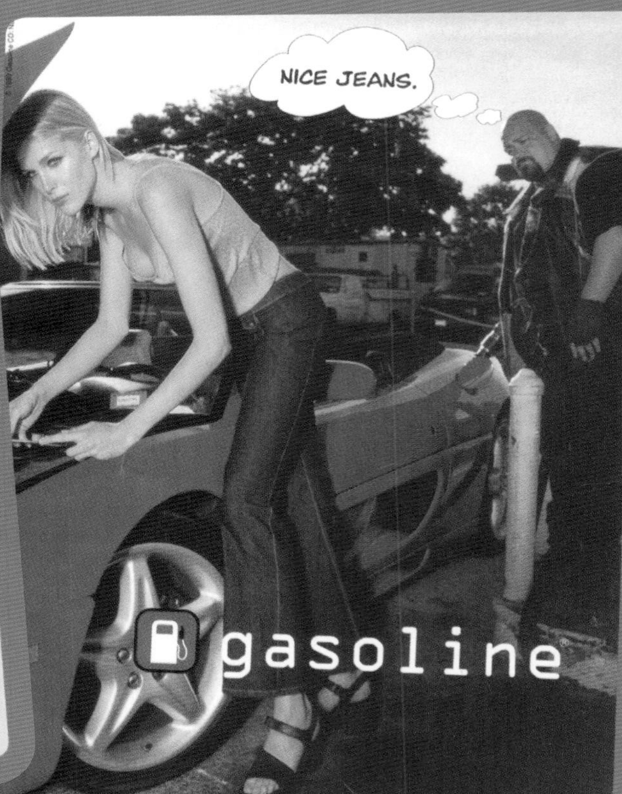

Visual feature	Key questions
Facial expression	How would you describe the expression on the model's face? Are the eyes looking directly at the viewer or at something else? What feelings do you think the photographer hoped to conjure up in the viewer through these facial expressions?
Character type	The model will have been chosen to represent a particular type of person. How would you sum up the character type? How does this choice support the message of the advertisement?
Gesture or posture	The model will have been given detailed instructions on exactly how to stand or sit, where to place their hands, the precise way to hold their head, etc. What do the postures and gestures make the viewer think about the model?
Props	All the other objects, or props as they are called, will have been chosen because they support the overall message the photographer hopes to convey. What are the most important props? What connotations do you think each prop was intended to produce in the viewer?
Clothing	Every article of clothing will have been carefully selected. Why do you think the model is dressed in this way?
Setting	Whether the shoot took place on a specially constructed set in a studio or at an outside location, the setting will be used to add further to the overall effect of the advertisement's message. What connotations does the setting in your advertisement summon up in the viewer?

TIP

Try to imagine a totally different model in the advert. Maybe someone from a different age or ethnic group. Would the advert still work? Why/why not?

The following advertisement shows you, using the annotations, how the questions in the table above work in practice. Look at the advertisement, read the annotations, then have a go at the activity that follows.

The model isn't just anyone – it is Sarah Jessica Parker (SJP). Using a famous actress is an 'endorsement' – and the product actually carries her name on the label too. In a society like our own, which is obsessed with celebrity, associating your product with a celeb is a common advertising technique.

SJP's long flowing hair is shown off to good effect as it's being blown by a wind machine. This also adds life and movement to the image. Long flowing hair is associated with a certain type of conventional/ stereotypical beauty.

SJP's expression – gazing directly at the viewer, mouth slightly open, the hint of a coy smile – has a sexy edge to it.

The product is displayed prominently – and oversized! It needs to be easily recognisable in the shop.

SJP's posture is very carefully set up. Looking over her shoulder, half turned away from the viewer, she looks like she's being pursued.

The plain white dress given to SJP for the shoot suggests elegance, luxury and purity. The tight bodice emphasises her thin waist (stereotypical 'beautiful' figure). The flowing skirt adds glamour.

The long black gloves reinforce the elegance and sophistication. You only wear these for very special occasions.

SJP tells us, she 'had to have it'. Carefully chosen words to chime in with the product's name – 'covet', meaning an eager desire for something.

The ribbon adds an old-fashioned, feminine touch. It also balances the composition, complementing the product SJP is holding, both in colour and position.

The product label is reproduced here as a gold plaque, linking connotations of richness with the product.

The cool blue colour used for the background provides a good contrast for the warmth of SJP's skin tones and hair colour. It complements the colour of the dress and the ribbon – and especially the product's cap top.

The font used here is 'pre-computer', old fashioned, copperplate writing.

Having looked at the Sarah Jessica-Parker/ Covet advertisement (on page 156), it's your turn to deconstruct an advertisement.

1. *Look at the fragrance advertisement below and remind yourself of the key questions in the table on page 155.*

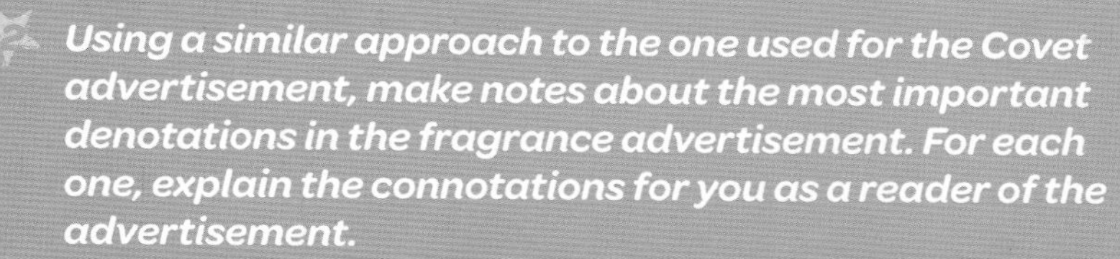

2. *Using a similar approach to the one used for the Covet advertisement, make notes about the most important denotations in the fragrance advertisement. For each one, explain the connotations for you as a reader of the advertisement.*

3. *When you have explored the various connotations, explain who you think the advertisement might have been aimed at and what helped you to make this interpretation.*
4. *If you were an advertising agency, which magazines would you try to place the advertisement in? Justify your decisions.*

Key terms

Representation How people, places, events or ideas are represented or portrayed to audiences in media texts. Sometimes this is simplistically through stereotypes so the audience can see immediately what is meant, and sometimes the meanings are less obvious.

Stereotyping Grouping people together according to simple shared characteristics, without allowing for any individual uniqueness.

Representation in advertising

The images used by advertisers to sell things constantly present us with a particular view of the world. Advertisements do not just sell us products: they constantly sell us a particular version of what is supposed to be desirable.

Stereotypes

Because they have a short time to grab our attention and drive home their message, advertisers often resort to **stereotyping**.

Once stereotypes are established, then advertisers can play around with them.

Like all other areas of advertising and marketing, the use of stereotypes is always evolving to meet changes in society. Recent research identified the following five distinct female stereotypes being used in advertising.

Examples of female stereotypes in advertising

The Beauty Bunny She believes that just because there is science in a beauty product, it will work. She is into every new invention in the beauty industry and reserves her greatest enthusiasm for the latest shampoo or face cream. L'Oreal's 'Because I'm worth it' could be her catchphrase.

The Alpha Female She's a powerful professional whose main focus in life is her career. She's definitely in control, but her entire life is work. She is not shown as a mother, a wife or a lover. She can be seen as rather scary.

The Fashionista She appears in every glossy magazine, such as *Vogue* and *Elle*, and is portrayed as someone who is only interested in the way she looks. She wants to know about the new clothes, the new shoes, the new bags and the new lip colour (but unlike Beauty Bunny is not old enough to worry about skin care). She has neither personality nor, by implication, intelligence.

The Perfect Mum We see her every time a household product or an everyday commodity is advertised. Her biggest concern is her children. She has pushed away every other need in her life. She's a mum, she's not an individual. She's not sexy or ambitious.

The Granny She is the Perfect Mum fast-forwarded 20 years or so. She has few interests outside her grandchildren.

Look at the five photographs that follow and remind yourself of the five female advertising stereotypes above.

Match the five photographs to each of the five female stereotypes.

Write a brief explanation for each photograph to describe how the connotations in the image suggested the stereotype.

A
B
L'ORÉA
TELESCOPIC
MASCARA
In a flash of a stroke...
up to 60% longer lashes and definition lash by la
Innovation: High-Precision Flexible Bru
Telescopic leng
The flat surfaces stretch the formula towards infin
for up to 60% longer lashe
Definition lash by las
The brush edges separate the lashes with precisio
Because you're worth
L'ORÉAL
PARIS
C
Dior
LONDON / BIRMINGHAM / MANCHESTER / DUBLIN / HEATHROW AIRPORT
WWW.DIOR.COM / TEL 020 7172 0172
D
Farley's Rusks. Four varieties they can't wait to try.
CROOKES Healthcare
Orange. Banana. Original and Low Sugar. They're all delicious.
And mashed up, you'd be hard pushed to find a better weaning food for your baby.
There are no artificial colours, flavours or preservatives. And there's certainly no added salt.
In fact, Farley's Rusks are packed with vitamins and minerals*. So they're sure to get them off to a flying start.
Farley's RUSKS
SO FARLEY'S SO GOOD
*Each Rusk contains 15% of the Recommended Daily Amount of most vitamins and minerals for children under two.
For further information on Farley's baby milks and weaning foods please write to Farley's Infant Nutrition, Department C, P.O. Box 12, West P.D.O., Nottingham NG7 2GB.
E
SUN LIFE
GUARANTEED
OVER 5
P L A N

ACTIVITY 7

Look at the advertisement for Gasoline below.

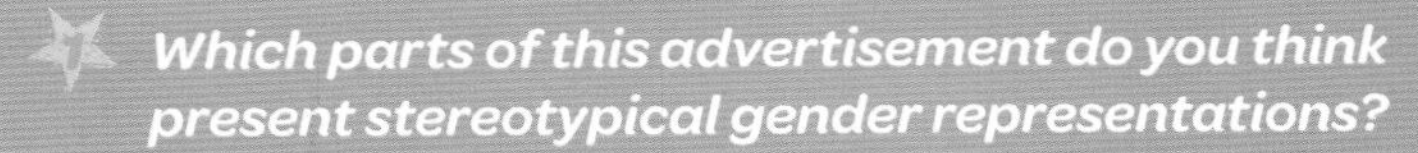

1. *Which parts of this advertisement do you think present stereotypical gender representations?*

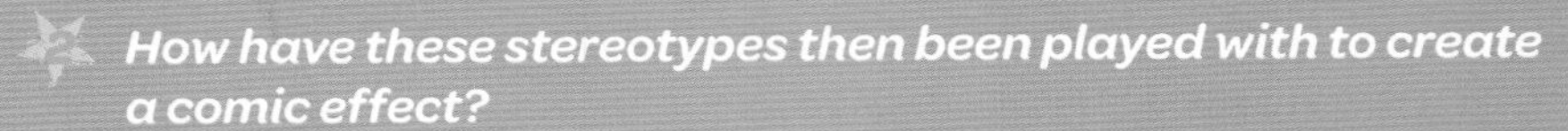

2. *How have these stereotypes then been played with to create a comic effect?*
3. *Who do you think the audience for this advertisement was and how do you know?*
4. *If you were the advertising agency placing it in a magazine, which one would you choose and why?*

Advertising: convergent media

This next activity focuses on convergent media aspects of advertising. This is where you are considering how advertising works across different media platforms.

ACTIVITY 8

You are going to carry out a content investigation.

1. *Choose one of the following areas to study:*
   - *gender representations – either male or female*
   - *ethnic representations*
   - *representations of the family.*

2. *Find ten different advertisements which feature representations of the group you are studying. These should be a range of print and moving-image advertisements. For each one, make notes on the types of representation shown.*

3. *Write a 300-word report on the extent to which there was a common pattern in the representations. Or did they offer a diverse view of gender, race or the family?*

4. *Compare your findings with a partner who studied a different area. Discuss whether stereotyped representations can be harmful in any way.*

EXAMINER'S TIP

When you are looking at advertising it is vital you consider the convergent nature of advertising today.

Intertextuality

Intertextuality is a term used to describe what happens when a producer deliberately makes a reference to another text to add a layer of meaning to the original. For example, to advertise a new cop series, the BBC used a *Radio Times* front cover to link it with a glamorous Hollywood crime movie and its stars. You can compare how similar the images are on page 162.

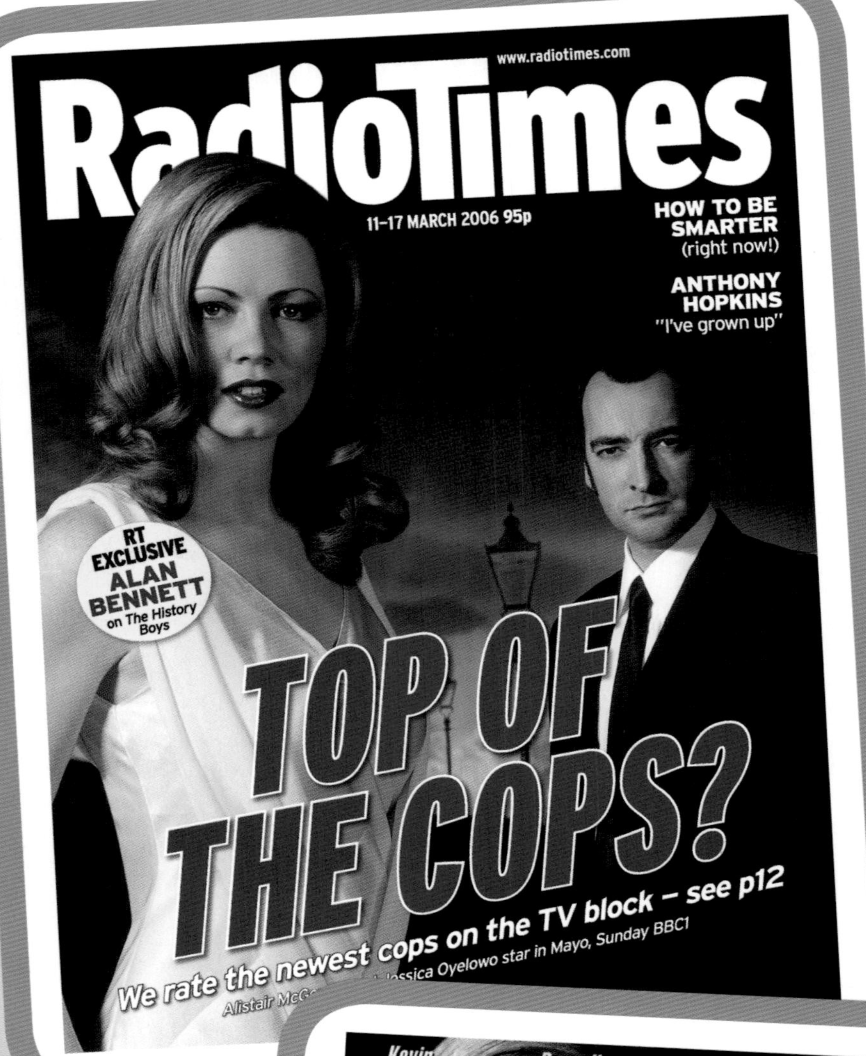
www.radiotimes.com
RadioTimes
11–17 MARCH 2006 95p
HOW TO BE SMARTER
(right now!)
ANTHONY HOPKINS
"I've grown up"
RT EXCLUSIVE
ALAN BENNETT
on The History Boys
TOP OF THE COPS?
We rate the newest cops on the TV block – see p12
star in Mayo, Sunday BBC1

Kevin SPACEY
Russell CROWE
Guy PEARCE
Kim BASINGER
Danny DeVITO
Everything Is Suspect…
Everyone Is For Sale…
And Nothing Is What It Seems.
L.A. Confidential
18

Intertextuality often adds a playful or humorous edge to an advertisement.

1. *Look at the advertisement for Typhoo Tea on the CD.*
2. *In what ways does this advertisement make references to other television shows, genres or previous advertising campaigns?*

CD-ROM
Extra!

Typhoo Tea advertisement

Open the CD in the back of this book and click on the icon below to see a Typhoo Tea advertisement.

Internet advertising

As in so many other areas of the media, the Internet has made a dramatic impact on advertising. With the exception of the BBC, which is entirely publicly funded, all other television channels rely on advertising revenue to survive. Commercial television channels can only make the programmes they do if advertisers continue to buy airtime.

Advertisers are spending increasing amounts of money on Internet advertising. This puts commercial television channels under threat. For instance, in 2008 Google received more income from advertising than Channel 4 did. Estimates also suggested that, in 2008, Google took 80 per cent of all new advertising revenue.

One reason why the Internet is threatening traditional television advertising is because there are now a lot of other ways people can entertain themselves. Research shows that, in particular, those under 25 years of age are spending much less time watching television and much more time playing games or surfing the Internet. If the television is on, it is often only on in the background.

Viral advertising

But it isn't just that not so much television is being watched. The Internet can get advertising messages to people much more cheaply. In particular, the use of **viral advertising** has grown very quickly. We are all familiar with the 'viral email' – online joke videos which individuals receive in their inbox and then spread them by sending them on to all the people in their address book.

Viral advertisements latched onto this practice. For instance, third in a recent 'chart' of the most frequently downloaded virals was actually an advertisement for Miller Lite beer. So instead of paying many thousands of pounds to place a slot in the middle of a television programme, an employee in an advertising agency just emailed the advertisement to everyone in his or her email address book. And the message spreads like wildfire.

Key terms

Viral advertising Spreading advertisements through the use of attachments to emails. It can give very wide coverage at no cost.

Buying Internet space

But you can't do it all through virals. Companies will also spend some of their marketing budgets buying space on the Internet. As you will have found out yourself when using a search engine, you will get many thousands of results for any Google search. Research shows that traffic drops by 90 per cent if you are on page 2 of search results – so people pay a lot of money to get themselves in the top three search results.

Direct hits

Advertisers always want to know that the money they are spending to market their product is hitting the target audience as directly as possible. Sophisticated new software is making it possible for Internet advertising to target niche audiences more directly than a broadcast format like television.

For example, Phorm is a system which tracks the types of site visited by individuals on their own computers. They then redirect advertisements linked to the types of site visited. So if you visit clothing, photography or travel sites, you can expect a lot of related advertisements to pop up in your inbox.

Broadcast to Reed networks

The big change for advertisers is the shift in audience consumption of media from a **Broadcast network** to a **Reed network**.

- **Broadcast network (television)** – this is where one or two big producers (like BBC or ITV) transmit television programmes which an unknown audience can receive individually. They can't respond and they don't know how many others are receiving the same communication.
- **Reed network (the Internet)** – this is where any individual can communicate with any other. In addition, they can also form groups. So YouTube and Facebook, for example, are ready-made interest groups who can be targeted by advertisers.

Key terms

Social networking site Examples are Facebook and Myspace.

For the Broadcast networks, like radio and television, the rapid rise of the Internet – a Reed network – is a threat. If they cannot make enough money from advertising, then they will go out of business. For marketing agencies, Reed networks offer a cheap alternative to paying for expensive media space.

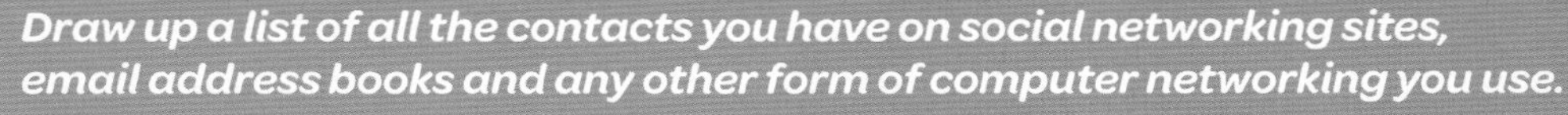

In this activity you will be exploring Internet networks.

1. *Draw up a list of all the contacts you have on social networking sites, email address books and any other form of computer networking you use.*
2. *Select six other people in your class to work with and add together the total number of contacts held by your group.*
3. *Now go back through your own list.*
   - *Identify all those contacts who you think will not appear in the list of anyone else in your group.*
   - *For every one of those contacts, assume they have the same total number of contacts in their network as you do.*
   - *Add up the total number of potential contacts who are two clicks away from you on the Internet – your secondary contact list. In other words, if you have 50 contacts in your network and you identify 20 of them as being your contact alone, that adds an additional 1000 people to your secondary contact list.*
4. *Now add together all the secondary contacts for the six members of the group.*

You now know the number of people you could potentially reach – at no cost and very quickly. So if you do happen to have anything to sell ... get clicking!

Public relations (PR)

Big advertising and marketing agencies will usually have a department which handles PR for their clients. The purpose of PR is to get the client's brand prominent media coverage by means of events or product placement. In advertising-speak, it is about 'creating brand endorsement and brand visibility' without buying expensive advertising space.

Events

The Events team in an agency will organise anything from a press conference for a football team who have just bought a star player to a major music festival linked to a brand – like the annual Virgin Move! festival in Manchester.

Getting the brief to organise a film premiere can be doubly useful to modern advertising and marketing agencies. It gives them the chance to bring together two clients. As well as working for the film producers who want to launch their latest movie with a blaze of publicity, a beer or soft drink client can link their product to the event by providing the refreshments. With good media coverage, both the film and the drink will get good brand exposure.

Product placement

In the past, film production companies often approached a range of businesses to offer them the chance to have their jeans, drinks, cars, etc. appear in a movie. This was good for the film company as it cut props costs and was good for the clothing or drinks company as it got their product on screen. This was the beginning of **product placement**.

Key terms

Product placement Giving brands or products to media producers for them to use as props so that the product is seen in a favourable way.

Thanks to effective product placement, James Bond has long been associated with the luxury car maker Aston Martin

Advertising and marketing agencies will have a Product Placement department that will actively seek out placement opportunities for their clients. The people in the department are dedicated to getting the product seen on the right people at the right time and in the right place.

TIP

Try to spot some product placement in a few films. You might be able to check if you spotted them all by looking at the list of suppliers in the credits.

Advertorials

Like product placement, the use of advertorials in print publications are a form of covert marketing. The term comes from a combination of advertisement and editorial copy. It is where a brand which places an advertisement in a magazine also gets an article written about it – usually in a complimentary way.

So, for example, if Apple advertise the iPhone in Q magazine, the deal might also include an interview with a prominent record producer who explains how the iPhone makes his working life so much easier and also provides him with instant access to all sorts of entertainment.

TOXIC Interview!

Wayne Rooney

TOXIC readers recently had the chance to ask Wayne Rooney a bunch of questions. Here's what he had to say about footy, FIFA 09 and more!

How old were you when you started playing football? James, aged 9

"As far back as I can remember! I used to play in the house, the street, and then I was seven when I played in my first competitive game."

If you weren't a footballer, what do you think you would you? Grady, aged 11

"I used to work for my dad years ago, but other than that, it's football that's my real passion!"

Which was your first professional club? Louis, aged 8

"It was Everton. I signed with them when I was 9 and was there until I was 18. I supported Everton growing up and so it was brilliant that I got to play for them. And then I moved to Manchester United!"

What's your favourite way to score in FIFA games? Max, aged 9

"I usually go out wide with Ronaldo, take three players on, and then cross it in to score!"

Do you think you look like your FIFA video game character? Taran, aged 8

"Yeah, it looks really good! I did some motion capture work for the character's moves a while ago. The graphics in the game are very realistic now. It's still a bit weird seeing a

It may not have been just coincidence that the interview with Wayne Rooney in games magazine *Toxic* features a photo of him wearing an EA Sports top, holding a copy of the magazine with the FIFA 09 game on the cover. The references to EA Sports and FIFA 09 will almost certainly have been 'placed' and then the journalist lined up to write the piece.

ACTIVITY 11

Working with a partner, imagine you are in the product placement division of an agency. You have been approached by the producers of a new energy drink to link their product with a young, trendy and fit lifestyle.

List ten people or places you would target to try and get positive exposure for the product. For example, a television chat show or backstage at a music awards ceremony.

Do you think it is acceptable for agencies to market brands in a covert way? Or should all forms of advertising be made obvious to readers/viewers? (For example, does it matter if Leona Lewis appears on a chat show wearing a t-shirt with a prominent brand logo on it?)

TIP

Consider how many branded items of clothing you and your friends wear.

Interactive advertising and marketing

As consumers become ever more sophisticated in their use of media, the advertising industry develops and refines its methods. The Internet has turned the people formerly known as 'the audience' into participants in and creators of media products and experiences.

The buzzword in the media these days is 'interactivity'. For broadcast television, for example, this translates into programmes which encourage viewers to text or email their opinions. For the advertising and marketing industry, **experiential communication** has become the way ahead.

Key terms

Experiential communication
Where consumers actually interact with the product rather than just look at pictures of it. (See the Nike case study on pages 168 and 169.)

CASE STUDY
NIKE SOLE PROVIDER

This case study discusses some of the convergent media aspects of advertising and marketing. In particular, it considers experiential communication as an advertising and marketing tool.

Experiential communication techniques

One company which has become a big player in experiential communication techniques is Nike. They have used various methods to bring their brand to life for young consumers. Their 'Run London' event provided runs of different lengths to encourage people with different fitness levels to enjoy running. Of course, by taking part in 'Run London', participants were also experiencing the Nike brand.

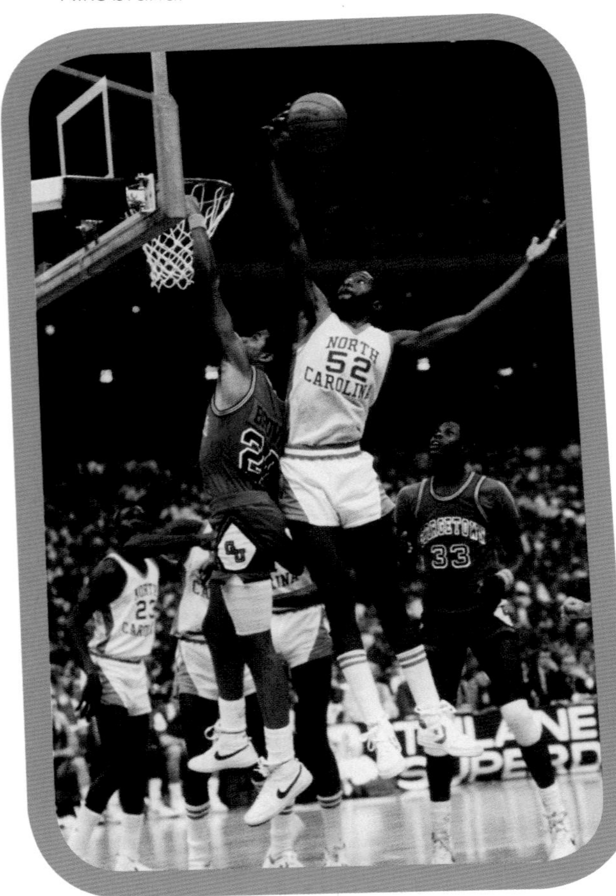

Nike has a long history of involvement in basketball.

Nike's Sole Provider event

To accompany their book on the history of Nike's involvement in basketball, which was called *Sole Provider*, Nike commissioned their agency to design an experiential event. The brief was to take the information in the book and turn it into a two-week exhibition at the Atlantis gallery in London's Brick Lane. The target audience for the exhibition was split into two distinct demographs:

- trainer fanatics
- basketball players/fans.

In the new experiential approach, the agency hoped that by involving people in the story of Nike's basketball history and interacting with the product, they would experience the brand rather than just being told what to think about it.

The exhibition displayed a lot of old trainers and advertising material, starting with the classic 1972 Blazer shoe right up to the most recent designs. One key problem the agency had to solve was to find an original way of displaying a heap of old trainers which would grab the visitors' attention. The answer they came up with was to put them in glass-fronted fridges!

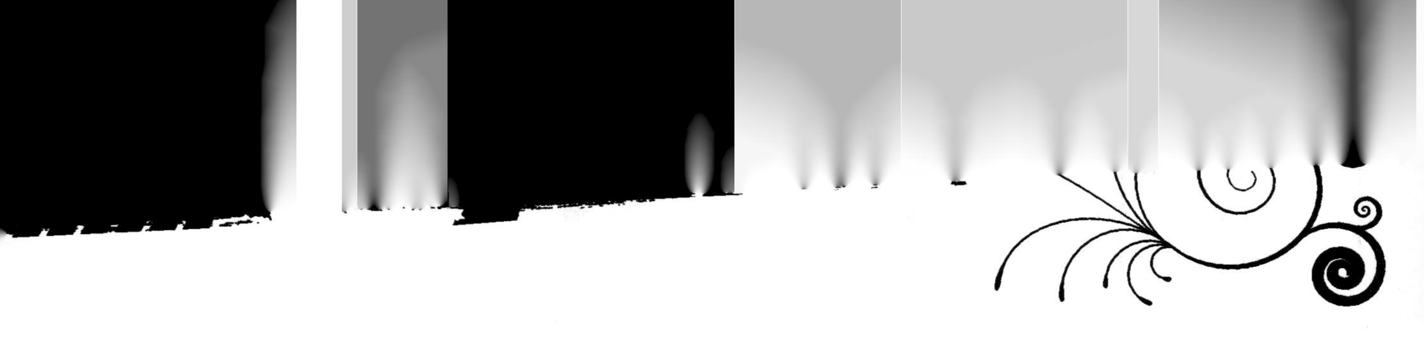

Some Nike classics were given special treatment. The Air Posit from the 1990s had taken some of its design ideas from insects. The agency decided it would be fun to display the 'bugged out shoe', as it was called in New York street culture, in an insect house filled with locusts.

The brief required that the exhibition should involve people in the sport and, by association, become engaged with the brand. So a basketball 'battleground' with two hoops was set up where people could actually play the game as part of the exhibition.

Of course, the experiential communication was supported by all the older techniques:

- The Events department organised an opening night to which important people in the trainer industry and basketball scene were invited. The intention was that they would tell their friends how good the show was, thus becoming 'brand ambassadors', as the industry calls them.
- The PR department secured the main designer of the exhibition an interview on BBC London's *What's On* slot.
- Print advertisements were taken out in the style press to hit the trainer fanatics and also in the basketball magazines to hit that part of the brief.
- A microsite was created to give Internet exposure to the exhibition and emails were sent to individuals within the target demograph to generate an online buzz about the exhibition.

TIP

Before you begin your planning for this activity, you should research the brief by looking at the Fairtrade website: www.fairtrade.org.uk.

★CASE STUDY★ ACTIVITY

Working with a partner, you are now going to design a digital and experiential campaign for Fairtrade products. The key brand value of Fairtrade is social responsibility to developing countries. Their aim is to promote ethical shopping.

In terms of the lifestyle groupings we looked at earlier in the chapter, the campaign will target:

- ***puritans: people who want to feel they have done their duty***
- ***utopians: people who want to make the world a better place***
- ***innovators: people who want to make their mark on the world.***

Campaign objectives. Fairtrade have asked you to concentrate on:

- ***raising awareness and visibility of their logo so that shoppers will recognise products which have been fairly traded***
- ***promoting bananas grown on the Caribbean island of St Lucia.***

1. ***Storyboard a 30-second viral advertisement which takes a humorous approach to delivering one or both of the campaign objectives.***
2. ***Create an experiential stand to be used at music events to enable fans to interact with Fairtrade ideas and meet the objectives of the campaign.***

What have you learned?

In this chapter you have learned about:

Texts

- How advertisements in a variety of different forms – printed and digital – communicate meaning

Media language

Genre

- How advertisements use intertextuality

Narrative

- The way stories around lifestyle contribute to advertising

Representation

- How women are often represented stereotypically in advertising

Audiences

- How audiences read advertising imagery
- How advertisers categorise audiences

Organisational issues

- The three main ways of marketing products or services: promotional campaigns, advertising and public relations events (PR)
- The changes that have taken place in marketing with the arrival of the Internet

Convergent media

- How marketing campaigns often use a range of media forms to promote their brands

8 Radio

Your learning

In this chapter you will learn about:

- how music, speech and sound effects are used by a radio station to create a recognisable house style
- how radio stations research and target their audiences
- how BBC and commercial radio stations are funded, and how this affects their schedules and content.

Talk about the answers to these questions in a group of three or four. Make notes of the decisions your group has come to.

1. *How important is each of these in your life: TV, newspapers, magazines, radio? Put them into a rank order as a result of your discussion.*
2. *When do you listen to the radio?*
   - *In bed at night*
   - *While doing homework on a computer*
   - *Radio alarm when waking up*
   - *While playing video/computer games*
   - *At school*
   - *Preparing to go to school*
   - *Having breakfast*
3. *Where do you listen to the radio?*
   - *Bathroom*
   - *Kitchen*
   - *Car*
   - *Other places, such as ...?*
   - *Living room*
   - *Bedroom*
   - *School*

EXAMINER'S TIP

Considering the convergent media aspects of radio is very important. Pod casting, advertising and news are just a few areas worth looking at.

TIP

Use a mnemonic to help you remember the five needs in the Uses and Gratifications Theory, e.g. ***I i****mmensely* ***e****njoy* ***s****ending* ***e****mails.*

Why do people listen to the radio?

The results of surveys show that people listen to the radio under many different circumstances. Why do people choose to put the radio on? The Uses and Gratifications Theory (see page 76) can be used to show that people consume media texts to satisfy a variety of needs:

- The need to be INFORMED and EDUCATED about the world
- The need to IDENTIFY with characters and situations to learn more about ourselves
- The need to be ENTERTAINED
- The need to use the media as a talking point for SOCIAL INTERACTION
- The need to ESCAPE from our 'daily grind' into other worlds and situations.

Work in your group again.

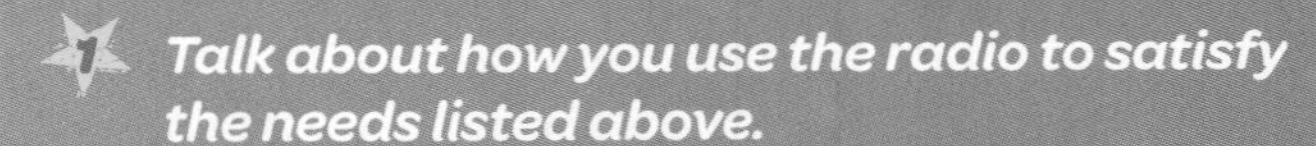

1. ***Talk about how you use the radio to satisfy the needs listed above.***

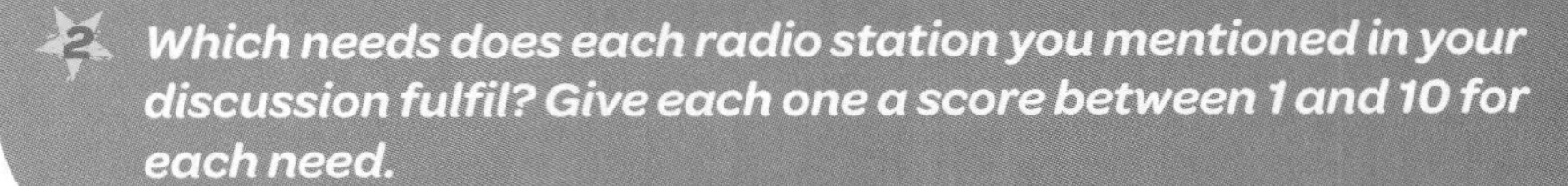

2. ***Which needs does each radio station you mentioned in your discussion fulfil? Give each one a score between 1 and 10 for each need.***

A short history of radio in the UK

1922 British Broadcasting Corporation licensed to transmit radio programmes.

1928 Radio audience of over 1 million.

1933 First commercial radio – Radio Luxembourg broadcasts popular music programmes on an unauthorised frequency.

1939 Nine million radios in the UK: most people listen to the Prime Minister, Neville Chamberlain, announcing war with Germany.

1947 First portable 'transistor' radios.

1958 Radio audiences dwindle as audiences for TV dramatically increase: BBC Radio's evening audience is down to 3.5 million.

1964 'Pirate' radio stations playing modern pop music start to broadcast to the UK from ships offshore, outside the broadcasting law. They attract large audiences of young people.

1967 Pirate radios closed down by law. The BBC opens pop station Radio 1.

1967 BBC Leicester, first BBC local radio station, opens.

1973 First legal commercial radio stations open: Capital Radio and LBC in London.

1980–2000 An increasing number of radio stations receive licences.

TODAY There are several BBC national network stations, over 40 BBC local radio stations, ten national commercial radio stations, more than 200 local commercial stations and large numbers of community radio stations.

People listened to radios like this in the 1930s

A modern hi-tech radio station

What makes radio stations different?

Funding: Beeb versus the rest

So what is the difference between a BBC radio station and a commercial radio station? The answer is very simple – who pays the bills.

The BBC gets the money to run its radio and television channels from a yearly payment called the *licence fee* (£139.50 in 2008) from everyone who owns a TV. The BBC is called a public service broadcaster because it is funded by the public. Although the BBC makes some money through selling its programmes, books and other merchandise, the public pay the largest part of the bill. So, no licence fee – no BBC.

Commercial radio has to cover its running costs by attracting advertisers who pay to market their products or services on air. No adverts – no commercial radio – or commercial TV!

CD-ROM

Extra!

News sources

Open the CD in the back of this book and click on the icon below to see an interview with a radio station news editor discussing news sources.

Talk versus music

Radio stations can also be divided into those that predominantly play music and those whose output is much more speech-based. BBC Radios 1, 2 and 3 and most commercial radio stations base their programmes around music. There is some speech – presenters talk between records, newsreaders give updates and weather forecasts – but the majority of airtime is taken up by music. In contrast, BBC stations like Radio 5 Live and Radio 4 are almost all speech-based, so that if you tune in to them at any time of day or night you are much more likely to hear people talking than music.

Sounding you out

Compared with television, radio is beautifully simple to produce. Although a great deal of thought may have gone into the sounds that come out of your radio and a team of people involved to get them 'on air', there are only three ingredients that programme producers can mix together:

- the human voice
- music
- sound effects.

But those three simple ingredients can be made to sound very different indeed. The look of a big-name trainer is about creating **brand awareness**. The sound of a radio station is also to do with **branding**. How many radio stations can you recognise the instant you hear them? It is vitally important for a station to create their own sound or **house style** because this will be the sound that they know their audience like.

Key terms

Brand awareness Making the product immediately recognisable to the public.

Branding The distinctive features by which we recognise products.

House style A radio station or publisher's preferred manner of presentation or layout which matches their audience.

The most important feature of a house style is the way the presenters talk to their audience. You know from your own experience that the way you speak to people depends on who they are and what the situation is. If you are caught breaking a school rule, the language and style you use when you tell a friend what happened are very different from those you use to a teacher. Radio presenters adapt the way they speak to suit the audience they think will be listening. Their job is to build up a relationship with each listener, to keep them listening to the station and – vitally important – to get them to tune in on a regular basis.

People who run radio stations often talk about presenters who have a 'good voice for radio'. This is a bit vague, but in his book *Broadcast Journalism: Techniques of Radio and TV News*, writer and broadcaster Andrew Boyd describes a 'good microphone voice' as one that is 'reasonably rich, crisp and resonant and free from obvious impediments'. In contrast, a voice that is 'piping, reedy, nasal, sibilant, indistinct or very young-sounding' would not work so well.

There are other factors that presenters must think about when presenting their programmes. The **tone** they adopt will be crucial. You could use any of the words in the following table to describe the tone of a presenter's voice:

serious	light-hearted	assertive	calm
scathing	soothing	humorous	pompous
aggressive	solemn	mocking	contemptuous
intimate	patronising	chatty	over-excited

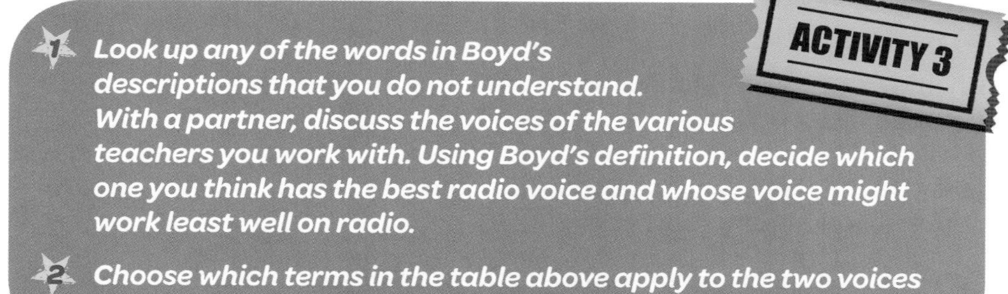

ACTIVITY 3

1. ***Look up any of the words in Boyd's descriptions that you do not understand. With a partner, discuss the voices of the various teachers you work with. Using Boyd's definition, decide which one you think has the best radio voice and whose voice might work least well on radio.***
2. ***Choose which terms in the table above apply to the two voices you have chosen.***

How would you describe the tone of voice used by the radio presenters you listen to most frequently? The tone they use will affect the way they come across to their listeners. Some presenters will want to sound friendly, as if they are talking to their friends. Others will be more formal, providing a 'voice of authority' on whatever it is they are discussing.

Another consideration will be the **pace** at which they talk – is it very slow and measured or is it rapid and quick-fire?

Finally, there will be the **accent** of the presenter's voice. At one time the BBC expected all its presenters to speak in *received pronunciation*, which was seen as a Southern, slightly posh way of speaking. Now it uses presenters who talk in a range of regional accents, reflecting the rich and diverse backgrounds of its listeners across the country.

Key terms

Tone The quality and character of a voice or piece of writing.

Accent The sound of the voice which tells us which part of the country the presenter is from.

Pace How quickly or slowly the presenter speaks.

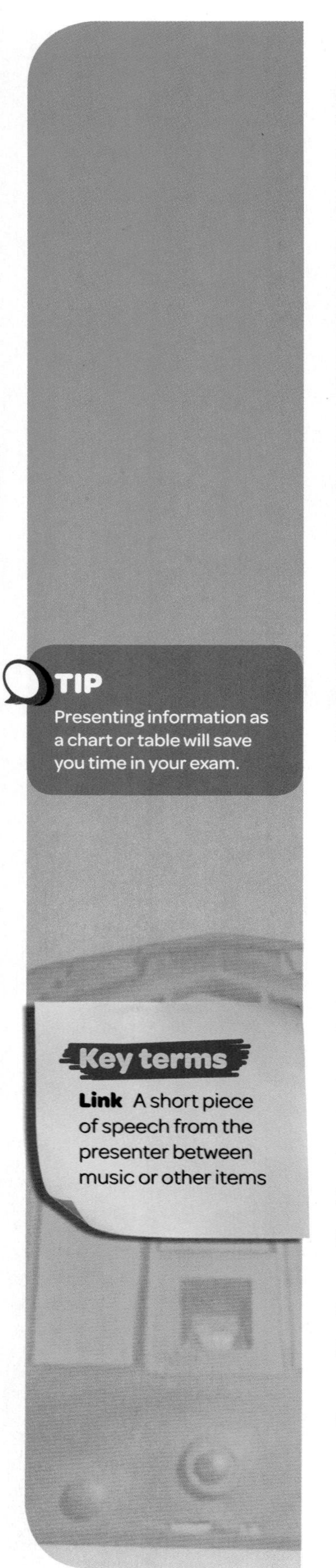

ACTIVITY 4

You are going to research the style and content of these radio stations:

- *BBC Radio 1*
- *BBC Radio 4*
- *Your local commercial radio station*
- *A radio station broadcasting in a foreign language.*

1. *Listen to the sound of each station. Use a grid like the one below to make notes of your findings so that you can discuss them with others afterwards:*
   - Presenters' voices: *use the ideas outlined on the previous page to help you make detailed notes about the style of the presenter's voice.*
   - Programme content: *describe the type of music played or the subject being broadcast by speech-based programmes.*

Radio station	Presenter's voice	Programme content
BBC Radio 1		

2. *Discuss your notes with a partner. Try to decide which type of listener you think each station is targeting with its house style.*

TIP

Presenting information as a chart or table will save you time in your exam.

Making the link

Chatting for 30 to 40 seconds and then playing a record may not seem like hard or difficult work, but making it sound that easy is the sign of a good presenter. Remember, most radio goes out live. Presenters try to make it sound as if what they are saying has just popped into their heads, as it would in a conversation with another person.

Some stations follow American research which suggests that presenters prepare their **links** by following these steps:

1. Choose an idea or topic which will interest or amuse your listener.
2. Mind map anything you can think of saying about that topic onto paper.
3. Choose one strong idea from your mind map and write an interesting first sentence which will hook your listeners into the link.
4. Identify two further ideas you will use to develop the topic.
5. Write a really strong sentence to end the piece (sometimes called a *power out*).
6. Make it sound unscripted when you actually do the piece live on air.

Key terms

Link A short piece of speech from the presenter between music or other items

ACTIVITY 5

1. *Record two links from a local radio station: one with just a single presenter talking and the other with two presenters talking to each other.*
2. *Play these back and make a written transcript of exactly what is said.*
3. *Discuss with a partner whether you think either link seems to have used the American approach.*
4. *Now try it yourself! Write a script for a 40-second link on any topic of your choice using the six steps. Swap scripts with a partner and edit each other's work to make it as powerful as you can. Practise presenting the link before recording it yourself and discussing the results with a group.*

Radio audiences

Radio is no different from any other media form when it comes to thinking about audiences. It needs to know clearly who it is talking to.

Every station wants to get as many people to listen to their output as they possibly can. The BBC Radio stations – local and national – have to prove that enough people listen to them to justify their public funding. Commercial radio stations only exist if they can persuade businesses to buy time to advertise. If no one is listening, advertisers will take their money to a station with big audiences.

So radio stations need listeners, but they cannot all have the same types of listener. What your mum or dad likes is probably a bit different from what you like – whether clothes, music, food or radio programmes. For a radio station, defining its **target audience** is very important.

Take, for example, Gemini FM, which broadcasts to an area of Devon that includes Exeter, Torquay and a lot of small rural towns and villages. This is what they think about their niche audience:

Key terms

Target audience
The types of people who a radio station deliberately tries to attract as listeners

> To talk about a 'typical listener' it is easier to refer to a single example. In terms of Gemini FM this is a twenty-five-year-old female who lives in the mainstream of British popular culture, loves eating and drinking and holidays abroad. She is permanently based in the local area and always enjoys a good night out on the town. She loves to spend money – mainly on clothes and fashion, music, magazines, DVDs and other products she's probably seen advertised. This woman is more likely to be a family-driven individual, maybe with young children, and deals with the pressure this brings. She has a passion for television and particularly loves the soaps, celebrity gossip, *This Morning* and *Big Brother*.
>
> It is important to note that Gemini FM is not a female brand. Nothing at the station should alienate our male audience. So why do we specifically target females? Extensive research has proved that men will willingly listen to a station directed at women but it will not work the other way round. In most cases, women tend to be 'rulers' of the household and it is often their choice of station to which the household radio will be tuned! So, by targeting women, we automatically attract the husbands and kids.

Key terms

Audience profile The types of people who listen to a station

So Gemini will use this as a broad guide for what they will call their **audience profile**. But of course it is not as simple as that. They know that at different times of the day there will potentially be different sorts of audience profile. And so they divide their output up into a *clock* to match the things their audience are doing.

The Breakfast slot is an important start to the day, and a station's programming will reflect the fact that all the family are getting ready for work or school. So *survival information* – traffic reports, weather, regular time checks – is a prominent part of the programme content. By mid-morning, listeners will be at work or back home. In Gemini's case, thinking of a typical listener who is 25 and female will guide the type of presenter chosen and the content for that show. The early evening show tends to attract a younger listener, so the musical content and presenter's style will reflect this.

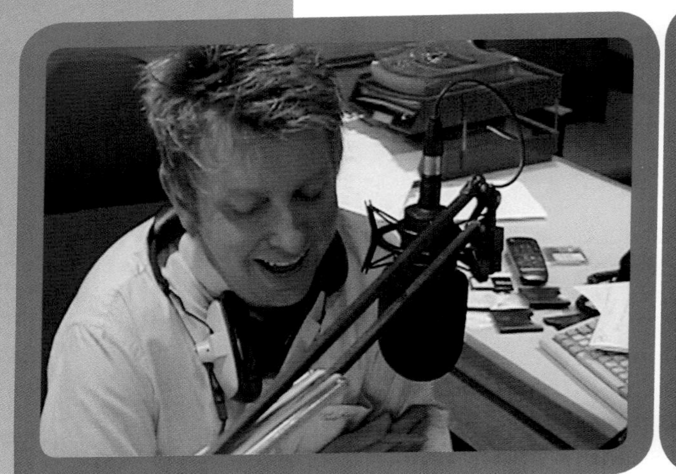

Gemini FM presenters

This broad outline of the types of programme played round the clock is called a *programme schedule*. Deciding on the programme schedule for the station is the responsibility of the *programme controller*.

Key terms

Audience share The number of listeners a radio station attracts compared to its competitors

Is there anybody out there?

Even though radio stations have a clear idea about the types of people they think are listening, they need constantly to check on their **audience share**. They do this by using the information provided by a company called RAJAR (Radio Joint Audience Research).

The sample of data from RAJAR in the following table shows the audience data for just one radio station. The same information is provided for every radio station in the country. Use the notes on page 179 to help you understand the table.

Station	Survey period	Population	Reach (000s)	Reach %	Average hours per head	Average hours per listener	Total hours (000s)	Listening share in TSA %
BBC Radio 1	Q	50,735,000	10,871	21	1.90	9.10	98,786	9.80

RAJAR survey data

Survey period: based on figures from a quarter (Q), half (H) or full (F) year.

Population: the number of people aged 15+ who live within the transmission area of a given station. BBC Radio 1 is a national radio station, so broadcasts to 50,735,000 people.

Reach (000s): the number of people aged 15+ who listen to a radio station for at least 15 minutes over the course of a week. For BBC Radio 1 this was 10,871.

Reach percentage: the weekly reach as a percentage of the population within the transmission area. For BBC Radio 1 this was 21%.

Average hours per head: the average number of hours that a person within the transmission area spends listening to a particular station. For BBC Radio 1 this was 1.90 hours.

Average hours per listener: the average length of time that listeners to a particular station spend with the station. For BBC Radio 1 this was 9.10 hours.

Total hours: the total number of hours that a station is listened to over the course of a week. For BBC Radio 1 this was 98,786 hours.

Listening share in TSA%: the percentage of all radio listening that a station accounts for within its transmission area. For BBC Radio 1 this was 9.80%.

Visit the RAJAR website. Look up your own local radio stations, both independent and BBC. Which do you think is the most successful station?

How do RAJAR find these figures?

Like all statistics of this sort, RAJAR's data is based on the response from a sample of listeners. RAJAR Limited was established in 1992 to operate a single audience measurement system for the radio industry. Results are published quarterly by monitoring a sample selection from every radio station's TSA (Total Survey Area).

- Listening diaries are distributed by RAJAR into selected households in each area of the country. They have to be completed within seven days.
- Diaries are placed with one selected adult over the age of 15 and up to two others in each household.
- The diary's pages are broken down into fifteen-minute intervals each day. The family fill in which radio station they listened to and for how long.
- Every radio station in the family's broadcast area is included in the diary.
- The diaries are collected by RAJAR at the end of the seven-day period. The data is collated and distributed to participating radio stations, and to the public via the RAJAR website.

What have you learned?

In this chapter you have learned about:

Media language

Genre

- How music, speech and sound effects are the common features of any radio station.
- How the ways in which each of those three components is used will give a distinctive house style.

Representation

- The events and ideas reported in radio news will be affected by the sources who provide the information on which the news reports are based (CD-ROM Extra! page 174).

Audiences

- How different radio stations target different audiences.
- How knowing exactly who is listening to a station is essential information for the programme controllers of radio stations.
- How very detailed information is provided to radio stations about their audience share.

Organisational issues

- Independent commercial radio stations only exist if they can attract enough advertisers – because advertisers pay the bills.
- The BBC is funded from the Licence fee and is able to run stations which might otherwise not exist.

Convergent media

- How radio incorporates a range of media forms such as pop music, news, advertising and so on. See also page 23 on podcasts.

What is the External Assessment?

The External Assessment is the written examination at the end of your course. It aims to test your thinking and creativity in Media Studies. It is worth 40 per cent of your GCSE.

The External Assessment will last for $2^{1}/_{4}$ hours. You will be allowed approximately 20–25 minutes to read or watch the stimulus material and to make your own notes based on the questions on the paper. You will then answer a series of questions on the stimulus material and the topic it relates to.

It will also test your creative media skills through a series of planning tasks for a media product. It will test your understanding of how these issues relate to the **convergent** nature of the contemporary media.

It is quite probable that you will enjoy the written External Assessment!

Key terms

Convergent When more than one media area come together, often in a business relationship – for example, comics and television.

Stimulus material

The paper is based on stimulus material chosen by WJEC that will centre on the topic area you have studied (note that the topic changes every two years). The stimulus material could be:

- an extract from a film
- a television programme or advertisement
- print-based material like newspaper front pages, magazines or comics
- web pages or CD or DVD covers
- many more!

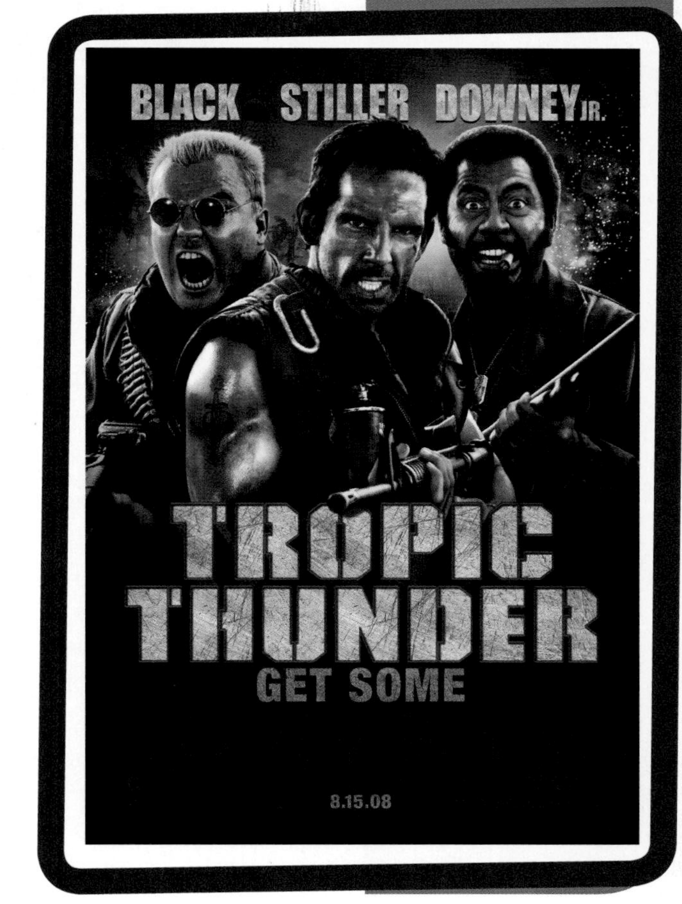

Media Concepts and Ideas

The External Assessment paper aims to test your knowledge and understanding of the Media Concepts and Ideas. These are:

- **media texts: genre, narrative and representation** – genre involves the study of how types of media text are grouped and clustered, their generic conventions, and the repetition and variation of a repertoire of elements
- **media organisations** – you will study the ways in which media organisations create, sustain and expand their markets and the ways they are regulated and controlled. You will also need to ask questions about the personal, social and ethical dimensions of creating media in an increasingly convergent world. Key areas for study will be:
  - marketing and promotion
  - regulation and control
  - conflicts between individual freedom and media organisations.
- **media audiences/users** – you will study the issues raised by the media for a range of audiences and users both in terms of audience/user engagement and audience/user response and interpretation. Essentially this will involve the study of:
  - the composition of audience/user groups
  - the everyday uses and pleasures audiences receive from media texts
  - how audience/users are targeted, appealed to and created
  - the impact of interactive and immersive environments on the nature of audience/user responses.

Section A: investigating

The paper is divided into two sections. Section A will test your thinking skills by investigating how the Media Concepts and Ideas are raised in the stimulus material. Questions will be based on the **codes and conventions** used in the stimulus material and how they make meaning for audiences.

You might be asked to:

- identify the types of camera shot or sound used in a film or television extract and to explain why they were used
- explain a character's role in a film extract or how men or women are represented in the extract
- explain, in relation to print media, how still pictures or language and font styles are used
- explain, in relation to the multimedia environment of web pages and computer games, how these codes and conventions are used in the convergent media.

Further questions will explore wider organisational issues such as how films or television programmes are marketed and promoted or why comics, newspapers or magazines are often linked to web pages.

Key terms

Codes and conventions
The things that make a piece of media what it is, i.e. the things that define it. For example, we associate horses, spurs, saloons and tumbleweed with Westerns and flashing lights, actors in shiny suits and lack of gravity with science fiction. Likewise, we associate a red-topped masthead, banner headlines and celebrity gossip with the popular tabloid newspapers.

Section B: planning and creating

Section B of the paper will enable you to demonstrate your creative media skills through a series of planning and creative tasks. These tasks will be based on creating for the convergent media. The types of task you will be asked to do will be based on a scenario . For example, you could be asked to plan a website to promote a new science-fiction film. This could include the following tasks:

- create a name for a new science-fiction film
- list three features that will appear on your web page such as a title, an image of the star and a moving image extract (for example, a trailer for the new film)
- create the web page with your chosen features
- explain why you have designed your web page in this way. This may involve explanations of the types of font used for your title, the type of picture chosen of the star of the film and a key sequence from the film in your trailer. You will also be asked to say how these features will attract an audience or how they will be used
- explain why a computer game could be included on the web page.

All of the tasks in the External Assessment will enable you to demonstrate the knowledge, understanding and skills that you have learned on your course. We hope that the written paper will enable you to do your best in a creative and exciting way and to think deeply about the texts you have studied.

A sample External Assessment

Sample topic: *Music*

During the two years of your GCSE Media Studies course you will have studied the External Assessment topic. This, for example, could be *Music*. In this example topic, your teacher will encourage you to:

- investigate and think about popular music texts in the media
- create popular music texts for the media
- explore these texts in relation to the convergent nature of the media.

These texts could include:

- popular music programmes on television
- music videos on television and the Internet
- websites for popular music bands, performers and stars
- popular music magazines.

There is a huge range of material for you to explore and investigate and for you to use when creating your music videos, web pages and music magazines through planning tasks in the classroom.

Sample written paper

In the exam of $2\frac{1}{4}$ hours you will be required to respond to a popular music text. For the purposes of this sample written paper, imagine that the stimulus material is a music video – the Take That video for their song *Rule The World* released in 2007.

Try to watch this video, perhaps by using a website such as YouTube. When you are watching it, think about the convergent nature of the media.

Now read the following sample External Assessment paper:

Section A: Thinking about the media – investigating music in the media

After viewing the extract (the music video *Rule The World* by Take That) answer the following questions:

1. (a) Identify two camera shots from the extract. [4]
   (b) Briefly explain why these two shots are used. [6]
2. (a) Identify two typical features of the music video from the extract. [4]
   (b) Explain how one of these features is used. [6]

3 Explore how men or women are represented in the extract. [10]

4 Outline two ways in which popular music is marketed in the media. Explain why it is marketed in these ways. [10]

Total [40]

Section B: Creating for the media – music and the convergent media

A record company which promotes and markets new bands and performers has asked you to create a website for their latest new band.

Complete the following tasks:

Task 1 Create a name for your website. Briefly say why you used this name. [4]

Task 2 List three features of your website. Briefly explain these features. [6]

Task 3 Plan the design for the homepage of your new website. You may annotate your plan. [10]

Task 4 Explain the plan of your homepage. [10]

Task 5 Many websites for music bands, performers and stars contain a wide range of still and moving images. Suggest at least two reasons why and explain those reasons. [10]

Total [40]

Sample student answers

Section A Question 1 (a) and (b)

Questions

1 (a) Identify two camera shots from the extract. [4]
(b) Briefly explain why these two shots are used. [6]

Student answer

The camera shots in the extract from Take That's music video ***Rule the World*** are well used. In the opening sequence there is a close-up camera shot of a person entering a recording studio. A long shot then shows all of the band singing at their microphones.

Explanation:

The close-up is used to show the audience that the story of the video is set in a recording studio so that this interests the target audience of Take That fans.

The long shot is used to show all the band together and introduce a story into the music video that they are cutting the first disc of the song.

Chief Examiner's comment

Part (a)

The student has identified two camera shots shown in the extract and used appropriate media language with 'close-up' and 'long shot' to achieve 2 marks for each camera shot.

The explanation is somewhat basic, and lacks thorough detailed description, but there is emerging media language in 'target audience' and 'fans' and there is some sense of identifying a story in the music video.

Therefore the mark for this candidate on question 1 (a) will be 2 marks for each camera shot = 4 marks.

Part (b)

The student has offered a reasonable explanation of why the camera shots were used and there is emerging media language in 'target audience' and 'fans'.

Therefore in part (b) a mark of 2 is awarded.

How to improve the answer

To improve the answer they should have written in far more detail on the explanation and used media language to explain their thinking in more sophisticated and confident ways.

What grade does the student achieve?
This will total 6 marks and will be equivalent to a grade C.

Section A Question 1 (a) and (b)

Questions

1. (a) Identify two camera shots from the extract. [4]
   (b) Briefly explain why these two shots are used. [6]

Student answer

There is a wide range of camera shots used in the extract. This helps the audience establish a narrative in this music video. The close up shot, which is in fact a tracking shot, with a roving hand-held camera behind a technician (who obviously works in the recording studio) tracks him through the studio creating a mise-en-scène of a typical recording studio with a wide range of symbolic codes shown to establish the scene and narrative. A long shot is then used to introduce the band members of Take That and establish for the audience that this is a privileged view of the first recording of their hit single 'Rule the World'. The narrative is then established and has intertextuality with a documentary style genre with its roving hand-held camera work in a cinéma verité style. This adds realism and verisimilitude to the special event. This acts as a wonderful selling point for both the music video and the CD, album or download.

Chief Examiner's comment

This is an outstanding answer. Sophisticated in its reading of the extract and how two camera shots are used to establish a narrative and a unique and privileged view for the audience through intertextual references to the documentary genre.

This would be typical of an A* answer and achieve 6 marks for the explanation plus 4 marks for the two camera shots identified, giving a total of 10 marks for this question.

What grade does the student achieve?

This will total 10 marks and will be equivalent to a grade A*.

10 Controlled Assessment

Introduction

Your Controlled Assessment package is worth 60 per cent of your final GCSE, which is a huge part of your final grade, so you should give each piece your very best effort!

On pages 194–228 there are individual topic suggestions that you could use in your Controlled Assessment package. However, these are only a guide – there are always so many avenues you could explore, and many will arise from reading the chapters earlier in this book.

In your Controlled Assessment package you need to:

- ensure it contains the right balance of tasks
- show your understanding of the convergent nature of the media as often as possible
- ensure that the supporting written material is appropriate
- ensure that the overall package meets the necessary assessment criteria. Your teacher will tell you more about these criteria – they are the standards by which your work is marked.

What is in the Controlled Assessment package?

Content	% of your GCSE	Guidance
Two investigations: • one based on **genre** • one based on either **narrative** or **representation**	20%	• These must be completed by you individually. • One investigation must be based on a print-based main text. • Only one investigation may be based on the examination topic. • You will aim to present around 400–850 words/word equivalent in total.
One production	40%	• This includes evidence of **research, planning, production** and **evaluation**. • Print and digital media productions must be completed by you individually, but audio/visual productions may be completed by small groups.

The textual investigations

The textual investigations can provide you with opportunities to explore your favourite media topics and texts. They also allow you to show your understanding of the convergent nature of the media and the ways in which media organisations are related to each other.

There are many ways to present your textual investigations. As long as you have the equivalent of a 400–850 word count, you may choose to create (amongst others):

- a multimedia presentation (such as PowerPoint, Flash, Windows Movie Maker, Windows Photo Story 3) with images, words, clips, voiceover and/or music
- an illustrated essay
- a series of annotated handouts.

Getting started

You need to begin by choosing a title, whether you are working on a genre, narrative or representation investigation. You will then choose a main media text to base the investigation around, with 3–5 relevant texts as support. These supporting texts will show aspects of convergence and relationships between texts. Your teacher will help you with this. The suggestions in each of the Controlled Assessment topics (pages 194–228 will give you examples to help you. The list below will also help you.

Example titles

Choose one title for **genre** and a second title for **narrative** or **representation** from the following:

Genre

- Explore how genre conventions are used in *Your Chosen Text*.
- Explore how far genre conventions are challenged in *Your Chosen Text*.
- Explore how far *Your Chosen Text* conforms to genre conventions.

Narrative

- Explore how the narrative is constructed in *Your Chosen Text.*
- Explore the structure of the narrative in *Your Chosen Text.*
- Explore how conventional the narrative construction or structure is in *Your Chosen Text.*
- Explore how far the narrative construction or structure in *Your Chosen Text* challenges conventional narratives.

Representation

- Explore how *Your Chosen Text* represents **either** gender, ethnicity, age, nation, place, events **or** issues.
- Explore how far the representation of **one** of the following is challenged in *Your Chosen Text:* gender, ethnicity, age, nation, place, events, issues.
- Explore how far the representation of **one** of the following reinforces conventional points of view in *Your Chosen Text*: gender, ethnicity, age, nation, place, events, issues.

The production

Your teacher and the examiner will be looking for four elements in the production task: research, planning, production and evaluation. The suggestions for production work in each of the Controlled Assessment topics (pages 194–228) will give you examples of exactly what to do.
The details below will also help you.

Research

This element asks you to provide 2–4 examples of the following:

- examining and annotating texts
- completed questionnaires and/or surveys
- the findings of focus groups and interpretations of information found through books and the Internet.

These examples can be presented as annotated sheets, tables, charts or in digital form.

Planning

This element asks you to provide 2–4 examples of the following:

- scripts
- character profiles
- flow charts for television/computer games/animations/websites
- running orders (for example, for news/documentary)
- shot lists
- location research
- mood boards
- set/costume/props/models/character designs
- storyboards
- 3D visualisations
- print mock-ups.

You should aim to make your planning activities relate to your research.

Production

This element asks you to provide 1–2 pages of print or digital media work, **or** about 3 minutes of audio-visual or audio work.

Evaluation

This element asks you to show how all your work so far demonstrates your understanding of:

- genre, narrative and representation
- your chosen target audiences/users
- organisational issues such as marketing and promotion, regulation and control issues such as copyright and the personal, social and ethical dimensions of creating media today.

Group work

You may decide to undertake a production as a group. The most important thing to remember is that group work is NOT an easy option! A useful first step is to ensure your group is not too big. Three is ideal, with four as a maximum, because you need to be able to account for your OWN contribution to the production. The two main roles which can be shared are camerawork and editing (this includes sound).

Whatever production role you are responsible for, you must also remember that your research, planning and evaluation are to be completed individually. A good tip here is to keep a diary/log of your choices (including elements you reject as well as those you include), so that when you write your evaluation you will have specific details to include.

Whatever you do, keep a lot of notes, save images, save drafts and copy out-takes. You may need them in an emergency.

GradeStudio

The tips on these pages should help improve your Controlled Assessment production and therefore your overall GCSE grade!

Tips for production research

Some research methods you may wish to use include:

1. Visit the websites of key media texts that you feel have elements relevant to your own production ideas.
2. For example, magazines have their own websites with valuable information about the way they research and engage with their target audiences, a sense of their demographic profile, and may even send you a media pack with even more detailed information, if you ask for one.
3. It is important to make use of the information you uncover. If you simply list or download material, you will not earn many marks.
4. Investigate a range of texts. This will give you a sense of the similarities between mainstream, niche and independent texts. This may well also give you inspiration about how you can create original versions of these texts.
5. Conduct surveys and questionnaires with members of your target audience. This will give you excellent feedback about how effective your ideas are likely to be.
6. Read up on your lesson notes, textbooks and relevant websites to make sure you have a good command of media theory relevant to the production process.
7. You must use your teachers to check you are on the right track! They will be an invaluable source of advice and encouragement to you as you seek to create an impressive Controlled Assessment package.

Tips for making print productions

1. Create the right number of pages of print production work – the equivalent of 2 pages.
2. Always proofread any drafts – and especially your final production – for simple errors in spelling and expression.
3. Think about your margins – all too often they are too narrow. Remember to set margins wider in order to make the most of the space on your page.
4. Some print pages use white space as a background for their layout design, but many do not. They use blocks of colour cleverly positioned next to each other with different-coloured fonts over the top. Do remember to check your white space and make sure it is there because you chose it that way.
5. Make sure your choice of font colour is sufficiently dark (or light) to be read clearly over whatever background you have chosen. A simple check is to print a sample section of the page to check the font colour can be read clearly.
6. Avoid Word art fonts if you can! They can look a little childish – it is much better to use a well-chosen font from the long list in the Word library.

Tips for making audio-visual productions

1. Create the right number of minutes of audio-visual work – the equivalent of 3 minutes.
2. When setting up a shot, always start the tape rolling slightly before you call 'action' and let it continue rolling slightly after you call 'cut' to allow for the tape start delay and also to make editing easier.
3. Think about lighting – never set up a shot with a strong light source behind your subject – it will make the shot very dark. Try to have the strongest light source behind the camera.
4. If you can use an external microphone, do! If you do not have one, then insist on absolute silence on set, and try to avoid filming in large rooms which make sound echo. Your editing package may also allow you to dub or tape over sections of the production after shooting. This is recommended if you are making a music video.
5. It can be difficult for a narrative to make sense in a very short time. Make sure you trial the planning stage of your production with a focus group or your teacher to make sure it is understood by your intended audience.
6. Students often want to make 'grand' productions, about intense and profound issues. Think carefully about how convincing your production might be, given your time constraints. For example, a short film that tries to deal with the nature of tragic love may well come over as rather stereotypical and even silly.

Tips for making audio productions

1. If you are making an audio production such as a radio item or podcast, then the obvious focus is going to be on sound quality – make sure you are familiar with the technology needed to layer sounds on top of each other.
2. Sound on radio works by foregrounding and backgrounding audio sources at different times (when you want them to be heard) on different tracks. If you want a sound to be heard clearly, you must bring it 'forward', whereas if a sound is simply meant to provide atmosphere, then you should place it further 'back'.
3. If someone is speaking, they should be heard clearly above any other sound.
4. Experiment with sound sources – aiming for codes of realism may well mean creating the sounds that accompany a real situation. For example, if a character is meant to be walking, then the sound of footsteps may well be important.
5. Rehearse – your actors may well be 'microphone shy' and even though they have great voices, they might become awkward and quiet as soon as you call 'action'. Practise the microphone-to-mouth distance for the best sound quality.
6. Encourage speakers to pause before, and after, speaking in order to help with editing (see audio-visual tips above).
7. Record small sections of your production at a time, then edit them all together.
8. Music often plays an important part in audio-visual productions. Choose backing music that will add to what you want to say in terms of genre, mood, character, narrative, etc. without dominating your script.

Controlled Assessment: Film

Below are some ideas for approaching textual investigations and the production task in the media area of film. For your own controlled assessments, you will be working on a different topic for your two textual assessments, you will be working on a different topic for your two textual investigations and your production but we've grouped our suggestions into media areas. These ideas are intended as a guide only.

Textual investigation: genre

Explore how far the Indiana Jones and the Kingdom of the Crystal Skull *website conforms to genre conventions.*

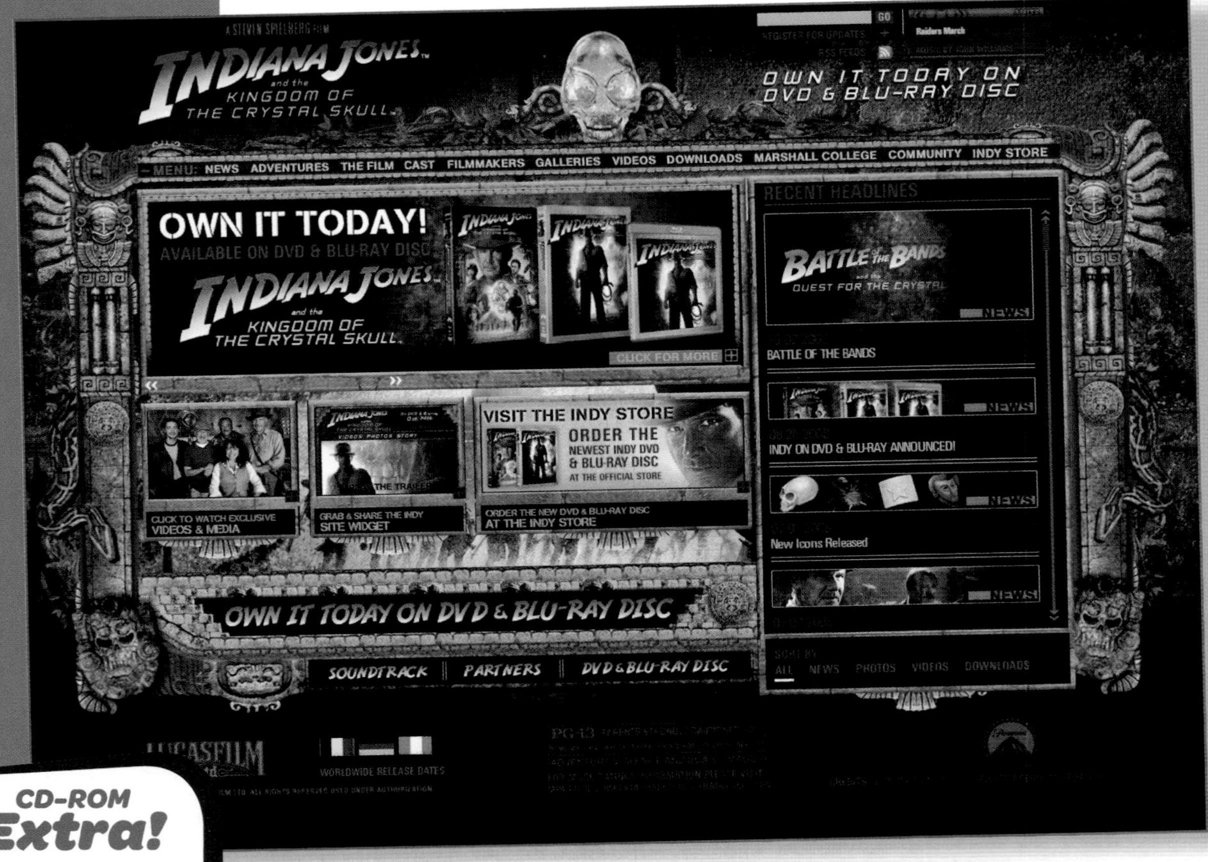

CD-ROM Extra!

Indiana Jones website

Open the CD in the back of this book and click on the icon below to open a link to the Indiana Jones website.

HTML

Support texts for this investigation

These might include:

- the film poster
- the XBox 360 game cover for *Indiana Jones* which uses Lego characters
- the film trailer or clips from the film or from earlier *Indiana Jones* films
- other examples of action adventure films and film-related texts.

Approaches to this investigation

These might include:

- Refresh your memory of techniques and terminology needed to analyse genre codes and conventions earlier in this book, then make a list of what you consider to be the main conventions of action adventure films. Use a printout of the *Indiana Jones* website and annotate it to show its key conventions as a text related to an action adventure film.
- Explore the website thoroughly – you will notice there are 'adventures' to play as well as information about the film.
- Make notes from the trailer for the film or the opening sequence of the film and explain why this film series has been so popular with audiences. What links can you see between the website and the trailer/sequence?
- Look at other examples of action adventure films – including earlier Indiana Jones or Harrison Ford films. Can you see similarities and differences in the way the texts each represent the action adventure genre?
- Now decide how you are going to present your textual investigation findings. Look at tips for this on page 189.

Textual investigation: narrative

Explore how conventional the narrative construction or structure is in the opening of Iron Man.

Support texts for this investigation

These might include:

- other media texts relating to *Iron Man* such as the poster and DVD cover
- a range of openings of other superhero films, for example, *The Incredible Hulk* (2008), *Dark Knight* (2008), *Fantastic Four: Rise of the Silver Surfer* (2007), etc. You may wish to look again at the activity on superhero openings in the Marvel comics case study on page 113 in Chapter 5.
- superhero comic strips
- documentary on creating Batman comic narratives on the CD in the back of this book.

Approaches to this investigation

These might include:

- Refresh your memory of narrative structure and the role of superheroes (page 9). Watch the opening of *Iron Man* and make notes on how the narrative is constructed, and how the character of Tony Stark is represented in the video. Try to decide how typical the opening of the film is, as a superhero movie. What expectations might an audience have about Tony's journey in the film?
- Look at the *Iron Man* website and trailer. What clues do they give about the narrative that the opening of the film does not? What does this tell you about the purpose of film websites and trailers?
- Look at other superhero films and consider how *Iron Man* establishes its narrative compared to the others – what are the main similarities and differences?
- Compare superhero comic strips and the documentary on Batman comic narratives (on the CD) to help you decide how conventional the *Iron Man* opening is.
- Now decide how you are going to present your textual investigation findings. Look at tips for this on page 189.

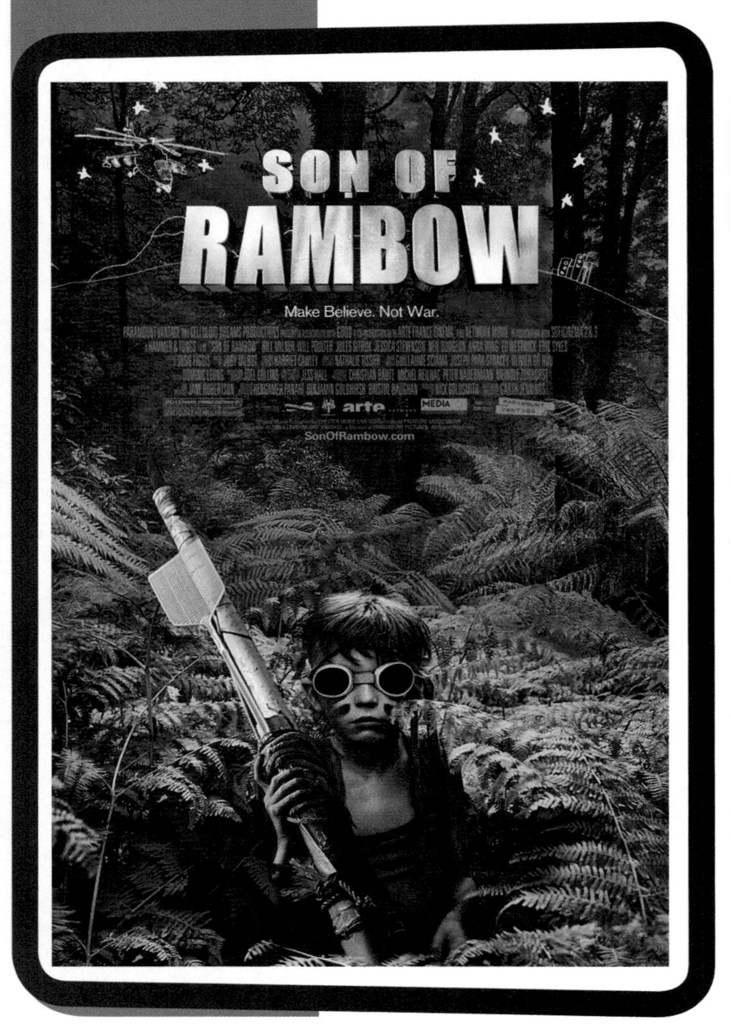

Textual investigation: representation

Explore how far the representation of age reinforces conventional points of view in Son of Rambow *(2007).*

Son of Rambow is the name of the home movie made by two young boys with a big video camera and even bigger ambitions, set in the early 1980s at the time when Sylvester Stallone's *First Blood* was first released.

Support texts for this investigation

These might include:

- magazines/comics aimed at young boys and girls such as *Girl Talk, Toxic, Match of the Day*
- television programmes featuring young boys/girls, for example, *Tracy Beaker, Eastenders, Neighbours*
- scenes from *Son of Rambow*
- a range of film texts focusing on age, such as *Home Alone, Matilda, Billy Elliot, Juno* and *This Is England.* These films all represent age in different ways, some more conventional than others.

Approaches to this investigation

These might include:

- Establish how young boys and girls are represented in the media – making notes and charts on print and audio-visual texts.
- Focus more closely on the representation of boys in films, making notes and suggesting how the representations are similar and different.
- Look closely at scenes from *Son of Rambow*, using the notes you have made on representations of young boys in the media. How conventional do you think the representation is of the two lead boys? Try to use examples from other texts in your answer, as well as specific details from the film itself.
- Now decide how you are going to present your textual investigation findings. Look at tips for this on page 189.

The production

Create a comic strip that introduces a new superhero. You may wish to explain how the superhero gets his/her powers, and maybe introduce a villain who the superhero will fight against.

Research

Start by looking again at the chapter on comics, cartoons and animation. Then collect as many comics as you can, including superhero-style comics, to help you research thoroughly. Some of the activities you may like to consider are:

- Remind yourself of comic techniques and how comic frames are drawn in order to tell a story. You may like to look again at the CD, which includes an interview with an illustrator from the new Batman comics/graphic novels.
- Remind yourself of the representation of superheroes in films – perhaps investigate a superhero film poster.
- Choose one of your superhero comics and scan one page in order to stick it onto an A3 sheet. Investigate it to show its comic techniques and how features such as movement, sound and emotion are used to create a narrative.

- Look at how comic characters demonstrate convergence. There are often links between comic characters and television, films, websites and games.
- Interview twenty to thirty people of different ages and ask them about the comics and superhero stories they enjoy now, or enjoyed in the past. Put your findings in a chart or graph to help you plan your own comic story.
- Think about the regulation of children's comics – find out what restrictions you may have to bear in mind when designing your comic and telling your story.

Planning

You should now have some ideas about the character and comic you want to create. Use your research notes and findings to help you plan out your production. This might include:

- Create and label a character profile of your superhero – this may involve two drawings if your character has an alias like Peter Parker and Superman. Label the profile showing any powers the character may have, features of appearance and dress.
- Don't be anxious about your drawing ability here – remember that you don't even have to use human characters. If you are able to draw vegetables, robots, aliens or simple animals like bees, caterpillars or penguins, then create a character around one of these!
- Create a series of drawings of your character in different poses and with different expressions.
- Think about how your character became a superhero. Write down what happened.
- Is there a villain who will oppose your hero? Write down his or her story, and draw a profile of his or her appearance.
- Decide on the key moments of the narrative and how you will show them in a still frame.
- Sketch out the frames/panels for the comic – try to aim for variation and interest – making it clear how to draw the reader's eye from one frame to the next.
- Decide on a striking title block for your comic story that will make the comic grab the attention of a potential reader.

Production

Look again at the tips for making print productions on page 192 in the introduction to this section. Remember that you must not work in a group for print production pieces. Create your comic to the highest standards, making sure that you refer to your planning closely. Aim to make it as colourful and eye-catching as possible.

Evaluation

Your evaluation can be in the form of a presentation or illustrated report. It should be 400–850 words or its equivalent and should try to show at least some of the following:

- How your research into comics and superhero characters helped you plan the structure of your own text.
- How your research into audience helped you create the meanings and representations in the text.
- Who your audience is and how you hope they will respond to your text (don't forget to try it out on your audience to help with this).
- How and why you created your frames to best effect – draw attention to your favourite sections of the comic.
- An explanation of how you would want to market your comic character (perhaps using convergent technology such as creating a game for a Wii console where the user has the chance to become your character in different scenarios).
- Any issues of regulation you had to consider (for example, if your comic targets very young children, you may have had to limit violence and conflict – perhaps restricting facial expressions of anger between the superhero and villain).

Controlled Assessment: Television

Below are some ideas for approaching textual investigations and the production task in the media area of television. For your own controlled assessments, you will be working on a different topic for your two textual investigations and your production but we've grouped our suggestions into media areas. These ideas are intended as a guide only.

Textual investigation: genre

Explore how far genre conventions are challenged in the opening sequence of Scrubs.

Support texts for this investigation

These might include:

- the *Scrubs* interactive website
- the openings of other medical dramas such as *Casualty*, *Holby City* and *ER*.
- the openings of comedy programmes such as *Friends*, *Gavin and Stacey* and *This Life*.

Approaches to this investigation

These might include:

- Investigate the opening to *Scrubs* in depth, considering music, title credits and graphics, character and narrative clues in the first scene.
- Explore the openings of medical dramas to find evidence of key genre conventions.
- Explore the openings of comedy programmes to find evidence of key genre conventions.
- Create a chart to show the genre conventions of medical drama compared with the conventions of comedy, then use it to show how *Scrubs* is an unusual medical drama, and is a true cross-genre with comedy.
- Now decide how you are going to present your textual investigation findings. Look at tips for this on page 189.

Textual investigation: narrative

Explore how the narrative of The Simpsons *comic relates to the narratives of* The Simpsons *television programme.*

Support texts for this investigation

These might include:

- other editions of *The Simpsons* comic
- episodes of *The Simpsons* television programme
- examples of comics
- examples of other animated television comedy programmes such as *Family Guy* or *South Park*.

Approaches to this investigation

These might include:

- Choose a comic story and scan it into your computer. Size it so that it fits into a page with enough room to add annotations around it, and make notes on its main comic conventions. Write a paragraph to show how the narrative has been constructed.
- Choose an episode from an animated television series and make notes on how it presents character, tells stories and encourages audiences to laugh.
- Choose a story in an edition of *The Simpsons* comic and one of your favourite episodes of *The Simpsons* and investigate them in depth, making notes on characters and narrative structure. Make a chart to show similarities and differences between the narratives.
- Now decide how you are going to present your textual investigation findings. Look at tips for this on page 189.

Textual investigation: representation

Explore how heroes are represented in the graphic novel of the television series Heroes.

Support texts for this investigation

These might include:

- the official *Heroes* website with links to pages from the graphic novel
- other graphic novels such as *Gotham Central* or *X-Men*
- Jock talking about designing for *Batman* on the CD in this book
- episodes of *Heroes* television series.

Approaches to this investigation

These might include:

- Watch some episodes of *Heroes* in order to 'get a feel' for the show and how its narrative is organised. You will notice the show has many characters, both male and female, who have special powers, and narratives are constructed around each character.
- Look at pages from the *Heroes* graphic novel – either in print form or online via the website. Make notes on the representation of a range of characters, then widen your analysis by looking at pages from other graphic novels – and try to decide how heroes are generally represented.
- Create a chart to show how the representation of heroes in *Heroes* is similar or different to the representation of heroes in other graphic novels. You may find that *Heroes* is quite unusual in the way it portrays heroes, in that it goes against gender stereotyping.
- Now decide how you are going to present your textual investigation findings. Look at tips for this on page 189.

The production

Create a two-page spread for a television listings magazine that gives information on a new television drama series aimed at teenagers on Channel 4. The programme could feature a central group of four to six characters and could be set in a sixth-form college or high school.

Research

You may like to consider the following:

- Find out what dramas already exist that are aimed at teenagers and feature a group of characters as the stars. Examples might include *Hollyoaks*, *One Tree Hill* and *Skins*. Trace their development, scheduling and ratings to analyse their success. Also look at how the title block of each programme has been designed.
- Make a chart to show the different conventions of the shows you have researched.
- Undertake an audience survey to find out who enjoys teen dramas and what an audience might expect from a drama set in a college or high school.
- Collect some magazines that include television listings and features on programmes and analyse how new programmes are 'advertised'.

Planning

You should now have some ideas about the main appealing features of your own television drama series. You should use your research notes and findings to help you plan out your production. This might include:

- Create a profile of each of the central characters by taking photos of them 'in character' and writing short descriptions of them to give clues about their character type and role in the series.
- Plan the first episode of the series by thinking of three to five storylines that will introduce the characters and be interwoven and end on a tense moment or cliff-hanger.
- Design the title block for your programme – this will act as a logo for the programme and go on to decide the layout of the double-page spread. How will you present images of, and information about, the programme and its stars?
- Create some draft pages of the magazine spread and show them to members of your intended audience to help you decide which of your ideas are most effective.

Production

Look again at the tips for making print productions on page 192 in the introduction to this section. Remember that you must not work in a group for print production pieces. Create your magazine pages to the highest standards, making sure that you refer to your planning closely. Aim to make it as appealing and eye-catching as possible.

Evaluation

Your evaluation can be in the form of a presentation or illustrated report. It should be 400–850 words or its equivalent and should try to show at least some of the following:

- How your research into television drama series and features on programmes in magazines helped you plan the structure and layout of your own text.
- How your research into audience helped you create the meanings and representations in the text.
- Who your audience is and how you hope they will respond to your text (don't forget to try it out on your audience to help with this).
- How you used technology to best effect – draw attention to any mixing of technology, such as using a mobile phone or digital camera to generate images, then manipulating them in a package such as Photoshop and embedding them in your text using a desktop publishing package such as Publisher to create the page.
- Your production is rather like an advertisement within another text. Explain how the magazine your production is placed in is marketed, and also explain how you hope to attract attention to your new drama series within the magazine.

Controlled Assessment: News

Below are some ideas for approaching textual investigations and the production task in the media area of news. For your own controlled assessments, you will be working on a different topic for your two textual investigations and your production but we've grouped our suggestions into media areas. These ideas are intended as a guide only.

Textual investigation: genre

Explore how far the **Politics & the City** *website conforms to genre conventions of news.*

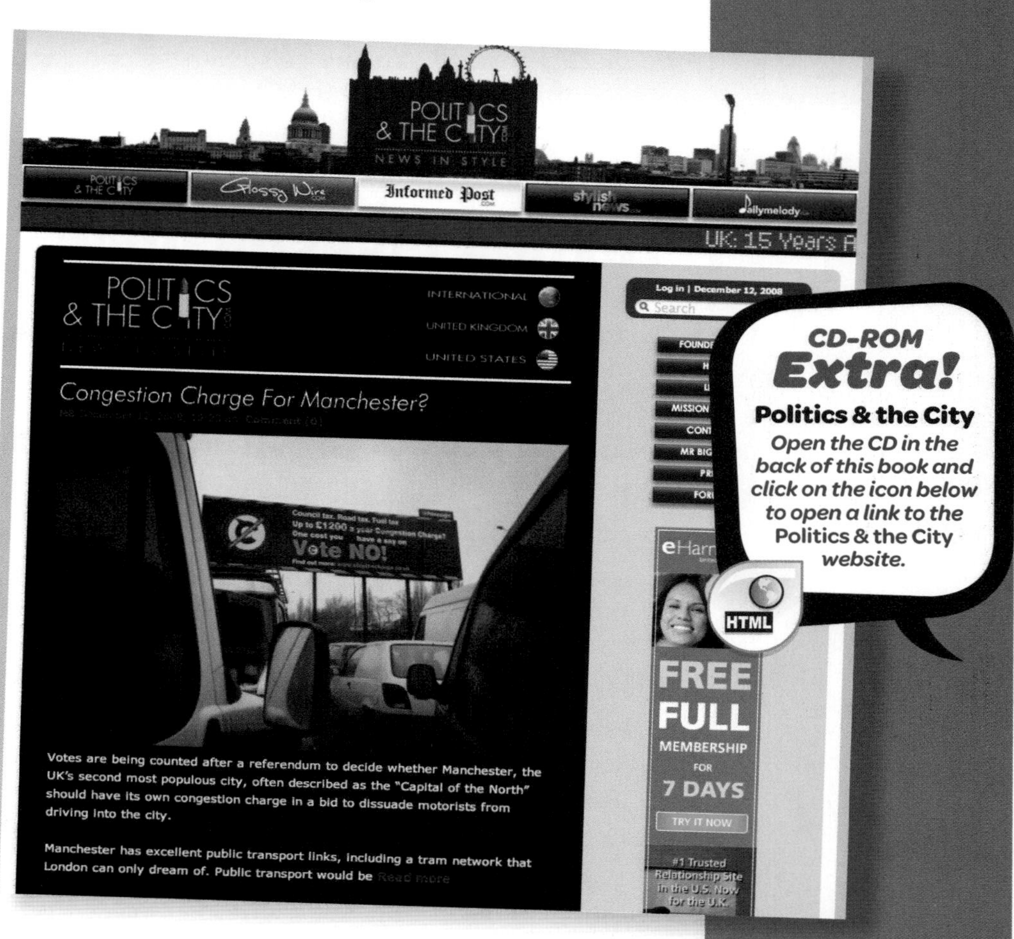

CD-ROM Extra!

Politics & the City

Open the CD in the back of this book and click on the icon below to open a link to the Politics & the City website.

Support texts for this investigation

These might include:

- other news websites, for example, bbc.co.uk or news.sky.com
- celebrity and other news coverage in weekly magazines such as *Heat*, *OK*, *Reveal* and *Now*
- news coverage in tabloid newspapers such the *Mirror*
- the opening to *Sex and the City* television series or film version.

Approaches to this investigation

These might include:

- Refresh your memory of the techniques and terminology needed to investigate genre codes and conventions in Chapter 3. Then make two lists – the first of the main conventions of general news coverage and the second of the coverage of celebrity news coverage.
- Examine the *Politics & the City* website closely. You will notice it is divided into sections that include UK news, world news, celebrity news, fashion news and human interest stories. The question you need to answer is – how typical is this of a news website?
- Look at a range of other news websites. What similarities and differences can you see? How do they compare to your focus text? Create a chart, mind-map or pie graph to show your findings
- Look at other media areas that cover the same kind of news that *Politics & the City* covers. Compare it also with the opening of *Sex and the City*. What does this suggest about the target audience of the website?
- Now decide how you are going to present your textual investigation findings. Look at tips for this on page 189.

Textual investigation: narrative

Explore how the narrative is constructed in 60–90-second news bulletins such as the BBC News 90 Seconds Update.

Support texts for this investigation

These might include:

- other news bulletins
- examples of news stories that generate audience interest from newspapers, television, mobile phone and website news sources.

Approaches to this investigation

These might include:

- Refresh your memory of narrative structure in Chapter 1: Film and Chapter 2: Television of this book. Also remind yourself of how stories are organised in a range of news sources to appeal to audiences and make them feel involved.
- Watch several 60–90-second news bulletins. Choose two to three stories that you think will create a high level of interest on the part of audiences – investigate how they use language, voice, images and perhaps sound clips to encourage audience appeal through story-telling
- Now decide how you are going to present your textual investigation findings. Look at tips for this on page 189.

Textual investigation: representation

Explore how far the representation of news stories reinforces conventional points of view in the CBBC Newsround *programme or website.*

Support texts for this investigation

These might include:

- either the website or programme – depending on which you have chosen as your main focus text
- other news programmes such as the main evening news on BBC1, ITV or Channel 4 or other news websites
- newspapers aimed at adults, for example, the *Mirror* or the *Guardian*
- newspapers aimed at children, for example, *Headliners* or *First News*.

Approaches to this investigation

These might include:

- Refresh your memory about representation, including the representation of gender and age in Chapter 1: Film; Chapter 2: Television; and Chapter 4: Magazines.
- Look at a range of news representations in adult newspapers or websites and compare them to representations of news in children's newspapers or websites. Present your findings in an interesting way.
- Analyse one or two CBBC *Newsround* programmes or daily website updates. Create a mind-map showing how *Newsround* uses typical representations of news and also moves away from typical representations.
- Now decide how you are going to present your textual investigation findings. Look at tips for this on page 189.

The production

Create the opening sequence for a new current affairs/news update programme, targeting a youth audience, that will be broadcast on your regional ITV news channel after the main evening news as an alternative to the local news channel.

Research

You may like to consider the following:

- Watch as many news bulletins, current affairs and news programmes as possible. Record the main conventions of the bulletins including:
  - how the title sequence is created
  - how music is used to give the programme a distinctive identity
  - where the presenters are when they 'deliver' the news
  - how presenters are dressed, and how they speak
  - the order of news stories listed in the opening line-up
  - the language used in telling the news stories
  - how news stories are made to seem 'dramatic'
  - how news stories target a specific audience.
- Conduct a survey amongst teenagers in order to find out what kind of news programme about their local area they would most like to watch. Make notes to help you with your planning.
- Find out about the key issues/problems/projects going on in your local area. You will want your programme to be as relevant and 'real' as possible.

Planning

You should now have some ideas about the news programme you want to make. You should use your research notes and findings to help you plan out your production. This might include:

- creating a profile of your presenter(s) with photos and annotations about the features that will appeal to a youth audience
- deciding on the content of the news programme to be featured in the opening line-up – make sure you have a range of issues to cover, and a variation of setting, speakers and 'importance' of stories
- storyboarding the opening sequence, making it clear how titles, music, on-screen text and images work together to create meanings for your target audience
- making a shooting script to indicate how you will set up your locations and individual shots.

Production

Look again at the requirements for the production length, and look at the tips for making audio-visual productions on page 193 in the introduction to this section. If you are going to work as part of a group, also check the tips for group work (page 189). Create your opening sequence, making sure that you refer to your planning closely.

Evaluation

Your evaluation can be in the form of a presentation or illustrated report. It should be 400–850 words or its equivalent and should try to show at least some of the following:

- How your research into news programmes, current affairs and bulletins helped you to plan the structure of your own opening sequence.
- How your research into audience helped you to create the meanings and representations in your opening.
- Who your audience is and how you hope they will respond to your text (don't forget to try it out on your audience to help with this).
- How you used technology to best effect. This will include your choices regarding music, on-screen text font and design, montage of images and representation of news presenters.
- How you hope to raise awareness of your new news programme. How will you advertise on ITV? Do you intend to have a spin-off website? Will there be a deal to advertise with a youth newspaper?
- Any issues of privacy you may have to discuss. Your images may well feature people under 16. Why might this present problems?

Controlled Assessment: Magazines

Below are some ideas for approaching textual investigations and the production task in the media area of magazines. For your own controlled assessments, you will be working on a different topic for your two textual investigations and your production but we've grouped our suggestions into media areas. These ideas are intended as a guide only.

Textual investigation: genre

Explore how far Bliss *online conforms to genre conventions*.

Support texts for this investigation

These might include:

- copies of *Bliss* magazine
- other relevant online magazine sites, for example, *Sugar*, *More*, *Elle* and *Girl*.
- console games targeted at teenage girls, for example, Girl Game
- film trailers targeted at teenage girls, for example, *High School Musical 3*.

Approaches to this investigation

These might include:

- Refresh your memory of the techniques and terminology needed to investigate genre codes and conventions in Chapter 4, then make a list of what you consider to be the main conventions of teen girls' magazines. Use a printout of the front cover of an edition of *Bliss* magazine and annotate it to show its key conventions as an example of a typical teen girls' magazine.

- Look at some other examples of teen girls' magazines and choose the key features that they share with *Bliss* magazine.
- Now print out a screen grab of the *Bliss* online magazine page (see page 210 for part of a typical web page). Make a list of the main similarities and differences between the magazine and the web page.
- Explore the website and visit some of the links, for example, to games and film trailers appealing to a teenage girl audience – decide what the website offers that the magazine does not.
- Now decide how you are going to present your textual investigation findings. Look at tips for this on page 189.

Textual investigation: narrative

Explore the structure of the narrative in the article 'Hollywood UK' on Simon Pegg from the September 2008 edition of Total Film.

THE STAR SIMON PEGG

IF SIMON PEGG'S CAREER HAD A TAGLINE, IT would be 'Making Geekdom Cool Since 1999'. That's the year, of course, that Pegg evolved from stand-up and TV comedy bit-parter into the star-creator (with Jessica Stevenson and Edgar Wright) of *Spaced*. After 14 perfectly formed episodes, Pegg pulled the plug on his cult slacker sitcom and, with his muckers Wright and best friend/*Spaced* co-star Nick Frost, proceeded to giddily, affectionately rip the piss out of the walking-dead genre in *Shaun Of The Dead* and buddy-copdom's bloated extremism in *Hot Fuzz*. In the process, he became Britain's finest comedy export.

Today, *Total Film* is tête-à-têting with Pegg in a far more glamorous environment than *Spaced*'s grubby bombsite flat or Pegg's beloved north London pubs – the beachside Century Club in Cannes, where the 38-year-old writer-actor is tapping into the global media pipeline on behalf of his new comedy *How To Lose Friends & Alienate People*. Directed by *Curb Your Enthusiasm* veteran Robert Weide, Brit journo Toby Young's memoir of his disastrous stint at *Vanity Fair* has been turned into a comedy that shifts the non-stop anecdotal parade of humiliation of Young's tome into a more charming romp about a cynical Brit in America. It's the perfect role for Pegg, who has superseded Hugh Grant as the quintessential British everyman...

bit of a control freak so it was nice to let that go for a change"). Strongly playing on Pegg's vein of slapstick, some are pitching it as the *Hot Fuzz* version of *The Devil Wears Prada*. It's not a comparison that sits easily with Pegg. "*The Devil Wears Prada* for blokes? I don't know if that's right. I suppose the premise is similar in that it's like an outsider going to work for a big magazine but that's where the similarity ends."

And that's where one of the similarities with Young's book ends. The author endures a string of embarrassing situations trying to date fearsome New York career women who would never entertain a pudgy journalist without a high six-figure income and a house in the Hamptons. In the film, Pegg not only befriends Megan Fox's sexy ingénue, but he also bags Kirsten Dunst, who moves in the sort of Hollywood circles that are now available to Pegg. He adored his co-star.

"I love her to pieces," gushes Pegg. "She's brilliant. She's one of the most instinctively talented actresses I've ever worked with". Usually, when gush like this comes out of an actor's mouth, you know it's code for "I hated her fucking guts" but it sits at the core of Pegg's all-pervading charm that you know he's genuine. As for rubbing shoulders with A-listers, Pegg retains a healthy British cynicism to the star-fucker world.

'It's always nice to appreciate the craziness of everything'

SIMON PEGG

"The character, Sidney Young, is a sort of shameless self-publicist – I'm not really like that. Even though here we are in Cannes sort of demonstrating to the contrary," says Pegg, his khaki shorts-and-sandals combo helping to back up his point. "I made a decision early on not to play Toby but to treat the screenplay like a fiction. As much as he'd probably disagree, not many people know Toby, so it would be silly for me to try and ape him. It's like Nicole Kidman's prosthetic nose in *The Hours* – who knew Viriginia Woolf had a nose like that?"

How To Lose Friends... is the first script Pegg's ever read where he didn't want to whip out his red pen and start rewriting from page one ("I'm a

"It's always nice to appreciate the kind of craziness of everything," he muses. "But whereas Sidney adores it, I'm suspicious of it. I don't know if I really want to be part of that at all."

And that hasn't changed at all? Is the Pegg of today the same Pegg he was before JJ Abrams was emailing him, asking him to play Scotty in *Star Trek*? "I understand how you can change, but as long as you always appreciate that it's a facile thing, then you'll stay on top of it," he says.

"You want to continue to work and you want to continue to work with the best people and inevitably you sort of move up and start working on bigger films and it's very difficult to say, 'I'd better not do that because it will make me famous'".

>>

Support texts for this investigation

These might include:

- other film magazines, for example, *Empire*, *DVD* and *Blu Ray Magazine*
- magazine articles on UK stars and celebrities such as Simon Pegg
- fan sites such as www.peggster.net.

Approaches to this investigation

These might include:

- Refresh your memory of narrative structure (page 9). Read the article 'Hollywood UK' and make notes on how each section of the feature is broken into clear sections – The Star, The Mavericks, The Director and The Bright Young Things.
- Focus on the first section: The Star – Simon Pegg, and investigate how his story is told in the article. You may wish to make notes on the way the article is introduced and concluded, the way films are referred to, the way quotations are used to add to our understanding of Pegg as a star, etc.
- Look at the way other magazines write about UK stars – these could be print magazines or online magazines.
- Explore Simon Pegg's website and look for similarities and differences in the way Pegg's story is told.
- Now decide how you are going to present your textual investigation findings. Look at tips for this on page 189.

Textual investigation: representation

Explore how the magazine industry is represented in the television series Ugly Betty.

Support texts for this investigation

These might include:

- *Sex and the City*
- *Just Shoot Me!*
- *13 Going On 30* directed by Gary Winick
- *How to Lose a Guy in 10 Days* directed by Donald Petrie
- lifestyle magazines such as *Heat* and *More*.

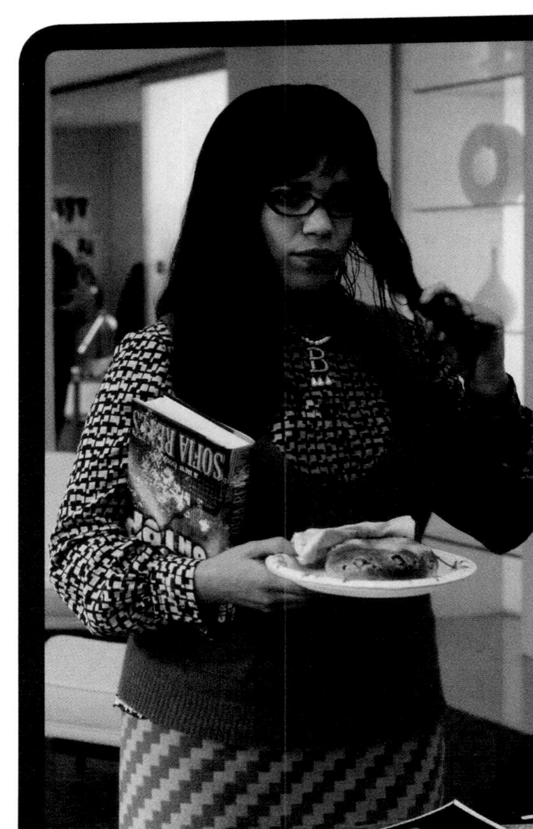

Approaches to this investigation

These might include:

- Refresh your memory about representation, including the representation of events and issues in Chapter 1: Film; Chapter 2: Television; and Chapter 6: Pop music. Then watch at least one episode of *Ugly Betty* and make notes on how the magazine industry and its workers are represented – you will notice immediately how the magazine industry is represented as being cut-throat and dependent on image and fame. The focus is very much on profit, meeting deadlines and beating competitors. How would you describe the impressions Betty herself has of the magazine industry?
- Look at a range of other texts that focus on the magazine industry – make notes on the similarities and differences between them.
- Choose key scenes from the main text that focus on aspects of the magazine industry and create a list of points in relation to the structure of the organisation, the jobs carried out by the employees and some of the main priorities of the magazine.
- Now decide how you are going to present your textual investigation findings. Look at tips for this on page 189.

The production

Create the front cover plus one other page (it could be a web page) of a magazine of your choice that will appeal to teenagers. This could be a lifestyle or specialist interest magazine – the most important thing is to tailor your magazine to reflect your own interests!

Research

You may like to consider the following:

- Find out what magazines already exist that are aimed at teenagers. Examples might include *Heat*, *More*, *Kerrang!* and *NME*. Explore their websites and visit the sections that tell you about the magazine's development and contents in order to help you investigate their success.
- Look at the title block and font style of each magazine, as well as typical front covers and contents pages. Make a chart to show the different conventions of the magazines you have researched.
- Undertake an audience survey to find out what teenagers might want from a new magazine.

Planning

You should now have some ideas for the design of a new magazine. You should use your research notes and findings to help you plan out your production. This might include:

- taking photographs for the central image on the front page and for small inserts on the contents page
- designing the title block for your magazine – this may act as a logo that you use at the top or bottom of each page
- creating drafts and designs for your chosen pages, then trying them out on your chosen audience to decide which ones are the most effective.

Production

Look again at the tips for making print productions on page 192 in the introduction to this section. Remember that you must not work in a group for print production pieces. Create your magazine pages to the highest standards, making sure that you refer to your planning closely. Aim to make them as appealing and eye-catching as possible.

Evaluation

Your evaluation can be in the form of a presentation or illustrated report. It should be 400–850 words or its equivalent and should try to show at least some of the following:

- How your research into magazines aimed at teenagers helped you to plan the structure and layout of your own production.
- How your research into audience helped you create the meanings and representations in the text – try to show how your understanding of audience led to the choices you made about your pages' content.
- Who your audience is and how you hope they will respond to your text (don't forget to try it out on your audience to help with this).
- How you used technology to best effect – draw attention to any mixing of technology, such as using a mobile phone or digital camera to generate images, then manipulating them in a package such as Photoshop and embedding them in your text using a desk-top publishing package such as Publisher to create the pages.
- An explanation of how your magazine will be marketed as a new title in a competitive market.

Controlled Assessment: Comics, cartoons and animation

Below are some ideas for approaching textual investigations and the production task in the media area of comics, cartoons and animations. For your own controlled assessments, you will be working on a different topic for your two textual investigations and your production but we've grouped our suggestions into media areas. These ideas are intended as a guide only.

Textual investigation: genre

Explore how genre conventions are used in the film version of the television cartoon series Scooby Doo.

Support texts for this investigation

These might include:

- the trailers and DVD covers for the films *Scooby Doo* and *Scooby Doo 2*
- episodes from the *Scooby Doo* television series
- the game cover for a *Scooby Doo* console game such as 'Scooby Doo! Unmasked'
- other television to real-action film comedies such as *The Magic Roundabout* and *Transformers*.

Approaches to this investigation

These might include:

- Refresh your memory of techniques and terminology needed to investigate genre codes and conventions in Cahpter 5. Then make two lists – the first of the main conventions of children's cartoons and the second of film adaptations of children's cartoons.
- Print out one of the DVD covers of the two *Scooby Doo* films and also a web page from the Cartoon Network website. Annotate them to show their genre conventions – try to show how they are similar and different.
- Look at the other support texts, for example, *Transformers* and try to identify what happens to a cartoon when it is adapted for film.
- Now decide how you are going to present your textual investigation findings. Look at tips for this on page 189.

Textual investigation: narrative

Explore how conventional the narrative construction or structure is in the comic Birds of Prey.

Support texts for this investigation

These might include:

- other DC comics – especially *Batman* comics
- the *Birds of Prey* real action television series
- the *Batman: Gotham Knight* animated television series
- other superhero comics, especially those featuring women superheroes, for example, *Rogue* and *Wonder Woman*.

Approaches to this investigation

These might include:

- Refresh your memory of narrative structure in Chapter 5: Comics, cartoons and animation. Also remind yourself of comic, storyboarding and storytelling techniques (see pages 106–110).
- Apply your knowledge by investigating the front cover and one story within *Birds of Prey* – how is the narrative organised and the story told? One striking feature of *Birds of Prey* is that it tells the stories of strong female, rather than male, heroes.
- Compare the narratives of *Birds of Prey* with one other superhero comic narrative based around female heroes.
- Widen your exploration to look at the narratives in the male-dominated *Batman* comics. What are the main similarities and differences in the way the narratives are constructed?
- Now decide how you are going to present your textual investigation findings. Look at tips for this on page 189.

Textual investigation: representation

Explore how far the representation of males is challenged in the Nintendo Wii animated game Rayman Raving Rabbids.

Support texts for this investigation

These might include:

- the free website Rayman Raving Rabbids game
- other animated games featuring male heroes
- other animated interactive websites, for example, *High School Detective.*

Approaches to this investigation

These might include:

- Refresh your memory about representation, including the representation of gender and characters in Chapter 1: Film; Chapter 2: Television; and Chapter 5: Comics, cartoons and animation. Then investigate the opening introduction to the Rayman Raving Rabbids Wii game.
- Widen your analysis to consider the representation of most male heroes in more real-to-life computer games – you may like to make a chart showing the main similarities and differences between other games and Rayman.
- Look at a range of free website animated games featuring male heroes – how do these help you to understand the representation of male heroes in animated games?
- Now decide how you are going to present your textual investigation findings. Look at tips for this on page 189.

The production

Create the first adventure of a new comic hero or superhero aimed at children under 10.

Research

You may like to consider the following:

- Find out what comic strips already exist that are aimed at young children based on strong hero or superhero characters. Examples might include *Justice League Unlimited*, *Super Friends* or *Teen Titans Go!*
- Choose one or two comic stories and investigate the techniques they use to make them eye-catching and appealing to their audiences. Also break the comic stories down into key points to find out how the narratives are organised and structured.
- Investigate comic title blocks are created – you will need to create your own soon!

- Make a questionnaire to find out what kinds of new character children might enjoy reading about.

Planning

You should now have some ideas about the main appealing features of your own comic story. You should use your research notes and findings to help you plan out your production. This might include:

- creating a detailed outline of your hero/superhero and possibly the villain who opposes him/her. Draw the character(s) and label their key features
- practising sketching your character(s) in different poses and showing different emotions
- designing the title block for your comic – this will act as a logo for the comic series and will be the first thing your audience will see and recognise
- planning your first comic adventure by thinking of 8–12 frames/panels that will introduce the characters, and also show emotion, sound and time passing
- drafting the page in rough, sketching out each frame and trying it out on members of your audience.

Production

Look again at the tips for making print productions on page 192. Remember that you must not work in a group for print production pieces. Create your magazine pages to the highest standards, making sure that you refer to your planning closely. Aim to make it as appealing and eye-catching as possible.

Evaluation

Your evaluation can be in the form of a presentation or illustrated report. It should be 400–850 words or its equivalent and should try to show at least some of the following:

- How your research into comic hero/superhero stories helped you construct your own comic story to be as eye-catching and exciting as possible.
- How your research into audience helped you create the meanings and representations in the text.
- Who your audience is and how you hope they will respond to your text (don't forget to try it out on your audience to help with this).
- How you went about creating the comic. You may have relied on your own graphic design skills, or you may have used a combination of digital and self-drawn frames – draw attention to any mixing of technology, such as using printed speech bubbles on hand-drawn images, or using computer filling for block colour. Note that, if you have hand-drawn your comic in A4, you can have it blown up to A3 at a local printer and the result will be a glossy, 'realistic' comic-style finish.

Controlled Assessment: Pop music

Below are some ideas for approaching textual investigations and the production task in the media area of pop music. For your own controlled assessments, you will be working on a different topic for your two textual investigations and your production but we've grouped our suggestions into media areas. These ideas are intended as a guide only.

Textual investigation: genre

Explore how far Rihanna's album art for 2007 release Umbrella *conforms to the genre conventions of RnB. You will need to obtain the album cover of* Umbrella *to complete this investigation.*

Support texts for this investigation

These might include:

- other covers for Rihanna's songs and albums, for example, *Disturbia* (2008) and *A Girl Like Me* (2006)
- the music video for *Umbrella*
- other examples of RnB album art, for example, Neo's *When You're Mad* and Usher's *Here I Stand*.

Approaches to this investigation

These might include:

- Refresh your memory of techniques and terminology needed to investigate genre codes and conventions in Chapter 6, then make a list of what you consider to be the main conventions of RnB. Use a printout of the album art for *Umbrella* and annotate it to show its key conventions as an example of RnB music.
- Make notes from the music video and explain why this RnB song has been so popular with audiences. What links can you see between the video and the album art?
- Look at other examples of Rihanna's album art – has the way she represents RnB changed over time? You may want to look at other examples of RnB artists' album art. Can you see similarities and differences in the way they each represent RnB?
- Now decide how you are going to present your textual investigation findings. Look at tips for this on page 189.

Textual investigation: narrative

Explore how the narrative is constructed in the music video Now You're Gone *by Basshunter.*

Support texts for this investigation

These might include:

- the sequel music videos *Please Don't Go*, *Last Night* and *All I Ever Wanted*. (These videos are embedded into the Basshunter website as well as Hard2beat.com and represent a continuation of the narrative in *Now You're Gone*.)
- the Basshunter website, which is highly interactive and links to the idea behind the narrative continuation of *Now You're Gone*.

Approaches to this investigation

These might include:

- Refresh your memory of narrative structure and the role of characters (pages 9 and 103). Watch the music video *Now You're Gone* (on the CD in this book), and make notes on how the narrative is constructed, and how characters are represented in the video. Try to decide how typical the narrative is and see if you can identify the purpose of the hero, heroine and helpers in the narrative.
- Widen your investigation and look at the supporting videos *Please Don't Go*, *Last Night* and *All I Ever Wanted*. They follow on from *Now You're Gone* – but how do they add further meaning to the main narrative? Also explore the Basshunter and/or Hard2beat.com websites. Think about the convergence of the media and how the music video is closely related to the website of the artist as well as the advertisements on Hard2beat.com.

- The use of technology is also an example of modern media convergence. How and why do the narratives use mobile phone, computer, webcam and camcorder technology?
- Now decide how you are going to present your textual investigation findings. Look at tips for this on page 189.

Textual investigation: representation

Explore how presenters of music programmes are represented in Chris Moyles' podcast: The Best of Chris Moyles.

Support texts for this investigation

These might include:

- BBC home website, which gives information on different ways to listen to the podcast and on how to download the podcasts successfully
- excerpts from the Radio 1 breakfast show
- clips from MTV programmes, focusing on presenters
- Sony Radio Academy Awards website, which gives details of other popular music programmes and their presenters
- an edition of a lifestyle magazine to focus on the representation of stars and celebrities.

Approaches to this investigation

These might include:

- Refresh your memory about representation, including the representation of stars and celebrities in Chapter 1: Film; Chapter 2: Television; Chapter 4: Magazines; and Chapter 6: Pop music. Then listen to one of Chris Moyles' podcasts and make notes on how Chris and the team are represented – you will notice immediately how little music features in the podcast, although there are many references to bands and artists. The focus is very much on Chris and his team. How would you describe the interaction between the presenters?
- Listen to the Radio 1 breakfast show to compare with the podcast. Is the team represented in the same way? Can you find any evidence of any of the team being represented in other media areas, for example, television?
- Look up one or two of the other award-winning radio music programme presenters. Do they have podcasts? Are they represented differently from the Radio 1 team? Also watch a television music programme presenter and make notes on how the representation might be similar or different.
- Now decide how you are going to present your textual investigation findings. Look at tips for this on page 189.

The production

Create a music video or trailer for a new television programme using a song of your choice from the alternative rock genre.

Research

Radiohead are considered by many to be the leaders of experimental alternative rock music videos, so they would be a good group to base your research around. You may like to consider the following:

- Start by looking at their discography and finding out about some of their albums: *Pablo Honey* (1993), *The Bends* (1995), *OK Computer* (1997), *Kid A* (2000), *Amnesiac* (2001), *Hail to the Thief* (2003), *In Rainbows* (2007). Print out or photocopy the covers of two Radiohead albums and annotate them to show genre conventions.
- Obtain a photo of Radiohead and investigate their band image.
- *In Rainbows* was, unusually, a free-to-download album. Watch the music video *Jigsaw Falling Into Place* which was filmed on a low budget, attaching cameras to the heads of the band for an interesting effect. Make notes on how the music video has been constructed and filmed.
- The Radiohead song *Nude* was also used in the trailer for the second season of E4's *Skins*. You can see the trailer on either the E4 or *Skins* website. Note how the music and lyrics are linked to the images seen in the trailer to communicate meaning.
- Undertake an audience survey to find out who enjoys alternative rock and what they expect from alternative rock music videos.

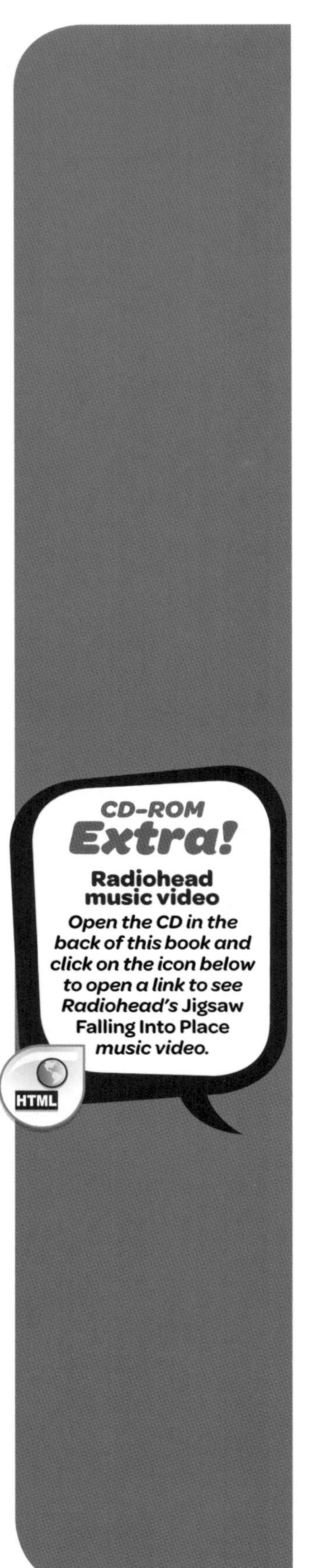

Planning

You should now have some ideas about the song you want to use to create your own music video or television trailer. You should use your research notes and findings to help you plan out your production. This might include:

- creating your band or artist image and taking a 'press photo' to give clues about the genre you belong to
- deciding on the content of the video/trailer and making sure it will meet the requirements of your target audience
- storyboarding the video or trailer, making it clear how music, lyrics and images work together to create meanings for your audience
- making a shooting script to indicate how you will set up your locations and individual shots
- creating a logo either for your music production company or for the television programme being trailed.

Production

Look again at the requirements for the production length, and look at the tips for making audio-visual productions on page 193. If you are going to work as part of a group, also check the tips for group work (page 191). Create your video/trailer, making sure that you refer to your planning closely.

Evaluation

Your evaluation can be in the form of a presentation or illustrated report. It should be 400–850 words or its equivalent and should try to show at least some of the following:

- How your research into music videos and the alternative rock genre helped you to plan the structure of your own text.
- How your research into audience helped you create the meanings and representations in the text.
- Who your audience is and how you hope they will respond to your text (don't forget to try it out on your audience to help with this).
- How you used technology to best effect – draw attention to any use of convergent technology such as a mobile phone in a music video or a shot of a newspaper headline.
- How you hope to distribute your text. Like Radiohead, you may want to use a free space forum like YouTube or bebo for Internet distribution, or to use more established paths such as a music production company.

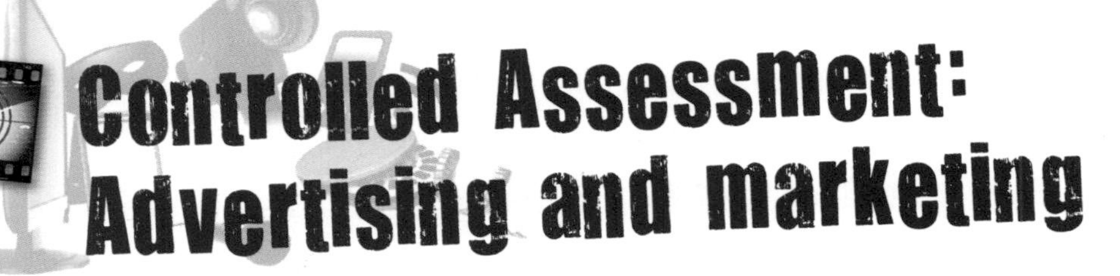

Controlled Assessment: Advertising and marketing

Below are some ideas for approaching textual investigations and the production task in the media area of advertising and marketing. For your own controlled assessments, you will be working on a different topic for your two textual investigations and your production but we've grouped our suggestions into media areas. These ideas are intended as a guide only.

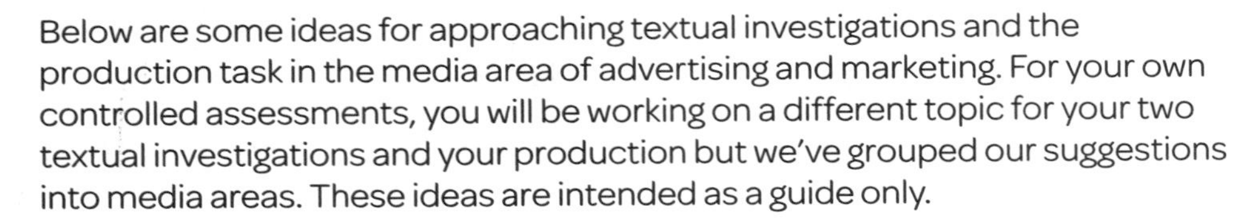

Textual investigation: genre

Explore how far genre conventions are challenged in the Sony Bravia plasticine rabbits advertisement.

Support texts for this investigation

These might include:

- versions of the rabbits advertisement in audio-visual and print form
- other Sony Bravia advertisements such as the bouncing balls and exploding paint advertisements
- examples of advertisements using animation techniques
- examples of advertisements using 'real' people and animals.

Approaches to this investigation

These might include:

- Refresh your memory of techniques and terminology needed to investigate genre codes and conventions in Chapter 7. Then make two lists – the first of the main conventions of audio-visual advertisements and the second of the conventions of stop-motion animation.
- Apply your analysis to a range of Sony Bravia advertisements – what genre conventions do their advertisements have in common? Make a mind map to show the main conventions of each advertisement you have studied.
- Widen your research to look at a range of both 'real' and animated advertisements. Make a chart to show the similarities and differences between them.
- Choose one advertisement you consider 'typical' of audio-visual advertisements, and make a bullet list of how the Sony Bravia rabbit advertisement both reinforces and challenges typical advertisement conventions.
- Now decide how you are going to present your textual investigation findings. Look at tips for this on page 189.

Textual investigation: narrative

Explore how the narrative is constructed in the eMusic Bluetooth advertisement.

Support texts for this investigation

These might include:

- other music download advertisements – print, Internet pop-up and audio-visual
- other Bluetooth Qwikker advertisements for a range of products – print, Internet pop-up and audio-visual
- the eMusic website .

Approaches to this investigation

These might include:

- Refresh your memory of narrative structure in Chapter 1: Film; Chapter 2: Television; and Chapter 7: Advertising. Also remind yourself of how audiences make sense of convergent advertisements that use, and can be found in, more than one technology.
- Explore the eMusic website, and go to the links on the homepage. Make lists of where the links take you, and what they give/show users.
- Investigate one or two examples of music download advertisements that use different media areas, for example, MTV, mobile phone, Internet pop-up. Try to explain how they have been made to give particular messages to audiences.
- Look closely at the focus eMusic Bluetooth advertisement. Stick it on paper and write annotations around it to show how it has been constructed so that audiences can see meanings in it.
- Now decide how you are going to present your textual investigation findings. Look at tips for this on page 189.

Textual investigation: representation

Explore how far the representation of the UK reinforces conventional points of view on the VisitBritain.co.uk website.

Support texts for this investigation

These might include:

- television and Internet advertisements for places in Britain
- newspaper and magazine advertisements for places in Britain
- a range of advertisements for other countries in the world
- representations of Britain in news bulletins.

Approaches to this investigation

These might include:

- Refresh your memory about representation, including the representations of place and events in Chapter 1: Film; Chapter 2: Television; Chapter 4: Magazines; and Chapter 7: Advertising.
- Look at a range of travel brochures, websites and newspaper advertisements and create a chart to show the most obvious features of how places/nations are advertised.
- Explore the VisitBritain.co.uk website thoroughly and list its key features. You will notice the changing images in the biggest panel of the homepage – these show a range of representations of Britain, and embrace a sense of beauty, ethnicity, class, tourist events, family and different ages.
- Use your research to look closely at general advertisements (in a range of media areas) for Britain. Make a list of the most commonly shown features of Britain.
- Compare your *VisitBritain* site notes with what you have learned about the representation of place/nation from your research.
- Now decide how you are going to present your textual investigation findings. Look at tips for this on page 189.

The production

Create a comic or photo story-style advertisement suitable for a magazine aimed at a teenage audience.

Research

You may like to consider the following:

- Look at as many magazines, photo stories, comic strips and 'traditional' advertisements as possible. Record the main conventions of these advertisements including:
  - how frames are created and shaped to tell an advertisement 'story'
  - how comic techniques are used to help tell the story, for example, narrative text boxes, speech and thought bubbles.
  - how characters are created to 'speak' to the audience about their role and function as well as the product in the advertisement
  - how photo story-style advertisements are made to seem 'dramatic', in order to draw attention to *the product*
  - how photo story-style advertisements *must show that they are advertisements* (often by using a small text box at the top or bottom of the advertisement saying 'Advertisement').

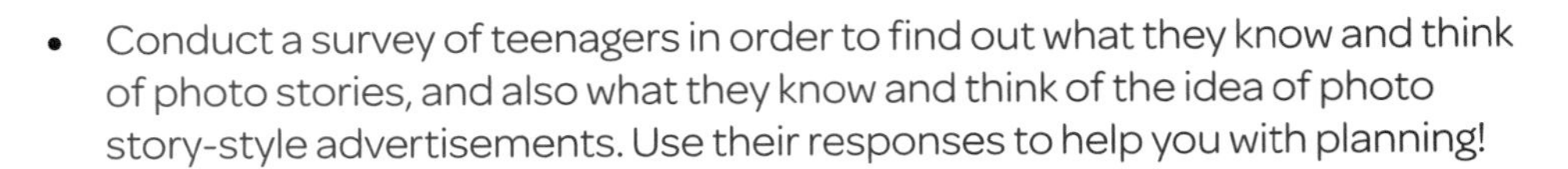

- Conduct a survey of teenagers in order to find out what they know and think of photo stories, and also what they know and think of the idea of photo story-style advertisements. Use their responses to help you with planning!

Planning

You should now have some ideas about the photo story magazine advertisement you want to make. You should use your research notes and findings to help you plan out your production. This might include:

- choosing the magazine you want to place your photo/comic strip-style advertisement in. Alternatively you may choose to create a new magazine to place your advertisement in
- deciding on the key moments of your advertisement, ensuring it will have all the messages about your chosen product that you think will be important to your target audience
- creating a storyboard of the advertisement you want to make, including a list of the features about it that will appeal to a youth audience
- choosing the key locations and actors to feature in your advertisement.

Production

Look again at the tips for making print productions on page 192 in the introduction to this section. Remember that you must not work in a group for print production pieces. Create your photo story advertisement to the highest standards, making sure that you refer to your planning closely. Aim to make it as colourful and eye-catching as possible.

Evaluation

Your evaluation can be in the form of a presentation or illustrated report. It should be 400–850 words or its equivalent and should try to show at least some of the following:

- How your research into advertisements in magazines and photo/comic strips helped you plan the structure of your own final advertisement.
- How your research into audience helped you create the meanings and representations in your advertisement.
- Who your audience is and how you hope they will respond to your text (don't forget to try it out on your audience to help with this).
- How you used technology to best effect. This will include your choices regarding each frame's set up (think about lighting and mise-en-scène especially), on-screen text font and design, layout of images and representation of key characters.
- How you hope to draw attention to your photo story within the magazine. How will you attract and KEEP audiences' attention even when they realise your text is an advertisement and not part of the magazine? How will you make links with other media areas that will advertise your product?
- How you considered areas of audience awareness. Is it important for the audience to realise that your product is a product? Why?

Accent The sound of the voice which tells us which part of the country the presenter is from.

Anchor To pin down a particular meaning of a drawing or photograph often by adding a caption.

Angle The particular point of view a newspaper wants its readers to take on a story.

Animations Audio-visual versions of comics that are used in a variety of media forms such as films and adverts.

Anime A Japanese animation form that combines camera movements with still frames.

Arch-villain The character who opposes the superhero and often has special powers too, that are used only for evil. The most memorable arch-villains are those who have a reason for turning to evil, for example, Doctor Octopus in *Spiderman*.

Aspiration When an audience sees fashion, accessories, a lifestyle, etc. in a magazine that they wish they could have for themselves.

Audience People who are reading, looking at, listening to or using a media text.

Audience profile The types of people who read, watch or listen to a particular media.

Audience share The number of people a particular media attracts compared to its competitors.

Back-catalogue All the previous work recorded by artists or bands.

BBC Charter The official permission from the government for the BBC to charge a licence fee in return for quality programming.

Blockbuster A film that has a huge budget and is expected to be a hit, so-called because of the long queues around the block to see successful films.

Brand A particular type of product, for example, Levi jeans.

Brand awareness Making the product immediately recognisable to the public.

Branding The distinctive features by which we recognise products.

Broadsheets Traditionally, newspapers printed in a large format (pages of 37 cm by 58 cm); they are considered to be more serious in content than tabloids.

Caption The descriptive words next to a picture.

Categorising Ordering or grouping similar texts, for example, magazines, according to the features they have in common.

Celebrity Someone who is popular in one country for appearing in one media field, such as a soap opera.

Central protagonists Key characters around whom the text and narrative are centred.

Circulation The number of copies of a newspaper or magazine which are sold.

Codes and conventions The things that make a piece of media what it is, i.e. the things that define it. For example, we associate horses, spurs, saloons and tumbleweed with Westerns and flashing lights, actors in shiny suits and lack of gravity with science fiction. Likewise, we associate a red-topped masthead, banner headlines and celebrity gossip with the popular tabloids.

Commercial broadcaster A channel funded by money from advertising, for example, ITV.

Computer-generated imagery (CGI) Using computer graphics, especially 3D computer graphics, in special effects.

Connotation The hidden meaning behind an image, word or sound that gives it depth.

Continuity editing Editing which is designed to make one event follow on naturally from another. Nothing unusual happens to make the viewer notice the fact that an edit has been made.

Consumers The people who buy, read, watch or lissten to media products.

Conventions The typical characteristics of a particular type of text.

Convergent When more than one media area come together, often in a business relationship – for example, comics and television.

Copy Material for articles that appear in newspapers or magazines.

Cover price The price charged for the magazine that is displayed on the front cover.

Cross-plot A way of tracking different storylines through a single episode of a TV drama series.

Deconstruction Taking a media product apart to see how it works and how it is constructed. It is more than just analysis.

Demograph The type of audience watching or reading a media product.

Demographics Another word for audience categories.

Denotation This is the understanding of media artefacts – what they look and sound like.

Disposable income The money someone has left to spend after they have paid for essentials such as housing and food.

Distribution method The way the music industry distributes music tracks to its audience.

Download Any file that is available on a remote server to be downloaded to a home computer. YouTube is an example of a file-sharing website.

Downmarket People who have smaller incomes and less money to spend on anything beyond the basic living requirements.

Endorsement Giving approval to something.

Experiential communication Where consumers actually interact with the product rather than just look at pictures of it.

Film pitch An idea for a new film which is presented to film producers. This usually involves ideas for a plot, possible actors, promotion and marketing.

Gatekeeping Where reporters or editors block certain issues but allow others through into newspapers or news broadcasts.

Genre A type of media text (programme, film, popular music, etc.) with certain predictable characteristics.

Glossies Magazines with thick, 'glossy' paper, expensive advertisements and a high cover price.

Hegemony The way people are influenced into accepting the dominance of a power group who impose their views on the rest of the population.

House style A radio station or publisher's preferred manner of presentation or layout which matches their audience.

Hybrid When at least two genres are brought together to create a new genre, for example, the superhero movie combines the genres of superhero comics and action films.

Ident Like a logo, an instantly recognisable feature of a film, character or company, for example, the Hulk's green fists.

Ideology A system of values, beliefs or ideas that is common to a specific group of people.

Intertextual reference When one media text refers to another media text in a way that many consumers will recognise.

Jump-cut Where the join between two shots is felt to be abrupt because what follows is something we don't expect to see.

Lifestyle magazines Magazines dealing with lots of topics and issues to appeal to a wide audience.

Lip-synching Where a person in a video mimes so that their lip movement matches the words being heard on a soundtrack.

Link A shot piece of speech from the presenter between music or other items.

Manga Popular Japanese comics that have influenced anime films.

Marketing The process of making customers aware of products, services and ideas in the hope that they will buy into them.

Market research Finding out what audiences like or dislike about aspects of the media through interviews, surveys and focus groups.

Masthead The title of the newspaper which appears in large type at the top of the front page.

Media conglomerates Large corporations who own more than one different media company and sometimes a large number of companies.

Media consumption The media texts you watch, listen to or read.

Media space Any space in newspapers, magazines, on the radio or television where advertising can be placed.

Mise-en-scène A French phrase which literally means 'put in shot'.

Model animation An animation technique using posable scale models.

Mode of address The ways that a text creates a relationship with its audience.

Multi-stranded narrative When a television drama follows more than one storyline and also interweaves them.

Narrative A story or account.

Narrative structure The way a story is organised and shaped in terms of time and events.

Network An interconnected group or system.

News values Things that help a story get into the news.

Niche markets Small groups who are targeted because they share the same interests, income, etc.

Opening (or title) sequence A series of shots and music or graphics that appear at the start of a programme or film.

Oppositional characters Characters who will play opposite the key central character, either in a relationship (for example, the hero/heroine) or in conflict (for example, the hero/villain).

Pace The speed at which something happens or a story develops.

Passive Not helping the narrative to move forward or not helping the hero.

Peak time The hours between 6.00 p.m. and 10.30 p.m. when most people are watching television and viewing figures are at their highest.

Picture editor The person responsible for choosing the photographs that go into a newspaper.

Post-production Activities at the end of the production process, e.g. editing, sound dubbing, credits, marketing and promotion, focus groups, trailers, articles and features.

Pre-production Activities at the beginning of the production process, eg. ideas, bids for finance, storyboards, scriptwriting, planning and designing, set construction, casting and rehearsals.

Primary consumer Someone who is focused on watching, listening to or reading a media text.

Producer The person who makes a product.

Production Shooting in purpose-built sets or in outside locations.

Product (or pack) shot A picture of the actual product, for example, a packet of Corn Flakes.

Product placement Giving brands or products to media producers for them to use as props so that the product is seen in a favourable way.

Public service broadcaster A channel funded by a licence fee that has to provide a choice of programmes to appeal to all social groups, for example, BBC1.

Readership The number of people who read a newspaper or magazine. This is usually higher than circulation, as several people can read the same paper magazine.

Red tops Tabloid newspapers with red mastheads.

Re-issuing When a record company releases songs recorded some time before and which have probably already sold well.

Representation How people, places, events or ideas are represented or portrayed to audiences in media texts. Sometimes this is simplistically through stereotypes so the audience can see immediately what is meant, and sometimes the meanings are less obvious.

Revenue The money generated by selling advertising space in a magazine or newspaper, on television, websites etc.

Secondary consumer Someone watching, listening to or reading a media text while doing something else, such as talking or homework.

Social networking site Examples are Facebook and Myspace.

Special effects Exciting and dynamic visual or sound effects used to create impact in films.

Specialist magazines Magazines focusing on a particular area of interest to appeal to a narrow or niche audience.

Spin-off Merchandise that uses characters from a media text.

Star A performer who is famous internationally.

Stereotypical Showing groups of people in terms of certain widely held but over-simplified characteristics, for example, showing women as nagging housewives.

Stereotypes People grouped together according to simple shared characteristics, without allowing for any individual uniqueness.

Stock character A supporting character who is often quite stereotypical and whose job it is to help the lead characters, to be saved by them or to die!

Stock footage Material held in a library which shows something relevant to the news story.

Storyboard The key moments of a story shown using images and notes.

Sub-editor The person responsible for the layout of a newspaper.

Sub-genre Genres can be divided into sub-genres, for example, teen comedies are a sub-genre of comedy.

Subsidise To reduce the cover price of a media text, such as a magazine or newspaper, by selling advertising space.

Subversion When a technique is used which does not fit a theory or the usual way of doing something (for example, when a twist takes the narrative in a new direction).

Superhero A heroic character with special powers and a lifelong mission.

Tabloids Traditionally, newspapers with pages half the size of broadsheets; they are usually more highly illustrated and can be less serious in their tone and content than broadsheets.

Target audience The specific group of people that a media text is aimed at.

Template A pattern which helps to shape the products that follow.

Tension The build-up of suspense or anticipation as a story develops.

Text This is not just the written word but a film text, radio text, etc.

Tie-in A media text that uses the characters, and possibly storyline, of a text in another form.

Tone The qualilty and character of a voice or piece of writing.

Typography The choice of font style and size, graphic design and layout.

Upmarket People who are comfortably off with a reasonable income.

Values and aspirations The ideas and goals that are important to people.

Viral advertising Spreading advertisements through the use of attachments to emails. It can give very wide coverage at no cost.

Watershed An agreement between terrestrial channels not to show explicit material until after 9 p.m.

Heinemann is an imprint of Pearson Education Limited, a company incorporated in England and Wales, having its registered office at Edinburgh Gate, Harlow, Essex, CM20 2JE. Registered company number: 872828

www.heinemann.co.uk

Heinemann is a registered trademark of Pearson Education Limited

First published 2009

12 11
10 9 8 7 6 5 4 3 2

British Library Cataloguing in Publication Data
A catalogue record for this book is available from the British Library.

ISBN 978 0 435404 21 5

Designed and produced by Kamae Design, Oxford
Original illustrations © Pearson Education Limited 2009
Illustrated by Tony Forbes
Cover design by Pete Stratton
Picture research by Ginny Stroud-Lewis
Printed in Malaysia (CTP-VP)

Acknowledgements

The author and publisher would like to thank the following individuals and organisations for permission to reproduce photographs:
© The Advertising Archives pp114, 149 (right), 156, 157, 159 (all photos), 224; ©Alamy/Alex Segre p71; © Alamy/AllOver Photography p77 (top); © Alamy/Chris Fredriksson p127; © Alamy/Coaster p43 (bottom); © Alamy/DEK C p124 (middle); © Alamy/Frances Roberts p12 (bottom); © Alamy/INTERFOTO Pressebildagentur p124 (middle left); © Alamy/Jon Arnold Images Ltd p145; © Alamy/Jon Challicom p32 (bottom); © Alamy/Roberto Herrett p18; © Alamy/WoodyStock p77 (middle); © Art Directors and Trip/Helene Rogers p11 (bottom three photos); © Bettmann/CORBIS p128 (bottom); © Channel 4 pp36, 48; © Colin Jones/Topfoto 124 (top); © Corbis pp 3 (bottom), 87 (top),121; © Corbis/Angelo Hornak p14 (top); © Corbis/Bettmann pp15 (top), 124 (far left),149 (left); © Corbis/Challenge Roddie p104 (middle); © Corbis/Denis O'Regan p138; © Corbis/Neal Preston p124 (second from left); © Corbis/Reuters/Ray Stubblebine p24; © Corbis/Rune Hellestad p133 (bottom); © Corbis/Saba/Louise Gubb p58; © Corbis/Sygma p6; © Corbis/Wally McNamee p168; © Daniel Attia/zefa/Corbis p68; © David James/Warner Bros/ZUMA/Corbis p111; ©Getty Images p104 (right), 124 (second from right), 147, 153; © Getty Images/AFP pp22, 184; © Getty Images/Felbert+Eickenberg p32 (top); © Getty Images/Film Magic pp 88, 89 (middle left), 219; © Getty Images/Lichfield Archive p135 (second from bottom), 139; © Getty Images/Lonely Planet p59 (top); © Getty Images/Michael Ochs Archives p124 (third from left, third from right); © Getty Images/Photodisc p59 (bottom); © Getty Images/Popperfoto p124 (middle right); © Getty Images/WireImage pp124 (far right), 126; © Ian West/PA Wire/PA Photos p43 (top); © The Illustrated London News Photo Library p52; © Image Source Pink/Alamy p28; © INTERFOTO Pressebildagentur / Alamy p47; © ITV p38; © ITV Granada p42; © The Kobal Collection pp135 (bottom), 136; © The Kobal Collection/ABC-Tv/Danny Feld pp44 (bottom), 212; © The Kobal Collection/ABC-TV/Moshe Brakha p41; © The Kobal Collection/Allied Artists p4; © The Kobal Collection/Celluloid Dreams/Hammer & Tongs p196; © The Kobal Collection/Columbia pp115,135 (top); © The Kobal Collection/Destination Films/Gullane Pics p102; © The Kobal Collection/Dreamworks/Aardman Animations p116; ©The Kobal Collection/Dreamworks LLC p181; © The Kobal Collection/Focus Features p17 (top right); © The Kobal Collection/Focus Features/Greg Williams p33; © The Kobal Collection/HANNAH BARBERA PRODS / ATLAS ENTERTAINMENT; © The Kobal Collection/Marvel Enterprises pp17 (top left), 195; © The Kobal Collection/MGM/United Artists/Sony p165; © The Kobal Collection/Monarchy/Regency p162; © The Kobal Collection/NBC-TV p200; © The Kobal Collection/Polygram/Suzanne Hanover p11 (top); © The Kobal Collecton/STUDIO GHIBLI p120; © The Kobal Collection/20th Century Fox p104 (left); © The Kobal Collection/20th Century Fox-film corporation p5 (right) © The Kobal Collection/20th Century Fox/Marvel p112; © The Kobal Collection/United Artists p135 (second from top); © The Kobal Collection/Universal TV/NBC p202; © The Kobal Collection/Walt Disney Pictures p117; © The Kobal Collection/Warner Bros Pictures pp5 (left), 15 (bottom),17 (bottom right), 118; © The Kobal Collection/Warner Bros/Castle Rock Ent. P17 (bottom left); © Mandy Esseen p89 (bottom left, bottom right); © Martin Phillips p173 (left and right), 178 (left and right); © Matthew Birchall / Alamy p87 (bottom right); © Michael Germana/Starmax/EMPICS Entertainment/PA Photos p89 (top right); © NASA/HSTI; © PAPhotos p44 (top); © Paul Kane/Getty Images p134; © Pearson Education/Tudor Photography p172; © Photoshot/UPPA p35; © Rex Features p49; © Raymond Press Agency p65; © Rex Features p69; © Rex Features/FremantleMedia Ltd p143; © Shutterstock p133 (top); © Shutterstock/Andriy Doriy p12 (top); © Shutterstock/foto.fritz p30 (bottom); © Shutterstock/ifong p77 (bottom); © Shutterstock/LesPalenik p29 (left); © Science Photo Library/Sheila Terry p30 (top); © Shutterstock/Ljupco Smokovski p29 (right); © Shutterstock/rook76 p14 (bottom); © 2006 TopFoto/Ken Russell p123; © Wikipedia p131.

Every effort has been made to contact copyright holders of material reproduced in this book. Any omissions will be rectified in subsequent printings if notice is given to the publishers.

Chapter 1: Cover of *Empire* magazine © Empire, used with permission; BBFC logos: These classification symbols are the property of the British Board of Film Classification and are both trademark and copyright protected. Used with permission of BBFC; **Chapter 2**: Quote from the BBC charter is used with permission of the BBC; Ofcom Logo is used with permission of Ofcom; BBC 1 and BBC 2 TV listings used with the kind permission of the *Radio Times* magazine; Peter Fincham quote is used with permission of the BBC; E4 TV listings used with the kind permission of the *Radio Times* magazine; **Chapter 3**: Edward R. Murrow quote © Edward R. Murrow used with kind permission of the estate; Masthead from the *Sun* used with permission of NI Syndication Ltd.; Front page of the *Sun* ('It's the Sun wot won it') used with permission of NI Syndication Ltd.; Front page of *The Times* ('Major plans reshuffle today') used with permission of NI Syndication Ltd.; Front page of *The Times* ('When war came to America') used with permission of NI Syndication Ltd.; Extract and front page of the *Daily Mail* ('Time's up for happy hour') used with permission from the *Daily Mail*; 'You're Spuddy Clever Walter' from *Hold Ye Front Page: 2000 years of History on the Front Page of the 'Sun'* by John Perry & Neil Roberts, © 1999. Used by permission of HarperCollins Publishers; 'Monkey Nutter' from *Hold Ye Front Page: 2000 years of History on the Front Page of the 'Sun'* by John Perry & Neil Roberts, © 1999. Used by permission of HarperCollins Publishers; Extract from the *Daily Mail* ('Shameless') used with permission from the *Daily Mail*; **Chapter 4**: Cover of *Elle* magazine used by kind permission of *Elle*, Paris; Screen grab from *ElleUK.com* used by kind permission of *Elle*, Paris; Screen Grab from the BFI website used by kind permission of the British Film Institute; Cover of *Asiana* magazine used by kind permission of I & I Media Limited; Cover and contents page of *Shout* magazine used by kind permission of D.C. Thomson; Cover of *Anglers Mail* used by kind permission of IPC Media; Screen grab of *empireonline.com* used with the kind permission of *Empire* magazine. www.empireonline.com; Film review from *empireonline.com* used with the kind permission of *Empire* magazine. www.empireonline.com; Cover of *Empire* magazine used with the kind permission of *Empire* magazine. www.empireonline.com; Cover of *NME* magazine used by kind permission of IPC Media, a Time Warner company; Cover the *Radio Times* used with the kind permission of the *Radio Times* magazine; Cover of *Thomas and Friends* magazine used by permission of Egmont; IPC Media logo used by permission of IPC Media; Cover of *PC Gamer* magazine used by permission of Future Publishing Ltd.; **Chapter 5**: Cover of *Dandy* used by kind permission of D.C. Thomson; Cover of *Beano* used by kind permission of D.C. Thomson; Cover of the *Fantastic Four*: TM & © 2009 Marvel Characters Inc. Used with permission; Cover of *Shidoshi* magazine used by kind permission of Antarctic Press; **Chapter 6**: *Numa Numa* article used by kind permission of The Salzburg Academy on Media & Global Change; Two covers of *Mixmag* magazine, used by kind permission of Development Hell Ltd.; David Hepworth extract from *Mixmag* magazine used by permission of Development Hell; Keris Ferguson extract used by kind permission of This is Fake DIY; **Chapter 7**: Extract from the *Daily Mail* ('Free DVD inside') used with permission from the *Daily Mail*; Cover of the *Radio Times* used with the kind permission of the *Radio Times* magazine; Wayne Rooney article and photograph from *Toxic* magazine used with permission of Egmont; **Chapter 8**: BBC Radio 1 audience data for period ending September 2008 from Radio Joint Audience Research website: www.rajar.co.uk; **Chapter 10**: screen grab of homepage from www.indianajones.co.uk; screen grab of homepage from www.news.politicsandthecity.com; screen grab of homepage from www.mybliss.co.uk; Simon Pegg article found in *Total Film* magazine used by permission of Future Publishing Ltd.; Bluetooth advertisement used with kind permission of permission of Qwikker; Screen grab of homepage from www.visitbritain.co.uk reproduced courtesy of VisitBritain.

Single User Licence Agreement: WJEC GCSE Media Studies ActiveBook CD-ROM

Warning:
This is a legally binding agreement between You (the user or purchasing institution) and Pearson Education Limited of Edinburgh Gate, Harlow, Essex, CM20 2JE, United Kingdom ('PEL').

By retaining this Licence, any software media or accompanying written materials or carrying out any of the permitted activities You are agreeing to be bound by the terms and conditions of this Licence. If You do not agree to the terms and conditions of this Licence, do not continue to use the WJEC GCSE Media Studies ActiveBook CD-ROM and promptly return the entire publication (this Licence and all software, written materials, packaging and any other component received with it) with Your sales receipt to Your supplier for a full refund.

Intellectual Property Rights:
This WJEC GCSE Media Studies ActiveBook CD-ROM consists of copyright software and data. All intellectual property rights, including the copyright is owned by PEL or its licensors and shall remain vested in them at all times. You only own the disk on which the software is supplied. If You do not continue to do only what You are allowed to do as contained in this Licence you will be in breach of the Licence and PEL shall have the right to terminate this Licence by written notice and take action to recover from you any damages suffered by PEL as a result of your breach.

The PEL name, PEL logo and all other trademarks appearing on the software and WJEC GCSE Media Studies ActiveBook CD-ROM are trademarks of PEL. You shall not utilise any such trademarks for any purpose whatsoever other than as they appear on the software and WJEC GCSE Media Studies ActiveBook CD-ROM.

Yes, You can:
1. use this WJEC GCSE Media Studies ActiveBook CD-ROM on Your own personal computer as a single individual user. You may make a copy of the WJEC GCSE Media Studies ActiveBook CD-ROM in machine readable form for backup purposes only. The backup copy must include all copyright information contained in the original.

No, You cannot:
1. copy this WJEC GCSE Media Studies ActiveBook CD-ROM (other than making one copy for back-up purposes as set out in the Yes, You can table above);

2. alter, disassemble, or modify this WJEC GCSE Media Studies ActiveBook CD-ROM, or in any way reverse engineer, decompile or create a derivative product from the contents of the database or any software included in it:

3. include any materials or software data from the WJEC GCSE Media Studies ActiveBook CD-ROM in any other product or software materials;

4. rent, hire, lend, sub-licence or sell the WJEC GCSE Media Studies ActiveBook CD-ROM;

5. copy any part of the documentation except where specifically indicated otherwise;

6. use the software in any way not specified above without the prior written consent of PEL;

7. Subject the software, WJEC GCSE Media Studies ActiveBook CD-ROM or any PEL content to any derogatory treatment or use them in such a way that would bring PEL into disrepute or cause PEL to incur liability to any third party.

Grant of Licence:
PEL grants You, provided You only do what is allowed under the 'Yes, You can' table above, and do nothing under the 'No, You cannot' table above, a non-exclusive, non-transferable Licence to use this WJEC GCSE Media Studies ActiveBook CD-ROM.

The terms and conditions of this Licence become operative when using this WJEC GCSE Media Studies ActiveBook CD-ROM.

Limited Warranty:
PEL warrants that the disk or CD-ROM on which the software is supplied is free from defects in material and workmanship in normal use for ninety (90) days from the date You receive it. This warranty is limited to You and is not transferable.

This limited warranty is void if any damage has resulted from accident, abuse, misapplication, service or modification by someone other than PEL. In no event shall PEL be liable for any damages whatsoever arising out of installation of the software, even if advised of the possibility of such damages. PEL will not be liable for any loss or damage of any nature suffered by any party as a result of reliance upon or reproduction of any errors in the content of the publication.

PEL does not warrant that the functions of the software meet Your requirements or that the media is compatible with any computer system on which it is used or that the operation of the software will be unlimited or error free. You assume responsibility for selecting the software to achieve Your intended results and for the installation of, the use of and the results obtained from the software.

PEL shall not be liable for any loss or damage of any kind (except for personal injury or death) arising from the use of this WJEC GCSE Media Studies ActiveBook CD-ROM or from errors, deficiencies or faults therein, whether such loss or damage is caused by negligence or otherwise.

The entire liability of PEL and your only remedy shall be replacement free of charge of the components that do not meet this warranty.

No information or advice (oral, written or otherwise) given by PEL or PEL's agents shall create a warranty or in any way increase the scope of this warranty.

To the extent the law permits, PEL disclaims all other warranties, either express or implied, including by way of example and not limitation, warranties of merchantability and fitness for a particular purpose in respect of this WJEC GCSE Media Studies ActiveBook CD-ROM.

Termination:
This Licence shall automatically terminate without notice from PEL if You fail to comply with any of its provisions or the purchasing institution becomes insolvent or subject to receivership, liquidation or similar external administration. PEL may also terminate this Licence by notice in writing. Upon termination for whatever reason You agree to destroy the WJEC GCSE Media Studies ActiveBook CD-ROM and any back-up copies and delete any part of the WJEC GCSE Media Studies ActiveBook CD-ROM stored on your computer.

Governing Law:
This Licence will be governed by and construed in accordance with English law.